Green BIM:
Successful Sustainable Design with Building Information Modeling

Green BIM:
Successful Sustainable Design with Building Information Modeling

Eddy Krygiel

Bradley Nies

Wiley Publishing, Inc.

Acquisitions Editor: WILLEM KNIBBE
Development Editor: JENNIFER LELAND
Technical Editor: SCOTT JOHNSON
Production Editor: RACHEL MCCONLOGUE
Copy Editor: LIZ WELCH
Production Manager: TIM TATE
Vice President and Executive Group Publisher: RICHARD SWADLEY
Vice President and Executive Publisher: JOSEPH B. WIKERT
Vice President and Publisher: NEIL EDDE
Book Designer: FRANZ BAUMHACKL
Compositor: MAUREEN FORYS, HAPPENSTANCE TYPE-O-RAMA
Proofreader: JEN LARSEN, WORD ONE
Indexer: TED LAUX
Cover Designer: RYAN SNEED
Cover Image: © ASSISSI

LIBRARY OF CONGRESS CATALOGING-IN-PUBLICATION DATA

Krygiel, Eddy, 1972-
  Green BIM : successful sustainable design with building information modeling / Eddy Krygiel, Brad Nies.—1st ed.
    p. cm.
  Includes bibliographical references and index.
  ISBN-13: 978-0-470-23960-5 (paper/website)
  ISBN-10: 0-470-23960-3 (paper/website)
  1. Sustainable buildings—Design and construction. 2. Building information modeling. 3. Building—Data processing.
I. Nies, Brad, 1971– II. Title.
  TH880.K79 2008
  720'.47--dc22
                                    2008008357

Dear Reader,

Thank you for choosing *Green BIM: Successful Sustainable Design with Building Information Modeling*. This book is part of a family of premium quality Sybex books, all written by outstanding authors who combine practical experience with a gift for teaching.

Sybex was founded in 1976. More than thirty years later, we're still committed to producing consistently exceptional books. With each of our titles, we're working hard to set a new standard for the industry. From the paper we print on to the authors we work with, our goal is to bring you the best books available.

I hope you see all that reflected in these pages. I'd be very interested to hear your comments and get your feedback on how we're doing. Feel free to let me know what you think about this or any other Sybex book by sending me an email at nedde@wiley.com, or if you think you've found a technical error in this book, please visit http://sybex.cus-thelp.com. Customer feedback is critical to our efforts at Sybex.

Best regards,

Neil Edde
Vice President and Publisher
Sybex, an Imprint of Wiley

I would like to thank my family, especially Laura, Payton, and AJ for all their support and enthusiasm. Also, this book could not exist without the wonderful experiences we've shared with fellow BNIMers, both past and present.

—Bradley Nies

For Angiela, with and for whom all things are possible.

—Eddy Krygiel

Acknowledgments

This book, like a building, wasn't put together by a single individual. It was the work of many who came together to use their specialties to create what you have before you. We, the authoring team, get the opportunity to have our names on the cover, but this book would not have been made possible without the hard work of many others.

First, we'd like to thank our colleagues at BNIM Architects, who willingly let us tackle this endeavor and were generous in their support. A special expression of appreciation is extended to Steve McDowell, FAIA, for writing the foreword and leading the design and innovation of our firm.

We extend our gratitude to the artists and photographers whose artwork makes this book come alive. Special appreciation goes to Farshid Assassi, Lyndall Blake, Filo Castore, AIA, Jean D. Dodd, Paul Hester, Timothy Hursley, David W. Orr, Richard Payne, FAIA, Mike Sherman, and Mike Sinclair.

We would like to offer some huge thanks for the excellent support we received from the team at Sybex. Truly, not a more crack group could be had to constantly poke and prod us to use the Queen's English, write in complete sentences, and start writing at the end of a long day.

Thank you's are particularly due to our developmental editor, Jennifer Leland, who will hopefully still like us after this project is complete. Thanks to Scott Sven for his technical expertise, and to Rachel McConlogue for making us use something we've heard about called *grammar*. Thanks as well to Pete Gaughan, and last but not least, a hearty thanks to Willem Knibbe, without whose undying support, generous praise, and constant prodding none of this would have, well, they won't let me print the rest.

About the Authors

With over 10 years of professional experience, Eddy Krygiel serves as a project architect for BNIM Architects. As a well-rounded professional, his experience includes the many facets of design, construction documentation, and construction administration. In addition, Eddy is familiar with the advanced integration of technology in practice, including the latest software and program systems, which ensures maximum performance on all of his projects.

In his role as project architect, Eddy is responsible for developing the design into working details, leading the production of construction documents and specifications and construction administration. His participation is constant throughout the project, particularly during the construction documents and construction administration phases.

Eddy is responsible for implementing BIM at his firm and also consults for other architecture and contracting firms looking to implement BIM. For the last three years, he has taught BIM to practicing architects and architectural students in the Kansas City area and has lectured around the nation on the use of BIM in the construction industry. Eddy has coauthored a number of books and papers on BIM and sustainability.

Eddy's representative project experience with BNIM includes the Internal Revenue Service Kansas City Service Center, the H&R Block Service Center, Art House Townhomes, Freight House Flats, and Shook Hardy & Bacon law offices, among others. While at other firms, he has also been involved with large housing projects at Whiteman Air Force Base and Benedictine College.

Bradley Nies, AIA, LEED AP, is director of Elements, the sustainable design consulting division of BNIM Architects. He received his bachelor of architecture from the University of Kansas.

Brad has 13 years of experience and has worked on silver, gold, and platinum USGBC LEED Certified projects. He was the sustainable design consultant for the LEED Platinum Certified Heifer International Headquarters in Little Rock, Arkansas, which won a 2007 AIA Top Ten Green Project Award and a National AIA 2008 Institute Honor Award. Brad also led the team that created Implement, Seattle's online Sustainable Building Tool.

In 2005, Brad founded a Kansas City–based volunteer construction waste management forum, which led to the development of RecycleSpot.org. Brad has served two terms on the AIA Kansas City Committee as the Environment Chair and is currently serving his second year on the Greater Kansas City USGBC Chapter Board. Brad often speaks at regional design and construction conferences throughout the Midwest and is an annual guest lecturer at the University of Kansas School of Architecture.

Contents

Foreword

The great pyramids remain beautiful marvels of design, engineering knowledge, fabrication ability, and precision. The architect builder(s) of the great pyramids achieved seemingly impossible feats. They imagined, visualized, and realized structures of stacked stones, dwarfing design construction accomplishments still to this day. Stones were shaped and placed one by one with rudimentary tools and slave labor. It was slow-going, and each layer of stone became the scaffold for the next. Gravity was overcome with each stone as the laborers lifted and carried it to its predetermined place in the composition. Finally, every stone was at rest and carried the weight of those above, stone by stone down to the sand.

Many mysteries remain about exactly how these complex and precise structures were accomplished. How were ideas documented and communicated among the tens or maybe hundreds of thousands of laborers? In the case of Giza, what tools ensured that the lengths of the four sides varied by only 58mm? What process was in place to organize the fabrication and installation of millions of stones over decades of time by thousands of workers and achieve the parti with degrees of precision that would be considered extraordinary today?

The pyramidal form is simple and beautiful. These structures are even more beautiful as monuments to the ingenuity of the designer builders. Each is a three-dimensional diagram of the forces of gravity at work, cementing every stone in its exact position in balance with nature. We will never know if the builders understood the science of the design or simply selected the shape for its form and because it was buildable with the tools available.

Eero Saarinen understood the forces of nature. Many centuries after the pyramids, he collaborated with colleagues, engineers, a mathematician, and builders to achieve balance with gravity to realize his competition-winning design. Rising from the banks of the Mississippi River is the monument to the vision of Thomas Jefferson. The St. Louis Arch, as it is widely known, stands today as an inverted catenary curve resting in pure compression and void of all shear. Accomplishing such an undertaking demanded innovation in all aspects of design and construction.

His team approached the design utilizing mathematical formula to determine the form, sectional design, and dimensions of the entire building. High-carbon steel and concrete were combined to create a balance of form, structure, durability, aesthetics, and constructability. New elevator and other building systems were invented to provide usefulness and comfort. The design accommodated a construction approach relying on the incomplete structure to carry the weight of the workers and their tools and materials as they progressed toward the keystone piece joining the two legs of the curve. The meeting of the two legs that rise from a distance 630 feet apart to a height 630 feet above the earth demanded precision. An error greater than 1/64 inch could not be tolerated if the legs were to meet. The final section would only be allowed to slip into place with the help of nature. The only force powerful enough to align the two legs exactly into position was the sun. Solar radiation landing on the opposing legs of the arch the morning of October 28, 1965, widened the gap enough to insert the keystone section precisely and complete the arch.

The pyramids and the arch were large-scale breakthroughs in design and construction. Our era is in need of similar-scale advancements in how we realize our needs for enclosure and inspired design. We are facing a construction boom like no other in history. Over the next 20 years, we will more than double the amount of built space occupied today. Innovation is the foundation for sustaining life on earth. We are at a critical point, and the right innovations must be incorporated in the environments of the future.

Nature provides the answers—it is up to us to ask the right questions. Like the great pyramid builders centuries ago and Eero Saarinen centuries later, the authors of this book are doing just that. Eddy Krygiel and Bradley Nies are practicing a new approach to design and building that utilizes the power of building information modeling tools and integrated design thought and process with profound results. Their work has developed within BNIM Architects, a firm with a long history and commitment to sustainable design. Many new questions about the process of design and building have emerged from that experience. Those questions cover topics of sustainability, design, and construction process efficiency, construction quality, method of fabrication, roles and responsibilities of designers and builders, human health and comfort, durability, and the future of our industry.

By answering those questions and more, Krygiel and Nies have provided leadership within our firm, enabling design teams to begin the journey along a new approach to design and construction. Utilizing BIM side by side with green design principles, our projects and research undergo scientific modeling during the earliest stages of design as the parti is refined. User comfort is evaluated and the design is modeled, helping client, designer, and builder understand the quality of space and experience. Daylight and energy is studied throughout the process. Energy needs are minimized and renewable strategies found to serve the needs of the building. Water use and waste are minimized or eliminated through the modeling and design of the building and site. Fabrication and construction process is anticipated and guided as critical elements of design. Construction waste is identified and redirected as a source for other uses and products.

As a beautiful and powerful landmark for the vision of Thomas Jefferson, the St. Louis Arch is also a reminder of our need to always improve our approach to design and construction. The arch is in balance with nature's force of *gravity*, but also very dependent on resources that tax nature in the form of pollution, waste, global warming, and resource depletion. It is time to move forward.

The proposition of Krygiel and Nies will result in more beautiful, greener buildings, regenerative buildings, and triple bottom line results—good for all people, good for the environment, and responsible to the economics of their clients and communities. As perpetual leaders in sustainable design and building information modeling in design and construction applications, Krygiel and Nies have integrated the principles and benefits of each with innovative, high-performing results.

Today, collaborative design and construction teams are creating buildings with new aspirations. The result has been a new approach to designing and building that has given birth to buildings that strive to achieve balance with nature. These structures harvest energy, capture and clean any water that is needed, use resources efficiently, and exude maximum beauty. The term *Living Building* is associated with this approach to design and construction. These sustainable structures rely on innovation and collaborative design teams. They benefit from scientific processes to understand and model high-performing results in balance with nature and achieve the contemporary needs of building occupancy. The designer and builders are achieving these results using BIM and other design and construction tools to maximize beauty, efficiency, and functionality while minimizing or eliminating impact of the environment. This is possible utilizing the tools and design approach revealed in this book—at the scale necessary to address the impending construction boom spreading across the globe.

Steve McDowell
Principal, BNIM Architects

Introduction

Nothing is as dangerous in architecture as dealing with separated problems. If we split life into separated problems, we split the possibilities to make good building art.

—*Alvar Alto*

Welcome to *Green BIM: Successful Sustainable Design with Building Information Modeling,* which offers a look at two current and growing movements in the architecture, engineering, and construction industry: sustainable design and building information modeling (BIM).

As with any project, architectural or textual, or for that matter, any project that you want to turn out well, it was a lot of work. We won't lie. That said, it was also great fun, and we enjoyed the synergy as designers and collaborators to bring this project into reality. Most importantly, we were driven by a desire to do something that could help the industry universally understand how to better tackle the growing concerns about our impact on the earth's climate by using tested design methodologies together with BIM software.

As we consider the sustainable design strategies in this book, it's important to understand some key concepts about how those strategies integrate with BIM. Relative to architecture and sustainability, BIM is a fairly recent technology. Many of the tools used to measure the impact of sustainable design strategies, old or new, are not directly accessible within a BIM model itself; therefore, data needs to be exported to another application or imported from a data source.

Analysis tools can range from something more complicated like Integrated Environmental Solutions Virtual Environment (IES <VE>), a whole building energy and daylight analysis application that can take months to master, to a universal application like Microsoft Excel. In some cases a team may need to import information to the BIM model from an outside source, such as a database of weather data or material properties. Better and more seamless integration between BIM and sustainable design will come with time as the industry continues to standardize file formats, as data sets are developed, and as owners, clients, and designers begin to demand more from application developers.

We have tried hard throughout this book to avoid promoting one green building rating system or software application over another. Our purpose in this book has been to promote best practices for sustainable design and show how to use BIM to achieve the most sustainable solution. However, as it is not realistic to become an expert on every software application or rating system available on the market, it's important to note that within our own practice we do standardize on a few software programs that support our office's workflow. It is also important to acknowledge that many of our clients prefer the U.S. Green Building Council's (USGBC) Leadership in Energy and Environmental Design (LEED) green building rating system.

Many of the screen shots in this book are software specific. In our own practice, for BIM, we use Autodesk's Revit Architecture (http://www.autodesk.com/Revit). For applications that aid in informing our designs for sustainable solutions, we utilize a host of them at different levels and different phases of design, such as:

- IES <VE> (http://www.iesve.com)
- Ecotect (http://www.ecotect.com)
- Green Building Studio (http://www.greenbuildingstudio.com)
- eQUEST (http://www.doe2.com/equest/)
- EnergyPlus (http://www.energyplus.gov)
- Daysim (http://www.daysim.com)
- Radiance (http://radsite.lbl.gov/radiance/index.html)
- Climate Consultant (http://newton.aud.ucla.edu/energy-design-tools/)
- WUFI-ORNL/IBP (http://web.ornl.gov/sci/btc/apps/moisture/)

  And last but not least:

- Microsoft Excel (http://www.microsoft.com/office)

Yes, we know that looks like an extensive list, but there are even more options available. However, throughout this book, we will be discussing ways to streamline some of that list and find the answers that work best and solve the problems that you will be facing as you reach for more sustainable designs.

As you read this book, bear in mind that we tried to write this for everyone. Some in our industry are knowledgeable about sustainable design and rather new to BIM. Others know a great deal about BIM but might be a little *green* regarding sustainable design. There are also some who feel as if they might need a good overview of both. In this book, we try to address all of these groups.

In the first chapters, we begin with an overview of sustainable design and an overview of BIM, discussing how the design and construction industry has arrived at this crossroads and why we need to look to new approaches and methodologies to solve the problems we've inherited. These problems are based on a number of issues that have evolved over the course of time, such as process problems like information management on larger team sizes or the specialization of the labor force and how that can negatively impact efficiency. Other issues revolve around sustainability, such as climate change, the globalization of materials, and human health and productivity. Because implementing either sustainable design or BIM or both can be drastic changes in a firm's culture and approach to design and delivery, we discuss best practices regarding workflow, integrating project teams, and offer an order of operations approach to sustainable design.

The book continues with core concepts and a deeper understanding of keys to sustainability in building design, touching on building envelope, systems, materiality, and orientation. By adding water and energy, we round out a building's needs, impacts, and opportunities for existing with the natural environment, both on a macro scale (globally) and a micro scale (locally).

Finally, we create the synergies with BIM and discuss how to use the information hosted in the BIM model to better inform the building design and share benefits with the project team.

We conclude with a brief look to the future of all the things we imagine and hope can soon be accomplished because of the value BIM brings to sustainable design.

We hope that you enjoy *Green BIM* and can capitalize on our knowledge and experience to help advance your practice and share innovations with others as we move forward to a more sustainable future.

Best,

Eddy Krygiel

Bradley Nies

Green BIM:
Successful Sustainable Design with Building Information Modeling

1

Introducing Green

The best way to predict the future is to invent it.
—Alan Kay

What you'll find in this chapter is an introduction to what it means to be green *or* sustainable *in the architectural profession and why this has become such an important topic both in the design and construction industry and global culture.*

Sustainability

We, the authors, started our professional careers near the beginning of what Bob Berkebile, FAIA, a founding principal of BNIM Architects, refers to as one of the greatest changes in the profession of architecture in his professional lifetime. The year was 1995 and architects were starting to use terms like *green* and *environmentally friendly* to describe their projects and project approaches. Dialogue, experience, and marketplace transition have allowed the people not only in the profession of architecture but also other professions involved in the design, construction, and operation of the built environment to garner a better understanding of what *green* means. Generally speaking, however, today we think in terms of *sustainability*.

A Brief History of Sustainable Design

The practice of sustainable thinking is in many ways ancient. If we look at the buildings from some of the North American indigenous cultures, we can see that they were highly skilled at adapting the location and materials of their structures to climate and place. For example, igloos constructed in Greenland's Thule area and by the people of Canada's Central Arctic, which were made of materials found on site, were built in a way to create thermal mass and wind resistance. Another example is the Native American teepee, built from both natural plant and animal materials found in the region. The teepee was lightweight and easy to transport for reuse and was designed utilizing natural convection flows for heating and cooling. The ancient Pueblo peoples of the southwest (who are often referred to as the Anasazi) utilized naturally formed cliffs and caves as the location for some of our first sedentary civilizations, adding structures made of earthen materials found on site (Figure 1.1). They understood the sun and natural rock formations enough to utilize passive solar techniques for cooling, heating, and lighting.

Figure 1.1 Cliff Palace at Mesa Verde National Park

Over time as civilizations grew static, buildings took on a different significance. Civic structure and time for play and leisure developed buildings of cultural and political significance. Humankind was no longer building for survival alone. Some examples of this transitional period were the inspiring and elegant structures built by highly skilled craftsmen to last lifetimes. Buildings like St. Peter's Basilica in Vatican City, St. Basil's Cathedral in Moscow, and the Alhambra in Granada, Spain, are now centuries old and still exist today (Figure 1.2).

Image courtesy of Brad Nies

Figure 1.2 St. Peter's Basilica, Vatican City

With the Industrial Revolution came the ability to mass-produce interchangeable building materials more quickly and inexpensively than skilled laborers of the past. The goal of the Industrial Revolution was to conserve human labor while increasing production of all things needed for human society. Herein lay the beginning of prefabrication and interchangeable parts. Natural resources, in the industrial model, were rarely valued at their true cost. Most natural resources were treated as if they were abundant, unlimited, and inexpensive.

As we turned the corner into the early twentieth century, humankind started to master premanufactured materials and components, transporting materials from around the globe. At this stage, buildings were still responding to natural light and natural ventilation with narrow footprints and tall operable windows. However, the invention of better technologies for electric lighting, elevators, and other mechanical systems soon changed our built environment for decades to follow (Figure 1.3).

Image courtesy of Brad Nies

Figure 1.3 The Wainwright Building, one of the world's first skyscrapers, 1891.

As technologies like heating, ventilation, and air-conditioning (HVAC) systems continued to flourish, the building industry moved away from design that was specific to climate, culture, and place and toward uniform standards for all situations. Our built environment relies on developed technology standards that for the most part have been turned into building codes and thereby linked to product warranties. Most of our heating and cooling is mechanical, most of our lighting is artificial, and we get our building materials from anywhere in the world. Starting in the middle of the twentieth century through today, humans, especially North Americans, have continued to develop buildings in each and every one of our major climate zones with no respect for local climate.

We believe the modern understanding of human impact on the natural environment started in the 1960s, with the exact event remaining unclear. The key milestones from that decade that we refer to are the 1962 release of Rachel Carson's best-selling book *Silent Spring*—a book Brad's high school chemistry professor assigned as required reading in 1987—and the passing of the Wilderness Act of 1964.

Silent Spring was the first open look at widespread ecological degradation from poisons, insecticides, weed killers, and other common products.

The Wilderness Act for the first time established a National Wilderness Preservation System and, according to the U.S. Department of Interior, legally protected almost 9 million acres of wilderness in the United States by designating it as preservation area.

Interest continued in the 1970s as a growing number of people realized that humans have a direct impact on the natural environment. Two creations from the 1970s that are still with us today are Earth Day and the U.S. Environmental Protection Agency (EPA).

A U.S. Senator from Wisconsin, Gaylord Nelson, called for an environmental teach-in, or Earth Day, to be held in the spring of 1970. It is estimated that on April 22, 1970, over 20 million Americans participated in demonstrations that year. Earth Day is now coordinated by the nonprofit Earth Day Network and is observed in 175 countries. Earth Day Network claims that Earth Day is now "the largest secular holiday in the world, celebrated by more than a half billion people every year."

The EPA was also founded in 1970 by then-President Richard Nixon. According to the EPA, its mission is "to protect human health and the environment."

Also during the 1970s a small group of design professionals and building occupants started to understand how standard design and construction practices had veered too far away from earlier reliance on natural principles. This short-lived portion of the *Green Building* movement began as a reaction to oil shortages and the political and environmental events of the time. This part of the movement was therefore focused primarily on energy conservation. However, after the oil embargo and the Arab-Israeli and Vietnam wars ended in the middle part of the 1970s, we went back to our path of ecological ignorance, staying in that pattern until the early 1990s.

The period just over a decade long where our thinking lapsed saw several major environmental events that provided plenty of reasons to create change in our human behavior. These negative events were Love Canal, the Amoco Cadiz oil spill, the Three Mile Island nuclear incident, the British/American discovery of the Antarctic ozone hole, and the Exxon Valdez oil spill. One positive event during late 1980s was the adoption of the Montreal Protocol, an international treaty designed to phase out production of substances responsible for ozone depletion.

Recent Trends Toward Sustainable Design

So where did the most recent dialogue about *green* start in the realm of building design and construction? We believe it started in the early 1990s with the formation of the American Institute of Architects (AIA) Committee on the Environment (COTE) and the formation of the U.S. Green Building Council (USGBC).

During the 1970s portion of the Green Building movement, the AIA formed the Energy Committee. According to AIA historical documents, committee members created documents that helped the AIA lobby Capitol Hill and collaborated with government agencies for energy efficiency. Unfortunately, the committee's efforts lost steam as the price of energy became more affordable. Leaders from this group strived to keep energy and environmental concerns as a major design topic, and support surfaced at the 1989 AIA Convention in St. Louis, Missouri. AIA Kansas City Chapter President Kirk Gastinger, FAIA (AIA Fellow), and president-elect Bob Berkebile, FAIA, presented Critical Planet Rescue (CPR), a measure calling for the Institute to sponsor research and to develop a resource guide to help architects and their clients to act responsibly. A combination of national support for CPR and more than $1 million of grant funding from the EPA led to the formation of AIA/COTE at the 1990 convention.

AIA/COTE

AIA/COTE continues to be a large part of the continuing dialogue with industry partners, communities, not-for-profit organizations, and government agencies about sustainable design. As a result of being a part of this dialogue, there are two key things that AIA/COTE has contributed to moving us all forward. First is AIA/COTE's original top priority, which was the creation and publication of the Environmental Resource Guide (ERG) from 1992 to 1998. Second is the creation of the AIA/COTE Top Ten Green Projects program in 1997, a program that still runs today.

The ERG was funded primarily by the EPA grant and produced by the early members of AIA/COTE and a Scientific Advisory Group on the Environment (SAGE), which was comprised of nonarchitectural partners. The purpose of the ERG was to provide architects and others in the building industry a basis for comparing the environmental impact of building materials, products, and systems. This was accomplished by a simplified method and consistent format for assessing the environmental impacts of building materials from their original extraction and manufacture to their final disposal or reuse. The ERG exemplified the following ideals that are foundational to sustainable thinking:

- The understanding that dialogue about solutions must be multidisciplinary
- The latest information even if developing should be shared for a broader perspective and understanding
- That everyone can contribute to a better understanding

The AIA/COTE's Top Ten Green Projects program (http://www.aiatopten.org/) was created to share built examples of successful integrated thinking so that others can learn. Both the Department of Energy (DoE) and EPA have been involved with support since the beginning of the program. Currently, the EPA Energy Star program, the DoE, and Building Green Inc. provide support for the Top Ten Green Projects awards (Figure 1.4).

Image courtesy of Richard Payne, FAIA

Figure 1.4 University of Texas School of Nursing AIA COTE Top 10 Winner in 2006

The program is open to any project that has been designed by an architect licensed in the United States and completed by a selected date. Project teams submit projects electronically plus one printed board to be judged according to AIA/COTE's following ten "Measures of Sustainable Design and Performance Metrics":

- Design and Innovation
- Regional/Community Design
- Land Use and Site Ecology

- Bioclimatic Design

- Light and Air

- Water Cycle

- Energy Flows and Energy Future

- Materials and Construction

- Long Life, Loose Fit

- Collective Wisdom and Feedback Loops

The multidiscipline invited jury reviews both the qualitative and quantitative information provided by the project team and then awards ten projects a Top Ten award, solidifying those projects as some of the greenest buildings that year. According to the AIA, the number of project submissions continues to grow each year. During the first year there were only around 15 entries. Then from 1998 to 2004 entries grew from just over 20 to around 45. From 2005 to 2006, entries hovered around 60–65, and in 2007 the number jumped to 100.

The USGBC

The USGBC (http://www.usgbc.org), a nonprofit organization, was formed in 1993 with the intent to help define and promote sustainable building practices. Several original steering committee members from AIA/COTE participated in the early steering of the USGBC. One of the primary differences between the groups is that the USGBC is not beholden to any one profession; it includes all building industry professionals. A main staple of the USGBC is the Leadership in Energy and Environmental Design (LEED) green building rating system, which we will cover in depth later in this chapter in the section "Green Building Rating Systems."

As a result of defining standards for measuring how green a building is, the USGBC has established itself as a recognized trade name that manufacturers, building designers, contractors, and owners use to compete for third-party recognition that what they do, offer, or produce is recognized as green. Much like the ERG, LEED has educated the building construction industry, building owners, and designers. It has also raised consumer awareness of better, greener buildings. A testament to this is the rapid growth of both the LEED program and the USGBC membership. As last reported by the USGBC in 2007, they have 12,400 member companies and organizations, quadruple the number from five years prior. Individuals from these companies participate in over 72 local chapter components, and attendance at the national conference, Greenbuild, has grown to more than 20,000 people. Through 2007, according the USGBC, over 3 billion square feet of building space are a part of the LEED program (Figure 1.5).

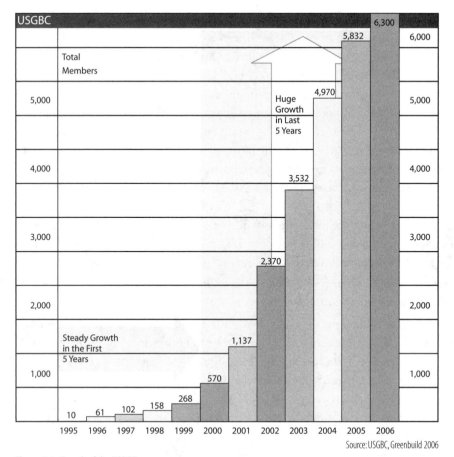

Figure 1.5 Growth of the USBGC

Groups like AIA/COTE, the USGBC, and others have defined what a *green building* is and tirelessly continue to educate the industry. Unfortunately, that definition is still widely debated even within the systems that have been created for our daily use. Is a green building sustainable? Can a building be considered green without achieving complete sustainability? As our knowledge has increased, rightly so have our questions.

Defining Sustainable Design

Before moving forward, we should be clear about the terms *green* and *sustainable*. What does being *green* mean to you? Undoubtedly it will mean something a bit different to you than the person next to you. In fact, in only the past few years has the term become common outside of the industry. In 2005 if you told someone that you were designing a green building, you would have to follow up with an explanation about how that meant it was environmentally friendly, not the color green. In a nutshell, that is how the term was and still is widely used—a green building has less of an impact on the natural environment than the traditional buildings the industry has completed over the last three decades. Only recently have we been able to quantify this impact.

Industry language has transitioned from using the term *green* to *sustainable*. This has made the definition of sustainable design more cumbersome but is definitely a vast improvement in how we think about our buildings. A *sustainable* design is better than a *green* one because sustainability takes into account a greater array of impacts than just those that burden the natural environment.

For example, whereas green building of the early 1990s might have contained some materials with some recycled content, a building of today that is approaching sustainability will consider the whole lifecycle of the product. Designers, contractors, and owners consider raw material extraction, manufacture location and processes, durability, reuse, and ability of the material to be recycled. We will cover more examples later in this book.

So what is the best definition for sustainable design? We find the World Commission on the Environment and Development, also known as the Brundtland Commission, offered the best definition in the 1987 report to the United Nations:

> *Sustainable development meets the needs of the present without compromising the ability of future generations to meet their own needs.*

According to the report, the commission was convened by the United Nations in 1983 to address growing concern "about the accelerating deterioration of the human environment and natural resources and the consequences of that deterioration for economic and social development." In establishing the commission, the UN General Assembly recognized that environmental problems were global in nature and determined that it was in the common interest of all nations to establish policies for sustainable development. The 1987 report, published as "Our Common Future," deals with sustainable development and the change of politics needed for achieving that change.

In his 1998 book, *Cannibals with Forks*, John Elkington offers a deeper look into the definition of sustainability. Elkington described a concept called *Triple Bottom Line* accounting. In this form of accounting, entities would take into account their environmental and social performance in addition to their economic performance (Figure 1.6). These three areas, which we refer to as People, Planet, and Prosperity, are commonly called the three legs of the sustainability stool. We believe that correctly balancing decisions over all three areas results in a sustainable solution.

With a broader range of thinking and understanding being developed about sustainability, the building industry is also exploring the deeper meanings. Language in the building industry still remains loose, using the terms green and sustainable interchangeably. As criteria for sustainable design principles have been explored, several leading thinkers have tested designs and written about the differences between green design and sustainable design. Two documents from the first decade in the twenty-first century address the difference.

People   Prosperity

Planet

Image Courtesy of BNIM Architects

Figure 1.6 The Triple Bottom Line

One document is "Building for Sustainability" (2002) by BNIM Architects in close collaboration with Keen Engineering, Oppenheim Lewis, Hawley Peterson & Snyder Architects, and the Facilities Steering Committee of the Packard Foundation. The document is freely available at `http://www.bnim.com/fmi/xsl/research/packard/index.xsl`. In two parts, *The Sustainability Report* and *The Sustainability Matrix*, this document describes the process and results of an exercise completed during the early design phase of the David and Lucile Packard Foundation's Los Altos Project.

The Sustainability Report and The Sustainability Matrix were created in response to the Packard Foundation's query about how to develop a decision-making tool to explain the impacts of different levels of green for the proposed project. Developing an answer to the question was accomplished by designing six solutions, based on the same program, same site, and meeting the required building codes, changing the design to increase environmental performance. The solutions are organized around meeting the four different green building certification levels of the USGBC LEED Rating System (more information later in this chapter), plus one standard market design and one beyond LEED that approaches sustainability. Impacts for each of the six solutions were quantified in the categories of Building Form, Energy, Pollution, and External Cost to Society, Schedules (Design and Construction), and Short- and Long-Term Costs (Design and Construction).

The design solution that went beyond LEED was conceptualized as a *Living Building*. In "Building for Sustainability," a Living Building is defined as having zero net annual impact on the environment from an operational standpoint. It provides its own energy and water, cleans its own wastes, and emits no pollution. The report authors also acknowledge that a truly sustainable building would mitigate impacts during design and construction.

When reviewing the report many professionals are primarily interested in the first cost premium for each solution. Compared to the market, building the green solutions of LEED Certified, Silver, Gold, and Platinum cost 1%, 13%, 15%, and 21%, respectively. The most sustainable solution, the Living Building, had an increased first cost of 29% compared to the market building, yet it was more cost effective to construct, own, and operate than the market building in less than 30 years' time. This is where the financially conscious person's attention should be focused—the total cost. The data showed that over a 100-year span, the Living Building wouldn't incur the costs associated with the market building over 30 years.

Today, just five years later, the state of California has updated its building codes, and the design solutions with the two lowest levels of environmental performance from "Building for Sustainability," the market building and the LEED Certified building, would not meet the current California Energy Code. This would change the premium between the market building and the Living Building to only 14%.

The other document addressing the difference between green and sustainable design is the Trajectory of Environmentally Responsive Design (2006) by Integrative Design Collaborative. The design pattern described in this document is shown in Figure 1.7 and follows the thinking described so far, but also takes it to the next level. The text refers to a truly sustainable design as neutral, or as this document attributes to Bill McDonough, a sustainable building is just "100% less bad." To truly have an environmentally and socially responsible design solution, we must go beyond sustainable design and start thinking about how our built environment can actively restore our planet or even work as an integral part of the system helping it regenerate.

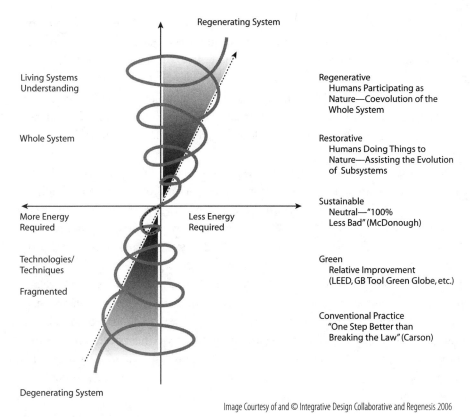

Regenerating System

Living Systems
Understanding

Whole System

More Energy
Required

Less Energy
Required

Technologies/
Techniques

Fragmented

Degenerating System

Regenerative
Humans Participating as
Nature—Coevolution of the
Whole System

Restorative
Humans Doing Things to
Nature—Assisting the Evolution
of Subsystems

Sustainable
Neutral—"100%
Less Bad" (McDonough)

Green
Relative Improvement
(LEED, GB Tool Green Globe, etc.)

Conventional Practice
"One Step Better than
Breaking the Law" (Carson)

Image Courtesy of and © Integrative Design Collaborative and Regenesis 2006

Figure 1.7 Trajectory of Environmental Responsibility

Why Is Sustainable Design Important?

Now that we have better defined sustainability, let's talk about why it is important. As stated before, the three widely accepted legs of the sustainability stool are People, Planet, and Prosperity. Given human nature, each of us might tend to value one a little bit more than the other two, but the more that we can make the three of them balance out, the better our design solution will be.

People

As designers, we have a code of ethics that includes our responsibility to protect life. Traditionally, this responsibility has been viewed as the lives of occupants within our buildings. In reality, the choices that we make also affect human life beyond a particular building or site. The impact of our choices ranges from those who manufactured the materials and products the building is composed of to the inhabitants in places up and downstream from the building.

There have been some commonly used materials in buildings that are suspected or known to have harmful toxins, carcinogens, endocrine disruptors, or other harmful chemicals. People can be exposed to these substances either during manufacture, an emergency event such as a fire, or in some cases just by occupancy. Also there are naturally occurring substances in materials that off-gas and accumulate in greater quantities when enclosed within the building envelope. As the industry learned from asbestos treated materials and chromated copper arsenate (CCA)–treated wood, the temporary benefits of these materials are not worth the long-term potential to harm building users. We must eliminate the use of such materials when there is an appropriate alternative. The industry must also strive to develop alternatives when a material has become suspect.

Other factors, and of no less importance, that influence the health and well-being of building occupants include noise, temperature, humidity, access to fresh air, daylight, and views and the ability to control them. Most owners should have the well-being of their employees in mind because oftentimes the cost of employees, not to mention attracting and keeping the best ones, outweighs the first cost and operational cost of the building. Sometimes people are the company's most expensive investment.

The USGBC has compiled many of the studies that have been done on the relationship between green buildings and people. They make them all freely available on the Green Building Research page of their website, http://www.usgbc.org. Studies have found that green buildings have human health and productivity benefits, such as better test performance in schools, earlier discharges from hospitals, increased sales in retail environments, increased production in factories, and increased productivity in the office environment.

Planet

With her book *Silent Spring*, Rachel Carson started making us aware of our impact on the planet. Since then many metrics have been developed to compare past, present, and future patterns against. The built environment has played a major part over the years.

According to the USGBC and the U.S. Census Bureau, buildings in the United States consume 30% of the world's total energy and 60% of the world's electricity annually for only 4.5% of the world's population. The energy consumption by buildings results in pollution, ozone depletion, and global warming, which in turn causes health problems for every living species. The natural resources used to make buildings are either nonrenewable, such as plastic or steel, or harvested more quickly than they can be replenished, like wood from the old-growth forests. According to the USGBC, buildings also consume 5 billion gallons of potable water per day to flush toilets, more than enough clean water wasted to provide every person in the world with clean drinking water. The USGBC LEED Reference Guide warns that the typical North American commercial construction project generates 2.5 pounds of solid waste per square foot of floor space.

In 2005, Capital E, a clean energy strategic consulting firm led by Greg Kats, studied all the buildings that had achieved LEED certification to that point. Capital E has calculated that green buildings have an average energy savings of 30%, a 35% reduction of carbon on average, a 30–50% savings in potable water use, and a 50–97% reduction in landfilled wastes.

A current metric that has garnered a lot of attention lately is carbon. The term *carbon* is actually used as a catchall for greenhouse gas emissions because it accounts for about 80% of all greenhouse gases. The built environment has many pathways for generating greenhouse gas emissions. First we think of the energy a building uses to operate. In the United States, that energy is primarily from a coal-fired power plant, one of our dirtiest sources of energy. Next are the emissions from constructing the building, which includes the harvesting, manufacturing, and transportation of the materials to the site. Finally there is the location of our building; if the building is located such that the majority of users must drive to it, we by default create an additional carbon load.

According to Architecture 2030 (`http://www.architecture2030.org`; a nonprofit, nonpartisan, and independent organization), data from the U.S. Energy Information Association (EIA; accounting for the embodied energy of materials and the operations of buildings) shows that buildings in the United States account for 48% of all greenhouse gas emissions.

Prosperity

The continued importance for role of the prosperity leg, which has traditionally driven most corporate decisions, often surprises some of the newest triple-bottom-line thinkers. Green design as we know it today has cost benefits, and the cost benefits of a sustainable design are rapidly developing shorter return on investment times.

Of primary interest to many building owners is the first cost premium traditionally associated with green buildings. As mentioned before, the 2002 "Building for Sustainability" document showed a rising cost premium with each level of green, culminating in a 29% first cost difference between a Living Building and a Market Building. While third parties verified all of that data, the building was never built.

In 2003 Capital E looked at 33 LEED-certified buildings in California and found that the average first cost premium across all levels of LEED certification was less than 2%. Davis Langdon, an international construction cost management consulting firm, reviewed both LEED and non-LEED projects nationally and found that the level of green doesn't necessarily determine the first cost. Davis Langdon first reported this in their 2004 report "Costing Green" and then again in "The Cost of Green Revisited (2007)."

Many of the strategies used to create healthier spaces for people have utility operational cost savings, but those savings are normally a drop in the bucket compared to the productivity gains mentioned earlier in this section. A 1% improvement in work-force productivity likely outweighs the utility cost savings because people are the most expensive investment a company has by the time you factor in the salaries and benefits.

Whichever leg of the stool you want to most align yourself with, make sure you honor the other two for balance and the most holistic return on your effort.

Green Building Rating Systems

The first building project Brad worked on was an elementary school. When the project team asked the owners if they had any environmental goals, they responded, "Yes, use 25% recycled plastic toilet partitions." By incorporating this trendy product of the time, they felt that they were doing their part for the planet. Little did any of us know that many of our other decisions addressed issues that today are considered green-building features. During that project, the team doubled the amount of windows in each classroom compared to previous models, provided operable windows, and designed daylight clerestories with shading and glare control in public and assembly spaces. These design features have since been proven by many researchers to increase the health, productivity, and learning of school occupants by making a better environment. They also represent criteria of the model green building rating systems.

According to Fowler and Rauch's "Sustainable Building Rating Systems Summary" in 2006, there were over 34 green building rating systems or environmental assessment tools available to the marketplace, and the number is likely to grow. In our opinion, here are the five primary developing players in green building rating systems:

- Comprehensive Assessment System for Building Environmental Efficiency (CASBEE)
- SBTool (formerly known as GBTool)
- Building Research Establishment's Environmental Assessment Method (BREEAM)
- Green Globes U.S.
- LEED (Leadership in Energy and Environmental Design)

Each of these in some part was developed to promote environmentally responsible design, construction, and operating approaches as well as transform the built environment and marketplace as we traditionally understand it. All of them offer some form of score so that the high-performance claims of projects can be compared openly, at least within each system.

In the following sections, we provide our review of the five leading systems based on our experiences and our study of documents available at the respective organizations' websites, rating system guides, and tools developed for using the systems. We've provided the website for each organization for your use.

CASBEE

CASBEE (http://www.ibec.or.jp/CASBEE/english/) is the newest of the systems and was developed in 2001 for use in Japan through cooperation of academia, industry, and government under the Japan Sustainable Building Consortium (JSBC). The system has been developed for New Construction (NC), Existing Buildings (EB), Renovations (RN), Heat Islands (HI), and Urban Developments (UD). Only the 2004 NC version is available in English, but it is downloadable from the CASBEE website for free.

CASBEE distinguishes itself from the others in that it is founded on a new principal of Building Environmental Efficiency (the BEE portion) as the major indicator of overall performance. The two parts to this principal are the Building Environmental Loadings (L), which is defined as the impact of the building on the outside world beyond a hypothetical project boundary, and Building Environmental Quality and Performance (Q), which is defined as improvements for the building users within a hypothetical project boundary. Users are encouraged to think about the project boundary as the division between private and public property. It is represented by the system as the following equation:

$$BEE = \frac{\text{Building Environmental Quality and Performance (Q)}}{\text{Building Environmental Loadings (L)}}$$

Overall, 100 subitems are scored within the three major categories of Q and L. Criteria for Q are developed from Indoor Environment, Quality of Service, and Outdoor Environment on Site issues. Criteria for L are developed from Energy, Resources and Materials, and Off-Site Environment issues. Each area is scored on a scale of 1 through 5, with 3 being average and 1 being the worst. Results from comparing the quality and the load reduction are plotted on the graph, as shown in Figure 1.8, and the better buildings will graph a scenario of high quality with the least environmental load. The final score of the project is put on a graph and graded C (poor) through B–, B+, A, and S (excellent). We have been unable to find a U.S. project that has used this system.

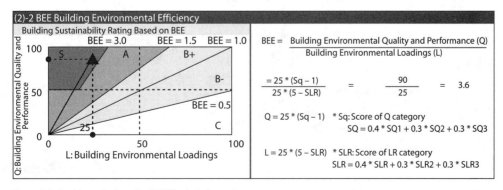

Figure 1.8 Graphic results from the CASBEE calculation tool

17

■ SUSTAINABILITY

SBTool

SBTool (http://greenbuilding.ca/iisbe/sbc2k8/sbc2k8-download_f.htm) is the current generation of GBTool, which was launched in 1998 as part of the Green Building Challenge (GBC), a program developed by Natural Resources Canada. In 2002, the International Initiative for a Sustainable Built Environment (IISBE) took over responsibility of running the GBC and has since renamed it to the Sustainable Building Challenge (SBC).

Similar to CASBEE, SBTool is a framework tool for assessing buildings based on environmental performance. The overall framework has 116 parameters spread over seven main categories. Those categories are:

- Site Selection, Project Planning, and Development
- Energy and Resource Consumption
- Environmental Loadings
- Indoor Environmental Quality
- Service Quality
- Social and Economic Aspects
- Cultural and Perceptual Aspects

One of the unique claims to this system is that it is highly adaptable to local needs and conditions. This is intentional and explains why more than 20 countries around the world are able to participate in the SBC and the development of the SBTool. As part of the adaptability, building performance is related to nationally established baselines or benchmarks. The IISBE notes that the scoring is meaningless unless the national team has established the baseline values. In other words, it only becomes a rating tool for a region if the performance baselines are agreed to. In an attempt to have further flexibility, the IISBE also touts that the SBTool can be used for projects of all sizes, commercial or residential, as well as both new construction and renovation.

The tool comes in three parts. First is the tool for noting and weighting the appropriate standards for the region the project is in. Second is a tool for the design team to describe all the project information. Last is the assessment form, which is based on information from the first two forms. At the current development stage, the IISBE recommends using the system for design assessments only.

BREEAM

BREEAM (http://www.breeam.org) has been most widely used in the United Kingdom and is the oldest of the five, getting its start in 1990. According to BREEAM, versions are updated regularly in line with UK Building Regulations. BREEAM assesses the performance of buildings in the following areas:

- Management
- Health and Well-Being

- Energy

- Transport

- Water

- Material and Waste

- Land Use and Ecology

- Pollution

An officially trained assessor assesses the project to develop the overall rating for the project. A first assessment can be done at the end of the design stage, with the final assessment coming after occupancy. Becoming an assessor is open to all building professionals who are trained by the BREEAM quality assurance body called BRE.

Credits are awarded in each area according to performance and then added together through a combined weighting process. Finally, the building is rated on a scale of Pass, Good, Very Good, or Excellent, and a certificate awarded to the project. Although BREEAM was originally available in two types, one for office and one for homes, it is now available in a range of building types: offices, homes, industrial, multiresidential, prisons, retail, and schools.

Achievement of BREEAM ratings is required by several UK organizations, including English Partnerships, the Office of Government Commerce, the Department for Children Schools and Families, the Housing Corporation, and the Welsh Assembly. BREEAM has caught on in other countries, and they have developed a tool called BREEAM International to assist with this. Additionally, BREEAM has been used as the basis for other assessment tools.

Green Globes

Green Globes (http://www.greenglobes.com) is one of the systems that grew out of BREEAM. Green Globes first appeared as an online version of BREEAM for existing buildings in Canada in 2000. In 2002 it was adapted for use in the design of new buildings, and then in 2004 it was converted to a U.S. version, which is distributed and run by the Green Building Initiative (GBI). Recently, GBI became accredited as an American National Standards Institute (ANSI) standards developer, and they are in the process of trying to establish Green Globes as an official ANSI standard.

The Green Globes tool itself is questionnaire based. To that end teams are expected to answer questionnaires and review recommendations developed from their answers at each stage of the design process. The rating system is based on the construction document questionnaire. The point system includes up to 1,000 points across the system's seven main sections:

Project Management—Policies and Practices	50 points
Site	115 points
Energy	360 points
Water	100 points
Resources, Building Materials and Solid Waste	100 points
Emissions and Effluents	75 points
Indoor Environment	200 points

The final Green Globes rating is expressed by a number of globes from one to four. The number of globes is based on the percentage of points successfully obtained:

1 Globe	35–54%
2 Globes	55–69 %
3 Globes	70–84%
4 Globes	85–100%

A unique thing about Green Globes is the focus given to lifecycle assessment (LCA); the majority of the Resources points are LCA related. According to GBI, "LCA considers materials over the course of their entire lives and takes into account a full range of environmental impact indicators—including embodied energy, solid waste, air and water pollution, and global warming potential." To assist project teams in developing a better understanding of these impacts, GBI commissioned the Athena Institute, one of the North American leaders in LCA, in association with the University of Minnesota and Morrison Hershfield Consulting Engineers, to develop the ATHENA EcoCalculator for Assemblies. The tool provides information on common building assemblies and has since been made available to anyone free of charge (http://www.athenasmi.ca).

An original goal behind the creation of the Green Globes system was to provide a simple, online, self-assessment tool. While this allows flexibility and cost savings compared to other rating systems, it can make the credibility of the assessment suspect. To that end, Green Globes has recently developed a third-party verification system. Verification is provided by a Green Globes trained licensed architect or engineer who has been approved by GBI. Precertification can be obtained after the construction document stage, with the final rating and ability to use the Green Globe certification coming after the Green Globes verifier reviews the completed project. Buildings that have been third-party verified for certification receive a plaque for display. Green Globes estimates the average total cost for all assessments to be $4,500 to $5,500. Currently no organizations require Green Globes ratings for their buildings.

LEED

The USGBC introduced the LEED (http://www.usgbc.org) green building rating system in 1998 as LEED for New Construction (LEED-NC), making it the second oldest system of the five described here. The rating system has two key fundamental attributes.

First it was developed with an open consensus–based process, with input from a broad range of building industry professionals and other experts, including the U.S. Department of Energy. Second, and common to the other systems, using LEED is voluntary. A goal behind creating the LEED system was to establish a measurement standard for what is considered a *green* building, comparing them on an even playing field. At the time of creation, some U.S. practitioners were finding it difficult to decipher the claims of their competitors and building product manufacturers who also had started campaigns about how environmentaly conscious their product or building was.

With its required third-party certification, LEED made it clear which buildings were high-performance green buildings and which ones were not. Under the LEED-NC system, buildings are judged via a 69-point credit system in five categories of environmental performance and one additional area for innovative strategies (Figure 1.9). The five major categories and credits available in each are:

- Sustainable Sites (14 points)
- Water Efficiency (5 points)
- Energy and Atmosphere (17 points)
- Materials and Resources (13 points)
- Indoor Environmental Quality (15 points)
- Innovation and Design (5 points)

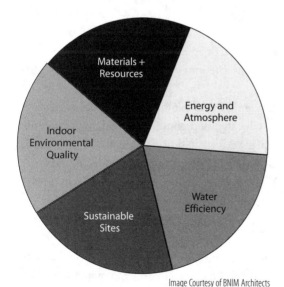

Image Courtesy of BNIM Architects

Figure 1.9 The five sections of the USGBC LEED rating system

In addition to the points, seven prerequisites must be met to participate in the program. These are considered the basics of a green building, such as construction pollution prevention, a recycling program, no smoking, no chlorofluorocarbon (CFC) refrigerants, basic building commissioning, minimum indoor air quality performance, and a baseline for energy performance. Up until June 26, 2007, once those seven prerequisites were met, the points attempted were left up to the team. It was at this time, in reaction to stakeholder cries for more progressive energy efficiency requirements, that the USGBC made achieving the first two Optimize Energy Performance points required as well.

To show credit achievement, the team must document in an online system per the LEED-NC Reference Guide how the project achieved each attempted credit. After the construction document phase, the team can submit design credits for a cursory review. Only after construction is complete can the team submit the project to the USGBC for certification. The total credits achieved in each category are added together for the final score to determine the level of certification awarded to the project. The four levels of certification are as follows:

LEED Certified   26–32 points
LEED Silver   33–38 points)
LEED Gold   39–51 points
LEED Platinum   52+ points

A plaque is provided to the building owner for display in the building upon successful certification. This clear, simple, verified system has been greeted with rapid adoption across the U.S. building design and construction industry. Originally developed for use in the United States, buildings have earned LEED in 13 other countries.

The USGBC has updated the LEED NC program three times since its inception, making the system more challenging and user friendly each time. Also, the USGBC has developed specific versions of LEED for Core and Shell Development (CS), Commercial Interiors (CI), Existing Buildings (EB), Homes (H), Schools (S), and Retail (R). As of June 2007, there are over 900 certified buildings and almost 7,000 more that are registered to seek certification.

As a result of LEED entering the marketplace, the building industry, building owners, and design practitioners have been educated and consumers made more aware. A key part of this education has been the LEED Accredited Professionals (AP) program. Individuals can show their proficiency with the LEED system and at understanding green building practices by taking the LEED accredited professionals exam. Individuals who succeed may use the designation LEED AP after their name. This is yet another level of competition among design and construction firms. One of our partners on the Building for Sustainability project, KEEN Engineering at one time had the largest amount of LEED APs. They celebrated each individual's achievement with a hockey jersey bearing the firms' KEEN Green logo. This can be a fun, inner-firm competition. We annually hold LEED Accreditation workshops open to all BNIM Architects' employees.

As a testament to how well received and beneficial the LEED program is, a number of federal government agencies, states, and local municipalities require LEED certification. The following facts were gathered from the USGBC website:

- The Department of Agriculture, Department of Agriculture-Forest Service, Department of Health and Human Services, Environmental Protection Agency, National Aeronautics and Space Administration, Smithsonian Institution, U.S. Army, U.S. Navy, and the General Services Administration all require LEED Certification, and some require achieving the Gold Level.
- More than half U.S. states have laws requiring project of specific sizes to meet LEED certification standards, six of them requiring actual certification. Ninety-two cities have adopted LEED standards of some form in ordinances, mostly for municipally owned developments.
- Washington, D.C. has provisions for requiring LEED Certification for private developments starting in 2008.
- In January 2008, the town of Greensburg, Kansas, became the first city in the United States to require LEED Platinum Certification for all city buildings.

As great as these rating systems are and have been for the industry, none of them are set up to produce or lead a team to a sustainable building—only a green one that is less bad than what we've seen over the past few decades.

Living Buildings: The Near Future of Sustainable Design

It was only a short nine years ago when the USGBC launched LEED into the marketplace and changed the course of design for many professionals. In 2006 at Greenbuild, the USGBC national conference, the Cascadia Region Green Building Council launched the Living Building Challenge (LBC) (http://www.cascadiagbc.org/lbc) with remarks from Jason F. McLennan, Cascadia GBC CEO, and Bob Berkebile FAIA.

Unlike the current green building rating systems, LBC is based on what the building does, not what it is designed to do. As the name suggests, the building must achieve living status in that it has zero net annual impact on the environment from an operational and construction perspective. Buildings are judged on 16 different achievements referred to as prerequisites. Simply put, the project either complies or it doesn't.

The 16 prerequisites are spread across six areas as follows:
- Site Design
  - Responsible Site Selection
  - Limits to Growth
  - Habitat Exchange
- Energy
  - Net Zero Energy
- Materials
  - Materials Red List
  - Construction Carbon Footprint
  - Responsible Industry

- Appropriate Materials/Service Radius
- Leadership in Construction Waste
- Water
  - Net Zero Water
  - Sustainable Water Discharge
- Indoor Environmental Quality
  - A Civilized Work Environment
  - Healthy Air/Source Control
  - Healthy Air/Ventilation
- Beauty and Inspiration
  - Beauty and Spirit
  - Inspiration and Education

In 1997 Brad worked with Bob, Jason and a highly diverse team of integrated professionals on the Montana State University Epicenter, a project which started defining the idea of a Living Building. Unfortunately, it was never built, but it did define a new benchmark to be reached. In our opinion, the Adam Joseph Lewis Center at Oberlin College, by William McDonough + Partners, currently represents the closest a completed building has come to achieving these high marks (see Figure 1.10). However, we believe in the near future there will be many actual Living Buildings as the LBC is where LEED stood only nine years ago. As the industry prevails as experienced integrated design teams, we will move on to achieve projects that are restorative and then ultimately regenerative.

Figure 1.10 Adam Joseph Lewis Center, Oberlin College

Building Information Modeling

2

A great building begins with the immeasurable, must go through measurable means when it is being designed, and in the end must be immeasurable.
—Louis Kahn

Building information modeling (BIM) is an emerging tool in the design industry that is used to design and document a project, but is also used as a vehicle to enhance communication among all the project stakeholders. This tool has already begun changing how designers work with their consultants and with builders, but it also has the ability to help guide the industry in a more sustainable direction by allowing easier access to the tools necessary to quantify a greener design approach.

In this chapter we will discuss what BIM can mean to the team as a whole and how it can help to inform the basis of a sustainable design workflow.

What Is BIM?

In the architectural, engineering, and construction (AEC) industry, there is a misconception by some that BIM is only a piece of software. Although the software is a necessary part of this process, it is much more than an application (we'll explain all this in more detail throughout this chapter). When we refer to BIM, we are discussing the methodology or process that BIM creates.

A BIM model, on the other hand, is a grammatically incorrect term that has become somewhat commonplace to refer specifically to the digital model created by the software in a BIM-based process.

BIM is a relatively recent switch in design and documentation methodology in the design and construction industries. BIM is information about the entire building and a complete set of design documents stored in an integrated database. All the information is parametric and thereby interconnected. Any changes to an object within the model are instantly reflected throughout the rest of the project in all views. A BIM model contains the building's actual constructions and assemblies rather than a two-dimensional representation of the building that is commonly found in CAD-based drawings (see Figure 2.1).

Image courtesy of BNIM Architects

Figure 2.1 A BIM model

BIM is defined as the creation and use of coordinated, consistent, computable information about a building project in design—parametric information used for design decision making, production of high-quality construction documents, prediction of building performance, cost estimating, and construction planning.

A BIM model can be holistically used throughout the design process and the construction process. For instance, it aids a design team by allowing parametric changes to a building design by speeding up the design process. If you move a wall in a plan, it is reflected in the elevations, sections, and other related views in a documentation set. After that model is brought to a level of completion by the design team, it can then be delivered to the contractor. She or he can use the model for on-site visualization of the design intent to get an understanding of what the space should look like when complete instead of the 2D abstraction provided in the drawing set. The contractor can additionally use the model for quantity take-offs and glean real-time material quantities. So, in a wall example, the contractor could tell instantly how much gypsum board or insulation is needed to build the wall. Eventually owners can use BIM for managing and operating the facility and all of the information that surrounds it by scheduling the materials and furnishings in the project.

BIM has shifted how designers and contractors look at the entire building process from preliminary design, through construction documentation, into actual construction, and even into postconstruction building management. With BIM, you create a parametric 3D model used to autogenerate traditional building abstractions such as plans, sections, elevations, details, and schedules. Drawings are not collections of manually coordinated lines, but interactive representations of the model. Working in a model-based framework guarantees that a change in one view will propagate to all other views of the model. As you shift elements in plan, those changes appear dynamically in elevation and section. If you remove a door from your model, the software simultaneously removes the door from all views and your door schedule is updated. This enhanced system allows unprecedented control over the quality and coordination of the document set while providing tools for quick analysis of energy use and material consumption. Figure 2.2 graphically demonstrates this concept.

In a CAD-based method, each view is drawn separately with no inherit relationship between drawings. The CAD-based drawings are simply a collection of all the manually generated files. In a BIM-based system, the focus and effort is placed within the BIM model. This BIM model then has the ability to generate the plans, sections, detail, and so forth.

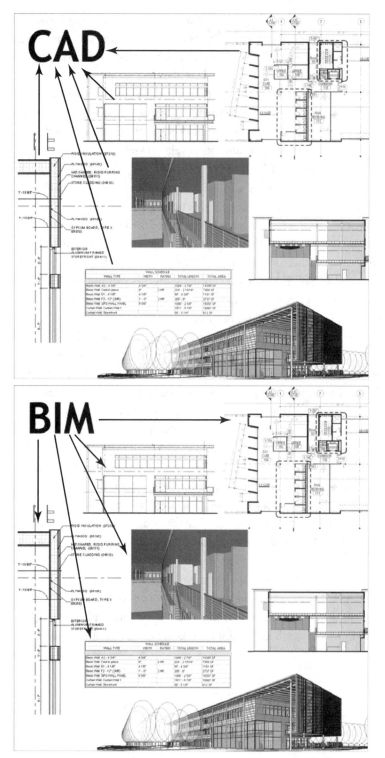

Figure 2.2 A graphical representation of a CAD- and a BIM-based system

Why Is BIM Important?

BIM is certainly not the only tool in the palette, but it is one of growing importance to help designers, contractors, and owners manage the ever-increasing amount of information and complexity in a project. Before we begin discussing BIM's role in detail, let's investigate some of the reasons that have necessitated a switch in our methodology and ways of thinking.

Over the past 100 years, the design and building industry has changed dramatically. Buildings have become much more complex with many more interrelated and integrated systems. During this period, we have added a number of building systems and other layers of design that either didn't exist to the same level of complexity they did before or simply didn't exist at all. If you consider the modern office building, in the last 100 years, we've added data and telecom, air conditioning, security, sustainability, underground parking, and enhancements to building envelopes, to name just a few specialties. Figure 2.3 shows some of the layers that now encompass a building design.

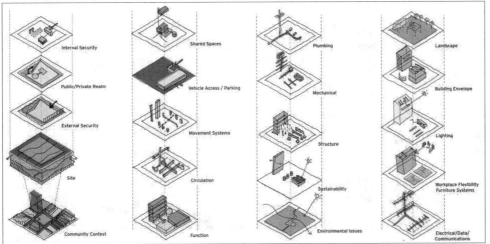

Image courtesy of BNIM Architects

Figure 2.3 Layers of design

With the added complexity, architects, owners, and contractors have all had to adapt to these changes. These layers have required more documentation on the part of the architect to design the project, with many more sheets and details added to the drawing sets. This has in turn demanded more time to coordinate all of these systems, coordinate and manage the additional trades and installers on site for the contractor, and demanded a more knowledgeable staff to maintain these systems on the part of the owner. These increases in specialization, scale, and complexity have added time and cost to the process and lifecycle of the building. These and other factors have led to an overall decline in building performance and an increase in energy consumption.

To analyze these factors in a bit more detail, it is necessary to get a wider picture of the design and construction industry over the past few decades. By looking at historic industry trends, we can see where we have been regarding time, energy, and other resources. If we don't consider a change in our methods to adapt to the changing environment of design and construction, we can only expect these trends to continue.

This analysis will allow us to glean a better understanding of where we need to focus our energy to implement change. Figure 2.4 is a chart that shows the material flow (in tons) in industry from the year 1900 until 2000. The upper portion of the graph shows materials that the construction industry uses, while the other areas represent other primary industries. Although all industries overall have shown an increase in the use of materials over this 100-year period, the construction industry's use has been the most significant. The construction industry's material use was fairly steady until the post–World War II era. After this timeframe, material use rises to an alarming level.

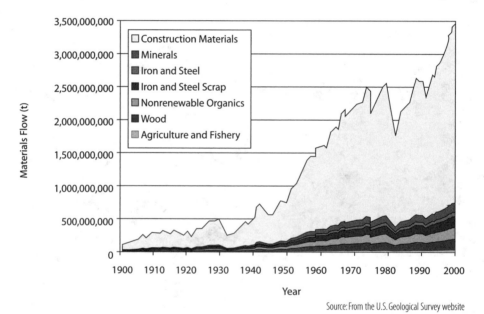

Source: From the U.S. Geological Survey website

Figure 2.4 Material use in industry over a 100-year period

Additionally, as we add more and more systems to a building, these systems demand more energy to run and operate. Figure 2.5 shows the average U.S. retail cost of electricity from 1970 projected to 2030. This shows a 764% increase in the cost of energy over this 60-year span. The addition of more systems to a building generates more materials, and those same systems demand more power to operate. The building owner eventually has to bear these costs not only in construction but also during the lifecycle of the building.

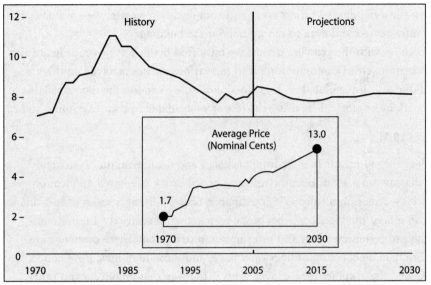

Average U.S. retail electricity prices,
1970–2030 (2005 cents per kilowatt hour)

Source: Energy Information Administration, Annual Energy Review 2003, DOE/EIA-0384(2003) (Washington, DC, September 2004). Projections: Table A8.

Figure 2.5 Energy use in U.S. buildings

The cost of labor in construction is also increasing. Figure 2.6 shows the National Construction Employment Cost Index taken over a 10-year period from 1995 to 2005. This graph shows increases in construction labor costs anywhere from 1.4% to 5.8% per quarter. Inflation, specialization, and building complexity are some of the reasons for these increases in costs.

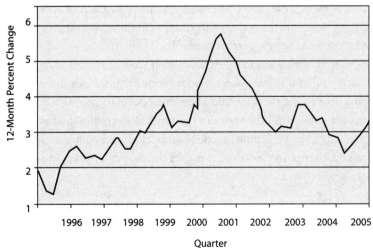

Quarter

Source: Department of Labor, Bureau of Statistics

Figure 2.6 National Construction Employee Cost Index

These trends show that buildings are becoming more complicated to build. They are taking more resources to construct and operate, and this translates to the increasing lifecycle cost for a building. As these costs and complexities escalate, we are flooded with more information and data to manage about the building.

To keep up with the growing trends, we must find better ways to coordinate all of this information, clearly communicate it to the various parties involved, and better understand our role in the global ecology. By doing so, we can use the tools available to make our work more efficient by using the resources available to their maximum value.

Understanding BIM

So, what does this all mean? In a traditional design and documentation system, a designer will draw up a set of documents using pencil or a CAD-based application. These drawings, either physically as printed paper, or digitally, as a series of individual files, have no inherit intelligence, either alone or together. It is strictly a representational method of communication and information distribution. These drawings are nothing more than a collection of lines on a page, and those lines have little added meaning beyond the graphics they convey. This is the way that architects and other designers have worked for countless centuries. Based on the building complexity of those times, the drawings paired with direct communication with the builder were sufficient to describe both the design intent and construction methodology. Figure 2.7 is a sketch that shows both structure and architectural detailing for the Alhambra in Granada, Spain.

A BIM methodology seeks to adapt to the added layers of information, allowing new methods of data exchange and communication amongst all the stakeholders in a project. This can be the design team (designers and consultants), builders (contractors and subcontractors), and owners (developers and facility managers). Each of these teams needs a methodology with which to share information about a project in greater quantities and more efficiently than their current method.

The goal of a BIM methodology is to allow an overall view of the building or project by including everything in a single-source model. With BIM, we can draw or modify building components in a single place and allow the system to propagate changes of those objects throughout all the views in the set of deliverables. So, as you model your plans, it is creating the elevations, sections and details, schedules and energy loads. If you make a change in elevation, it makes the change in plan, section, and so on—or the other way around.

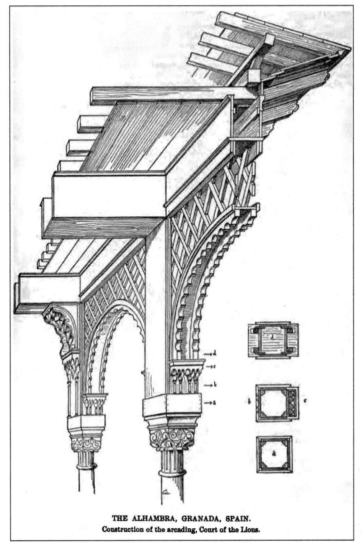

THE ALHAMBRA, GRANADA, SPAIN.
Construction of the arcading, Court of the Lions.

Source: A Dictionary of Architecture and Building, Russell Sturgis, The Macmillan Company, 1901

Figure 2.7 Alhambra structural and architectural detail

The point is that it doesn't matter where you initiate the change because the change is made to the underlying model. The system takes care of updating the other views and other displays of model information. In addition, BIM models are capable of embedding key building information into the model or into elements within the model. So, while a more historic system of building design would only allow you to add information about envelope performance through annotations on a drawing, a BIM model contains actual key data such as R-values, materiality, recyclability, and so on within the model itself.

Figure 2.8 shows an axonometric view that is similar to the previous sketch of the Alhambra column detail but created from a BIM model. Besides the annotations, dimensions, and constructability shown here in this view of the project, we can also derive sunshading, thermal properties, roof areas, and other overall project data.

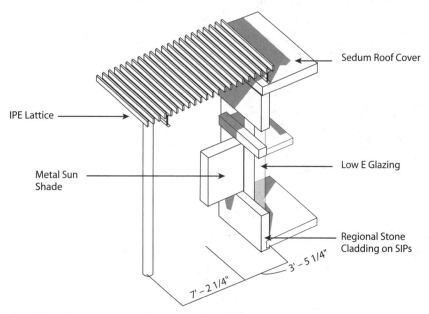

Figure 2.8 A BIM axonometric view showing materiality and shading

Basic Benefits of BIM

BIM is a methodology of continual refinement, not one of drastic change. Success will occur by evolution, not revolution. The basic benefits of a BIM-based methodology are simple:

3D simulation vs. 2D representation As stated before, a 2D drawing of a building is merely a representation of the final, built form abstracted into plans, sections, elevations, and sometimes perspective or axonometric views. BIM allows a 3D simulation of the building and its components. This simulation goes beyond demonstrating how different building assemblies can be combined in the project. It can predict collisions, show environmental variables on different building designs, and calculate material and time quantities.

Accuracy vs. estimation By being able to virtually construct the building before physical construction begins on site, BIM adds a level of accuracy to both building quantities and quality that supercedes historic processes of design and documentation. Building materials and environmental variables can be demonstrated in real time rather than manually estimated.

Efficiency vs. redundancy These benefits add a level of efficiency to a BIM project. By simply drawing building elements only once in the project in lieu of a drawing plan, then projecting elevation, then section, we can begin to capture time and focus that additional time on other design issues.

A Change in Method and Approach

The industry standard design and documentation process looks like Figure 2.9. To describe this better, we need to understand that design is a cyclical process and one of continual refinement. As we share ideas and coordinate information with the entire project team, we can begin to make adjustments to our own portion of the project. A standard architectural project might go something like this:

- The architect draws a building design and shares this information with consultants.

- Various consultants, working separately, will reuse parts of the architect's drawings to create a new series of their own drawings specific to their specialization.

- The consultant's drawings will be shared with the architect who will need to use them to further coordinate his or her own work. Portions that affect the architectural drawings such as building structure or mechanical ductwork are in a large portion redrawn within the architectural set.

- At a certain point in the project process, all of the drawings (typically in printed form only) are shared with a contractor or builder. The contractor disseminates the drawings to various subcontractors who will need to utilize their specialties to embellish the information in the original drawings.

- The contractor will create new sets of drawings with added detail, but all based on the original set of documents.

   With all of these separate teams making their own sets of drawings, a system of checks and balances is needed to ensure the information is communicated accurately and effectively. In our traditional model earlier, the subcontractors send their drawings back to the contractor to verify the work. The contractor duplicates the drawings (based on the number of parties who need to review the drawings) and passes them to the architect. The architect reviews his or her set while giving copies to various consultants to do the same. All of these changes are manually transcribed to one set before being sent back to the contractor to pass along to the subs for further revisions and clarifications.

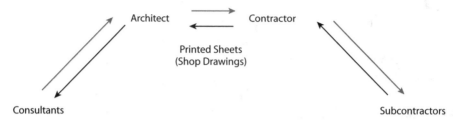

Figure 2.9 The traditional method of design review

This entire chain of information sharing has many opportunities for miscommunication, and much of the information is redundantly reproduced as a way of error checking. If we can utilize the advantages inherent in a BIM-based method (Figure 2.10), we can eliminate much of the redundant efforts, improve communication, and focus more time on improving the design and expediting construction.

In an ideal BIM-based system:

- The architect and consultants would work together on a single building model. This might be one model, or a model comprised of interconnected parts.

- After this model reaches a stage of refinement, it is passed on to the contractor and building team to further embellish with information specific to their trades and expertise.

- As they construct the physical building, the BIM model can be adjusted to reflect the changes that happen in the field.

- The revised model can then be shared with the owner and facilities operator. The model can contain the necessary product information about the systems installed to aid the owner's facility operator in maintaining the building. The model can also be used for future personnel moves or even building additions.

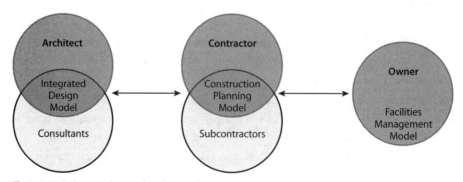

Figure 2.10 An integrated approach to design review

If we focus on the first model of a BIM-based method, the integrated design model, we can begin to look at all of the various components that can begin to make up that model. Figure 2.11 shows some of these models.

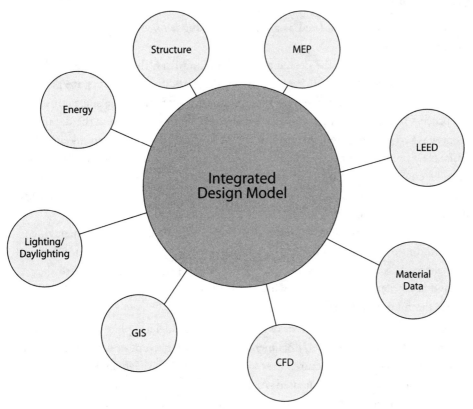

Figure 2.11 The integrated design model

As all of these various specializations interact and create the building model, we begin to see how structure, mechanical, energy, daylight, and other factors can begin to inform design direction. We can also begin to draw relationships between some of these elements that might not have been as obvious in a more traditionally based approach. While some of these specialties (such as structure and mechanical) are historically separate systems, integrating them into a single design model allows us to see how they can interact in relation to other systems with a building. Daylighting can begin to inform our building orientation and structure. Depending on our glazing, it can also affect our mechanical requirements (as solar heat gain). We can see some of these effects through a Computational Fluid Dynamic (CFD) model used to calculate airflow. Geographic Information System (GIS) data will give us our relative location globally and allow us to see how close we are to certain products and materials, how much sunlight we will be receiving, or what the local temperature swings will be. As you can see, all of these variables can easily affect building design.

Beyond Documentation

BIM was originally conceptualized as a way of *drawing it once* to speed the design documentation process.

Since its inception by the design and building industry, there have been a host of other benefits derived from a BIM model. All of these additional benefits are primarily due to BIM's ability to virtually realize the building through all of the stages of the design process in the form of a database. This allows us to simply *view* the database in different ways to gain different pictures of the building. These views can take the form of plans, elevations, sections, or schedules. Everything added to the building database can also be counted and quantified. By leveraging this method of reporting information, we can visualize the same project in a variety of ways to save time in communicating design information.

These benefits extend from conceptual design and documentation, through construction and into building occupancy. As the use of BIM gains momentum, more and more of these ideas are becoming realized and able to be easily integrated into the design and construction process. Let's look at some of these advantages and how they can affect the final building:

Integrated documents As all of the drawings in a BIM model are placed within the single, integrated database or model, document coordination becomes relatively automatic. Because BIM is a database structure, after views are added to sheets in a drawing set, the references are instantly coordinated. As buildings become increasingly complex, the number of sheets in a set of construction documents continues to grow. A building that might have once been documented with 30 or 40 sheets 50 years ago can now take four times as many. Being able to automatically coordinate all of that information is no small feat and can be time consuming to do it manually.

By integrating consultant information into the architectural drawings, we can derive additional benefits. Since the building is modeled in three dimensions, we can easily overlay architectural, structural, and mechanical models and check for interferences and conflicts within the building. Many BIM packages can also automate this process and provide reports of intersecting building components.

Design phase visualization Design phase visualization is another of the low-hanging fruits of BIM. Again, because the model is in 3D, we are able to almost instantly see the building from any angle. This can be a great tool not only to aid in the design process in visualizing space, but also to convey ideas about the design to team members, clients, contractors, or regulatory agencies. Not only does this help with simply communicating the design of the building, but also there are many other benefits. As

Figure 2.12 demonstrates, we can show the effects of the sun on the building during midday to help explain the importance of proper sunshading to an owner group.

Image courtesy of BNIM Architects

Figure 2.12 Design visualization

In another example, we have used a live BIM model to show the local fire marshal how access to the building will be available for fire trucks from various points surrounding the site in an emergency.

Materials database Again, because BIM creates a database of the virtual building, assemblies that are modeled can be created with their physical properties. When you add a *wall* in BIM, you are adding a 3 5/8″ metal stud between two layers of sheet rock, or 7 5/8″ CMU, or whatever else the wall is created out of in the design. Because the wall has a height and length, the database will allow you to create schedules of information about the wall or other objects within the model. You can quickly see how many linear feet or square feet of a given wall type you currently have in the design (Figure 2.13), or those walls can be broken down into their individual components and you can create a schedule showing how many square feet of gypsum board is in the project. All of these materials and areas automatically update their quantities as walls (or other elements) are added or removed from the model.

Wall Schedule				
Wall Type	Width	Rating	Total Length	Total Area
Basic Wall: A1 – 6 1/8" 2 HR	0'–6 1/8"	2 HR	724' – 5 5/8"	12151 SF
Basic Wall: A2 – 5 1/2" (1 HR)	0' – 4 7/8"	1 HR	1736' – 8 1/16"	16079 SF
Basic Wall: A3 – 4 3/4"	0' – 4 3/4"		4536' – 3 15/32"	37736 SF
Basic Wall: A4 – 4" - Soffit	0' – 4"		788' – 1 1/32"	1965 SF
Basic Wall: A4 – 7 1/4"	0' – 7 1/4"	1 HR	1247' – 0 3/8"	12090 SF
Basic Wall: Exterior – Cement Board	0' – 7 7/8"		187' – 3 1/2"	7360 SF
Basic Wall: Exterior – Glass Bay	0' – 7 1/4"		160' – 1"	3287 SF
Basic Wall: Exterior – Wood Slat	0' – 7 1/4"		207' – 3 7/32"	3972 SF
Basic Wall: Exterior – Zinc	0' – 8"		115' – 10 13/32"	3798 SF
Basic Wall: Exterior – Zinc – Cap	0' – 8"		217' – 9 29/32"	6336 SF
Basic Wall: F1 – 12" (1 HR)	1' – 0"	1 HR	919' – 7 13/16"	9353 SF
Basic Wall: F2 – 12" (2 HR)	1' – 0"	2 HR	262' – 3 5/32"	2961 SF
Basic Wall: N1 – CMU Wall	0' – 8"	2 HR	1270' – 2 15/16"	20075 SF
Curtain Wall: Storefront			550' – 2 3/32"	5631 SF

Figure 2.13 A schedule of wall types, lengths, and areas

Because we now have an idea about the quantities within the model, it is a simple matter to add unit costs to those quantities to derive an estimated project cost. It is important to understand that in any BIM model all of the components of any assembly won't be modeled. It is not realistic to model all of the screws, flashing, studs, sealant, or many of the other components in the project. Nor will any estimates take into account building complexity or any site-specific contingencies. However, by working closely with an estimator or contractor to derive unit costs, it is possible to get general ideas about the overall project cost. Although this will not be exact, it can certainly aid in design.

Sustainable strategies One of the unique benefits of BIM is the ability to use the building geometry from the model in other applications to speed some of the analysis that needs to occur for sustainable design principles. Examples of this would be energy analysis or daylighting analysis (Figure 2.14). We can also use BIM's ability to automatically report areas and quantities within the model to automate calculations for:

> **Rainwater harvesting** Being able to take roof areas in plan to size cisterns.
>
> **Solar access** Calculating orientation and roof area for solar panels.
>
> **Recycled content** By adding custom variables to schedules and materials within BIM, we can calculate the amount of recycled content within given materials or throughout the entire project.

Construction planning Demonstrating building visualization to builders can also save time on the job site. A contractor who is familiar with BIM can use it to identify areas of a project that traditional documents do not permit him or her to quickly visualize (Figure 2.15). These areas can also be quickly captured and returned to the design team to request further elaboration on that portion of the project. On site, BIM can be useful by breaking down the model into separate phases within regular time intervals to show construction staging.

Figure 2.16 is an enlargement of a 7′ × 7′ computer numerical control (CNC)-routed door panel. By feeding model information directly into a computer-controlled router, we were able to create complex patterns with a minimal amount of back and forth communication with the fabricator. The ability to go directly from design intent to fabrication is a higher level of control afforded directly to the designer than previously available. Additionally, less paperwork is involved in a digital workflow, thereby allowing these doors to be more affordable to the project.

Postoccupancy and facilities management Once the project is built, BIM can still be a useful tool for the building owner. Because it is possible to not only count but also locate any model elements with the building model, BIM can be a useful tool for asset management and equipment tracking.

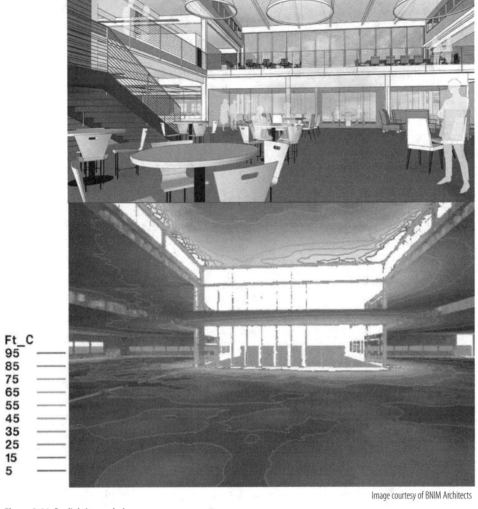

Ft_C
95
85
75
65
55
45
35
25
15
5

Figure 2.14 Daylighting analysis

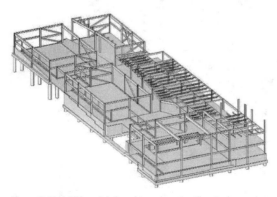

Figure 2.15 A BIM model phased to see construction staging

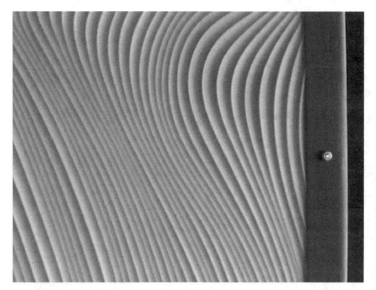

Figure 2.16 A detail of a CNC-routed door panel

Postconstruction Resources

While we have only 100 or so people in our Kansas City office, we relocate resources frequently to accommodate project changes and needs. We use a BIM model within our own in tandem with other applications to track hardware and furniture and locate employees. We can also perform moves, additions, and changes when it comes time to relocate staff based on ever-changing project needs. The next illustration shows the BIM model in the facilities software that we use to locate resources at a particular workstation.

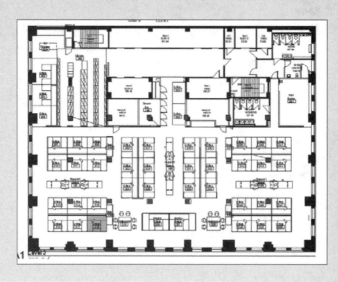

In all, there are a number of different uses for BIM beyond creating a good set of construction documents. If you are investigating any of these, here are a few core concepts that all of these uses have in common:

- BIM is a database application that can help to manage relationships between materials, assemblies, and views.

- Computers can count—and they can count more accurately than you. As simple as that seems and as long as computers have been doing this, being able to dynamically count and quantify materials and assemblies with a model is a huge benefit.

- BIM is 3D—BIM allows the viewer the ability to instantly visualize not only the design of the building but also the effects of sun on fenestration and building envelope. This also means the entire project's geometry is held digitally and can be transferred between applications for a variety of uses in design and fabrication.

Migrating to BIM

Because BIM is a relatively new approach to design and documentation, it has a great deal of potential for future industry advancements. BIM requires planning for implementation to achieve successful and predictable results. It needs to be approached not as a change in software, as that is the use of BIM in the most basic way, but approached as a change in method and workflow. Successful implementation of BIM can change how you structure your project phases and design expectations. Remember, BIM is a methodology of continual refinement, not one of drastic change. Moving to a BIM-based methodology can take time and many project iterations (Figure 2.17). By first understanding the process and workflow, you can begin to make gradual changes and enhancements to the individual project process to achieve better and better results. Repeat the concepts that work and innovate to improve that ones that can better perform.

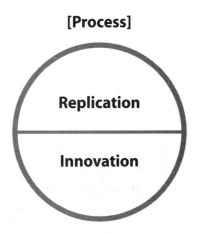

[Process]

Replication

Innovation

[Continual Improvement]

Figure 2.17 Replication and innovation

As with any methodological change, success will be had if all the factors can be addressed. Project success happens on more than a financial or chronological level. It is also determined by a team's ability to replicate successful results. A difficult aspect of transitioning to BIM is predictability. Any system or method, even if it is inherently inefficient, is at some level successful if the system is predictable. If you can say that x effort + y time will yield z result, there is an established comfort level with that system even if it is an inefficient system. When moving to BIM, the system automatically becomes unpredictable as team members need to experience the new system to establish a comfort level with the given results. No longer does x effort + y time yield z result.

There is a curve to any process change that looks like Figure 2.18. This is the Happiness over Time curve. Happiness represents your overall satisfaction with a change in process or method. This combines financial, personal, professional, and emotional goals into one category.

With any new innovation, there is an immediate increase in happiness at the start. Take the example of getting a new cell phone. You are immediately thrilled with the new features, be they camera or Bluetooth and happiness increases.

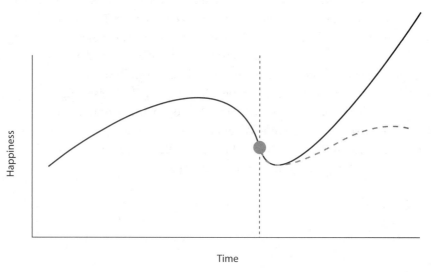

Figure 2.18 Happiness over time

Eventually, you will reach a point of temporary diminishing return. The amount of effort you feel like you need to put into understanding the new process or device seems as if it has begun to exceed the value you derive from the change, and happiness begins to decline. In our cell phone example, you might not be able to add contacts, or successfully synchronize it with your calendar or set the time and date. Eventually you reach the point on the curve where you need to make the decision to stay the course or roll back to your previous process or device (do you put your SIM card back in the old cell phone?).

Here your path can split. By regressing to your previous process, there will be an immediate increase in happiness with the familiarity and predictability of the former method, but this will only level out and never reach any greater heights than it did before you contemplated the initial change. If you stay the course with the new process, happiness will decrease (and frustration increase) as you struggle through the change. However, eventually as the new method becomes more predictable and comfortable, your happiness can achieve greater value.

While this might be an oversimplification of a process change, the core meaning is critical. Change can be challenging. However, to realize greater goals and adapt to an ever-changing environment both professionally and globally, we will need to rethink our process in order to achieve success.

Migrating within Our Own Offices

We tested our first project in BIM in 2001. At the time, we were faced with the largest project we had ever done to date: a 1.12 million-square-foot office building that contained some historic preservation, new construction, and enough underground parking to cover six football fields. We decided to see the challenge as an opportunity and push for a new document delivery process that was BIM. We had purchased Autodesk's Revit 5.1 and hired Autodesk's implementation service (the talented Phil Read) to come and train us on how to get the project off the ground. It was not without frustrations and challenges, many of which we just outlined, but we were ultimately successful. The project was completed seven months ahead of schedule.

With that success under our belt, we jumped into our second project in BIM. It was a disaster. At one point, the Revit development team had a pamphlet entitled *The 10 things NOT to do in Revit*. Eight of them were from this project.

Probably the biggest reason for the lack of success was we were simply overly zealous and tried to do too much with BIM too soon, and at the time there was no staff on hand or other firms available to offer support during times of crisis.

As you transition from two-dimensional to BIM, it's important to keep the process manageable. Since this project, we have done a better job of offering some predictability during change as we continue to push forward with experimental and largely untested methodologies.

BIM as a Workflow

To best understand the impacts of BIM on the larger project process, let's first discuss a design team's role in the project. The mainstream view of the architectural process is fairly basic. To the layperson, the designer's roles are simply:

- **Designing**
- **Building**

These two steps are the most obvious to the public eye. They typically consist of coming up with the brilliant, creative idea (concept) and then executing it in built form. Rarely in this limited scope do we see all of the other team members who are needed to take the idea off the drafting table to completion. In reality, a lot more happens in the design process. Good design becomes a more encompassing process, including:

- Listening
- Researching
- **Designing**
- **Building**
- Occupying
- Learning

Each of these steps becomes important in the project lifecycle. They can happen at the macro level where the entire project is idealized and constructed, or these same steps can help inform a more micro level on a project when it becomes a particular building component or system.

This process is not linear but iterative. We do not complete these steps only once as designers but we will do them over and over again. We begin thinking about the client's and building needs well before putting pencil to paper. As we research ideas and materials, the design begins to take form. As this design unfolds, we explore prototyping, modeling, and experimenting with some of these ideas in a built form. We test (or occupy in the case of a finished building), then ideally learn from the results and this cycle and begin it anew. As we repeat this process with various building components and systems, eventually a building begins to take shape. Once it's complete, we can then learn from the various successes in that project to begin the next one. *A successful project typically requires many iterations of these steps.* Although it might take several passes through this process to achieve the best result, plenty of projects don't afford that amount of time.

You might be thinking, "Well, I know all this. How does this relate to BIM or sustainability?" Both BIM and sustainable design take a slightly different approach to engaging the project process. A distinctive change in workflow is necessary if the results are going to be sustainable.

Lewis and Clark State Office Building

To demonstrate this process, let's explore a project that was done before BIM became widely available. While we are using examples from various projects, the process described can be viewed as fairly typical for a sustainable project designed in a more historical method of design and documentation.

As we revolved though various design iterations, the project team eventually created a series of *models*. We use the term fairly loosely at this point as they were not all true models in the physical or 3D, digital sense, but they were all a collection of specific ideas, thoughts, and concepts that were needed to create the project. Some were specifically visual, some analytical, and some were purely for documentation purposes. However, without any one of these models, the final built form would not have been realized and all the models were used in various parts of the project process. Let's discuss the importance of each model:

The physical design model This model was built to study the building geometry, exterior views, and building massing. Larger-scale physical models were created to study individual components of the building such as the sunshading. Figure 2.19 shows some of these models. As an example of a micro-level iterative process, the sunshades were physically modeled for their relationship to the built form, then digitally re-created in the digital design daylighting and energy models to test their performance and daylighting features.

Image courtesy of BNIM Architects

Figure 2.19 The physical design model

The solar analysis model This model was created to understand the value of shading against the building façade. A massing model was built to understand the sun against the building and various shading schemes were created to help architecturally articulate the effects of the sun against the building form. In this expressly nondigital format, the model was taken outside and rotated against the sun diagram shown on the left of each of these models in Figure 2.20. While seemingly basic, it accurately demonstrates the building's solar exposure.

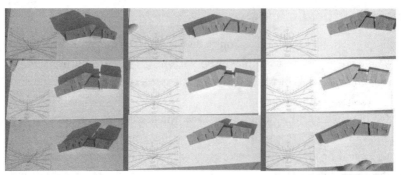

Figure 2.20 The solar design model

The digital design model This model (Figure 2.21) was a 3D graphical representation of the building used to communicate design direction to the client and owner groups. Typically, simpler versions of this type of model are used in early design phases and the more robust renderings are commonly used in presentation materials.

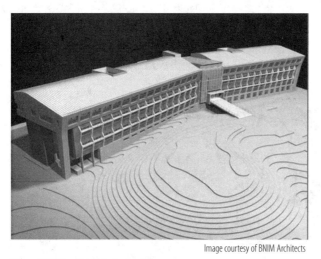

Figure 2.21 The digital design model

The energy model The energy model was created to understand the energy loads and demands on the building. This model begins to explain and help to predict not only power demands on a building but also how some of these systems are integrated. As we add more lighting and electrical service in the building, the need for cooling typically increases. People begin to play a role in this as well. Based on the number of occupants and their activity level, we need to adjust the amount of heat or cooling appropriately. Figure 2.22 shows a 3D energy model, and Figure 2.23 shows a graphical output of the heating loads during one of the earlier phases in the design process.

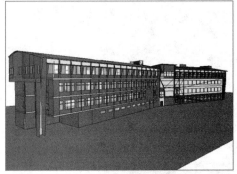

Image courtesy of BNIM Architects

Figure 2.22 The energy model

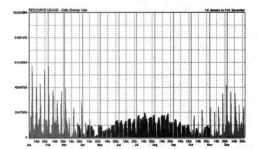

Figure 2.23 Energy data from the model

The daylighting model The daylighting model (Figure 2.24) is designed to study specific amounts of daylight in the building itself. This kind of model can analyze the levels of daylight that you will get at different times of year and with different types of sunshading devices integrated into the overall building design. Based on the amount of solar gain in the building, this can also affect the energy model and the heat loads. In this particular model, the lines represent isocontours that allow readings for different levels of foot candles within the space.

The construction documents model Although this example is not a true model, it is the communication tool used to get the project built. As various schemes and ideas are tried and tested with some of the models mentioned earlier, ultimately they need to be recorded in a system that is easy to understand and distributed to the construction team responsible for physically creating the building. The image in Figure 2.25 is an example detail created in CAD.

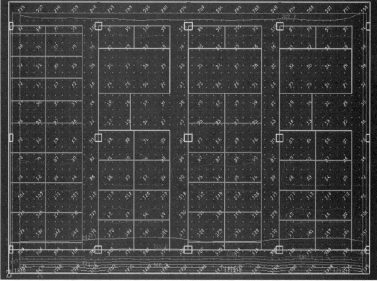

Image courtesy of BNIM Architects

Figure 2.24 The daylighting model

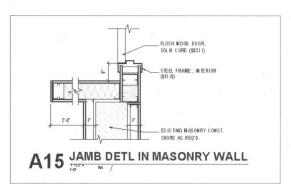

Figure 2.25 Construction Detail from the BIM Model

All of these models were necessary to successfully complete the project as it was designed; however, it became a whole separate set of tasks to simply manage the geometric information changes to the various models. Take the example of the sunshades. One model was created to design the look of the shades, one to test their functionality to keep out direct sunlight, one to measure and analyze the amount of light permitted inside the space, and the construction documents to convey that information to the building team. In each of these models, changes were made to the design, the shape, materiality, and location of the sunshades. As all of those features affect one another, you can begin to see the need for a tool to communicate and manage that information so all the changes are simultaneously kept up to date with one another.

Ranges of BIM

In projects since the Lewis and Clark State Office Building, we can use BIM to combine these separate analysis and design functions into one geometric model. Although most of these things cannot be done directly in a BIM model, the model can be used as a basis for much of this work, thus eliminating overlap in replicating changes made to the building geometry. Remember, a good BIM model is a database of building parts and assemblies with some rudimentary geographical information. Leveraging these database features and functionalities is what allows us to push past simple 2D design and documentation into new realms of possibilities. Some of the things a database-driven building information model can be used to do are:

Export model geometry We can take and reuse the building geometry from the BIM model by exporting it into different analysis packages for energy, solar, daylighting, and so forth. In our own work, half of the time needed to run an energy model can be consumed by simply re-creating building geometry in another application. Saving this time both speeds up the project and allows for more design iteration.

Count It's a computer, right? BIM software can be good at counting elements within the model. It can calculate not only the quantity of items within the model (such as doors) but also square feet of wall, cubic feet of material, or the volume of a space.

Sort It is not good having much of the data needed to create a building directly accessible if you can't drill down to the needed information quickly. BIM is a database, and the application can be quite good at sorting data.

Calculate (basic addition, subtraction, and so forth) After our data is counted and sorted, we can apply a number of calculations to that data to quickly get new information. As an example, if all our cast-in-place concrete in a project contains 15% fly ash and we need to know the volume of fly ash in the project, we can easily create a schedule in the model to report this quantity.

Communicate In all of these examples, the model is designed to quickly supply information about specific portions of the project. Reports can be included in the documentation of a project to better inform all the project team members about key issues in the design process.

Combining the functionalities listed here gives us an endless range of possibilities. Figure 2.26 explores some of these features and demonstrates the interrelationships possible between them. In the following chapters, we'll explore the elements key to sustainable design.

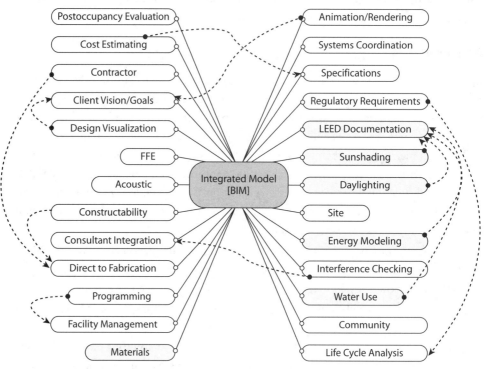

Figure 2.26 BIM roadmap

3

Integrated Design Teams

No one knows as much as everyone.

—Anonymous

The process and science of building design and construction has become increasingly more complicated in recent years. It has continually become less possible for designers to work without the aid of other specialists, be they consultants or contractors. The trend toward concentrated areas of expertise has led to a growing movement to combine the owner, designer, contractor, consultants, and key subcontractors into an integrated design team. Integrated design is founded on the ability to share knowledge across disciplines, the strength of project team commitment, and the power of project team passion. Collaboration, commitment, and passion are musts for developing the most sustainable solution.

The Shift in Responsibility

Due to the added complexities and specializations rampant in our field, we have drifted away from the holistic project view that we might have enjoyed as few as 100 years ago. During the time of the Renaissance, architects like Brunelleschi (Figure 3.1) were afforded the opportunity to operate as a master-builder. This paradigm allowed one person to hold complete knowledge of both the design and construction methodologies implemented in the building process, partially due to the relative simplicity of building systems at the time. Integration, so to speak, was automatic. After the Renaissance, the master-builder role split into the architect-contractor role.

Image courtesy of Brad Nies

Figure 3.1 Brunelleschi's Dome, Florence, Italy

As building technologies continued to evolve over the centuries, the industry continued to compartmentalize and fragment. As buildings became increasingly complex, building systems required greater levels of specialization. Concentrated specialization has led the design and construction professions to grow more fragmented and at times adversarial, with each specialization vying for primacy. Especially over the last century, fragmentation in our industry has resulted in a drastic decline in efficiency compared to other industries—efficiency within our own processes as well as within the buildings that we have created.

Why an Integrated Design

The purity of a master-builder construct (both architect and builder in one person) is no longer a tenable option. Although there is no real reason to lament the adulteration of the master-builder model, there is some benefit to understanding implications of its evolution to the more current model. The layers of design required in today's world are numerous—structure, landscape, plumbing, data, heating, cooling, security, power, lighting, controls, and accessibility, to name a few. The number of layers and the many complex interactions between them suggest the need for an integrated approach to design, just as they suggested the need for BIM (Figure 3.2).

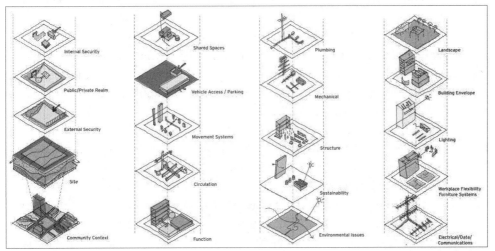

Image Courtesy of BNIM Architects

Figure 3.2 Layers of design

We still must endure many of the same, traditional design constraints that have been around for centuries, such as the following:

- Physicality of the site
- Availability of utilities

- Compliance with building code and zoning ordinances
- Respect for environmental regulations and aspirations
- Budgets

What the series of constraints suggests, even requires, is an ever-growing team of individuals, each carrying their own specialized library of information and solutions. The depth of knowledge within one individual is not a problem in and of itself, but it can be if the information collected from the disparate sources is not efficiently integrated.

If we are to understand and build upon the integration between nature and human nature, between the built and natural environments, we need to rethink our attitude toward the practice of design and construction. Today more knowledge and information lies within a team than a single individual. To capture the required knowledge, we must move toward an integrated design practice that involves all members of the owner group, the design and construction team, and the community at large in order to create a more holistic design and a more globally appropriate solution.

In his discussion paper "Toward a New Metropolis: The Opportunity to Rebuild America," Arthur C. Nelson reveals that, "In 2030, about half of the buildings in which Americans live, work, and shop will have been built after 2000." Consider the magnitude of Nelson's stunning prediction. The next generation of design teams and builders will have substantial impact on the global built environment in less than half a lifetime.

With the AEC industry's newfound sense of urgency, and the implied capacity for impact in mind, our discussion begins with the environment and the ever fascinating, yet often ignored, connections between nature and human nature. At this particular crossroads, we see our roadmap pointing primarily toward integration, technologically as well as culturally. We do not see where we stand today as a time for debate, only a time for changing our minds and our behavior and getting down to the business of solving what we perceive to be the ultimate design challenge: integration between nature and human nature, between the built and natural environments, between us and them, however this might be defined. If the primary responsibility of the architect is one of life safety, then consider this the ultimate concern for life safety.

We have come to a place where there is no longer any doubt that our actions as a society or as a collection of societies influence global economics, culture, and climate. A seemingly endless list of journal articles, television broadcasts, news stories, books, reports, environmental initiatives, and foundation programs bear witness to the planet's obvious and inevitable trajectory.

For example, articles about the human impact on climate change have stepped out of *Scientific American* in recent years to annually grace the covers of *Time*, *Newsweek*, and *Vanity Fair* Green issues. Al Gore's Academy Award–winning documentary "An

Inconvenient Truth" sparked a series of climate-change focused television specials on NBC, Discovery Channel, CNN, and HBO. For a while in November 2007, NBC Nightly News had a daily "Green in America" segment. PBS ("Building Green"), the Science Channel ("Eco-tech") and the Weather Channel ("Climate Code with Dr. Heidi Cullen") all have weekly programs dedicated to sustainability.

It appears that our ability to measure and track our own environmental demise has outpaced our ability or will to understand it, let alone do anything about it. Despite our inability, we remain encouraged by recent signs of hope that suggest a change in our industry's attitude. One could argue that it has been the arrogant and ignorant attitude of specialization, compartmentalization, and individualism that has brought us to this point, which might suggest a starting place for change. What about our own design and construction industry?

As other industries have found effective ways to balance resources, time, and productivity, the building industry has created more waste and less efficiency. We believe the inefficiencies and waste are due in large part to an industry trend of information hording. Often, teams working on the same project do not share data, forcing each other to redraw information or pay royalties for its use. Separatism has not solved the problems of litigation or quality control that it tried to cure, but rather adds to the inefficiencies and waste suggested next.

According to the U.S. Green Building Council, the contribution of buildings in the United States to the global environmental crisis is daunting. Buildings in the United States are responsible for the following:

- 70% of total U.S. electricity consumption

- 39% of total U.S. primary energy use (including fuel use for production)

- 12% of potable water in the United States

- 40% (3 billion tons annually) of raw materials use globally and they create:

- 38% of total U.S. carbon dioxide emissions

- 136 million tons of construction and demolition waste in the United States (approximately 2.8 lbs/person/day)

The solution must involve an opposing doctrine of connectivity, integration, and interdependence. It is a matter of changing not just the way we live, but the way we think and the way we work. It is not sufficient to use fewer raw materials and minimize emissions. A culture of change requires a spirit of teamwork and interconnectedness that is far different from our current state of isolation and adversarial tendencies.

Some examples where we have seen a lack of communication cause higher first costs and/or long-term inefficiencies are when the engineer designs the HVAC system on rules of thumb instead of the actual envelope that the architect designed. Another example is when the owner requires 4 watts/sq. ft. available for plug loads when their metered use is closer to 2 watts/ sq. ft. One of the most common communication failures that we see is the contractor suggesting value engineering items that don't meet the performance requirements of the architect or the engineer, such as cheaper window systems or less efficient mechanical equipment.

A fundamental tenet of true sustainability is integration of all building systems within themselves as well as with the external economic and environmental realities of the project. When the entire design team is able to actively share one another's work on the whole building, true integration becomes more real and compelling. Active sharing requires a method that allows free-flowing and constant communication.

The Team Members

Back in the mid-1990s, owner interviews for a project were primarily about the owner selecting an architect. While a good portion of that selection is about qualifications, in the end design fees influence many owners' decisions as well. Today, the architect is still the leader of the design team, and while some owners are still focused on the architect, the other disciplines on the team are gaining importance. Our experience shows that owners are also finding value in being more inclusive of internal staff, hiring contractors earlier, and listening to the community.

The Designers

Beyond the architect, project designers are traditionally made up of interior designers, landscape architects, and civil, structural, mechanical, electrical, and plumbing engineers. In the late 20th century, we added some specialty consultants, such as cost-estimating consultants, acousticians, food service, roof, masonry, fire protection, security, data and telecom, and so forth.

Specialization has continued to grow, fragmenting the design professions. We have newer specialties, such as façade engineers, lighting designers, renewable energy consultants, commissioning agents, and—one of the latest to join the party—the sustainable design consultant. Consider also that if the owner has selected the design team with the lowest fee, the dollars remaining to involve these specialties are also limited.

While those mentioned are all likely to be trained in architecture or engineering, some teams have brought in other professional disciplines like product manufacturers, chemists, biologists, ecologists, and other research specialists. No matter the professional origin, it is important to bring in these individual experts if they can add value to the project. Each area of expertise will have a different way of looking at the problem at hand and participating in developing a solution. Compared to building components and construction, ideas are inexpensive. Be open to getting the best ideas from anywhere. Today's technological innovations for communication allow team members to be far away from the project site.

An Integrated Team

One of BNIM Architect's early highly collaborative projects that expanded the traditional project team was the Montana State University Epicenter, an original U.S. Green Building Council (USGBC) Leadership in Energy and Environmental Design (LEED) Pilot project. It was also one of four demonstration projects sponsored by the National Institute of Standards and Technology. The team included experts from California to England setting new standards for capturing the best ideas from around the world. The list is too long to replicate in our book, but team members included architects, engineers, contractors, manufacturers, faculty, students, industry researchers, politicians, historians, ecologists, biologists, physicists, economists, and specialty consultants for materials, daylighting, renewable energy, biological waste treatment systems, systems integration, and others. You can download the full report to the National Institute of Standards and Technology about the project at `http://www.fire.nist.gov/bfrlpubs/build00/art112.html`.

Rendering of the Epicenter

Image Courtesy of BNIM Architects

The Owner

So far we've only talked about potential members of the design team who are available to the owner. Let's not forget the makeup of the owner's team. In the past the owner's team was small, perhaps consisting of some upper-level management and part of the facilities group if they had one. We believe it is important to have a wide array of stakeholders present from the owner's side. Stakeholders are the users and decision makers who will not have a day-to-day role on the project team. We recommend identifying and inviting stakeholders who stretch across the traditional organizational hierarchy, from the top commander to the building engineer. Having those stakeholders present to deliver their perspective on the organization's new facility and the operation of it will bring great solidarity to the team.

The Contractor

Another team member whose role we should discuss is the contractor. As is common today and for most of the latter half of the 20th century, the contractor is brought to the team after the design and construction documentation is completed. In this traditional delivery method, known as design-bid-build, the contractor is handed sets of drawings and specifications that represent the design intent, and with little to no direct communication with the architect or owner, is asked to submit a bid for doing the work. The owner in turn selects the best-qualified contractor with the lowest price. However, from our experience, the most common outcome is that the best-qualified contractor is forgotten and it is the lowest bidder who is selected. Because so much is riding on the comparatively short time allowed for interpretation of the construction documents, wouldn't it be better if the contractor was part of the design and documentation team as well? We believe in involving the contractor as early as possible in projects. Later in this chapter we will share examples of great green buildings delivered through the three primary project delivery methods of design: design-bid-build, guaranteed maximum price, and design-build.

The Community

We cannot forget about community participation. When an individual building project is important to a community or when the project is redefining the community or neighborhood, community members must be allowed to participate in the early stages of the project. If the project team waits too long into the process to integrate the community, support can be compromised.

The most sustainable solutions are completely integrated and if all perspectives are not at the design table when key decisions are made, chances for complete integration are greatly reduced. There is no doubt that the earlier the collaboration starts, the greater the potential for success. Figure 3.3 shows an integrated design team diagram. Now, consider, after you've decided on whom you need at the table, how do you integrate the power of all the experts?

Collaboration, Commitment, and Passion

A team that is collaborative, committed to the project goals, or passionate about finding the best solution can create something good. We believe that a team that embraces all three creates an opportunity for something great, perhaps a new standard that has not been set before.

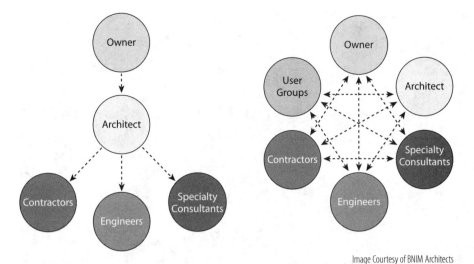

Figure 3.3 The traditional team model and an integrated design team model

Collaboration

One of the many tools available in all of our toolkits is the opportunity for dialogue. Given a chance to talk with one another we learn and develop a deeper understanding of a given design problem. Working hand in hand, not alone in each of our respective offices, we can develop the best solutions. Early dialogue with consultants is counter to the process that our early mentors taught us—to develop our base drawings and hand them off to the other professional disciplines so that they could start making our design work.

To start an open level of collaboration, each team member must know who the other team members are and what value they can bring to the table. Mutual respect for the expertise at hand is something we commonly cover in our first workshop or team meeting. We start by introducing ourselves as the individuals who will be on the team. It is important to state who you are, your role, why you are part of the project team, and what you hope to contribute.

This introduction is followed with some cross-team knowledge sharing so that everyone understands where each team member is starting from and where they think the project should be going. The knowledge-sharing part of the dialogue is best led off by the owner sharing first, because prior to hiring the project team, the owner already developed an idea of what they wanted, yet might not have communicated it to the team. For a successful end product, design and construction team members should understand what is expected from their efforts as early as possible. For many team members, the first workshop is likely the first chance to hear these thoughts from the owner and ask questions. Figure 3.4 shows exactly this: the integrated design team and owner group sharing initial thoughts during their first workshop.

Image Courtesy of BNIM Architects

Figure 3.4 Initial knowledge sharing session

Design and construction team members should build on the newly shared information by sharing the state of their profession. For these dialogues, we share our most recent thoughts on the state of design intermixed with our understanding of sustainability and how both of these relate to the particular project we are about to work on. Over the years the finer details of the state of design dialogue change, and the depth of which you go into each area should be adjusted for the specific audience.

Due to marketplace trends, owners have developed a deeper understanding of sustainability requiring less internal team education. Yet, there is often a part of the owner team that is being instructed to consider sustainable solutions, even though they have not bought into the concept themselves. We recommend the remainder of the project team meet that portion of the team where they are and help them understand the benefits of sustainable solutions within their own perspective. The more disciplines that can share the baseline type thoughts, the better the whole project team can challenge one another for developing a high-quality, sustainable building.

After all the team members understand the owner's vision for the project and each stakeholder has had the chance to share potential opportunities in the project, it is time to establish some clear principles for the project. Combining the owner's mission and vision with what is possible can develop principles for the project. Based on these principles, the team should begin to develop goals. The principles and goals should be strong enough, and simple enough, to refer to over the course of the project when making tough decisions. The goals should have measurable targets so that the team can clearly see where they stand regarding successful achievement. Keep in mind that during any project, some goals will be met, while others will not. However, at this early stage of a project, try not to be constrained. It will also become important to identify the barriers to these goals that must be addressed, and later overcome in order to achieve the desired results.

To look at an example of how project principles and goals can integrate into a sustainable strategy for a project, let's consider that our project team is working with an owner whose mission involves eliminating hunger. Water is a basic need for survival and most food sources require water as a resource; because of this our example project owner stated that they envision the building to be a model of water conservation. Based on this dialogue, the integrated team can develop a guiding project principle like, "Treat water as a valuable resource." A corresponding measurable goal for the project could be "Let no water leave the site."

Through the principle and goal-setting dialogue, the entire project team will understand which efforts can move forward quickly and which are going to need more time and energy to conquer. Developing clear principles and goals will also help to develop full buy-in from the key decision makers on the project team, which can become a critical asset later in the project when things are not going as smoothly as they did in the earlier phases. Going through the dialogue brings clarity about the owner's commitment empowering the design team. Next we will review the need for owner commitment and project team passion.

Owner Commitment

A handful of design firms have been striving for green solutions for several decades. With the invention and adoption of the USGBC LEED Green Building Rating System, additional design firms and contractors have rapidly joined in the challenge. More important, though, is the current market trend of developers and owners requesting higher performance solutions as well.

Identifying Goals Early

In 1998, after being short-listed to interview for a project, the owner's instructions "included leave your *green thinkers* at home." Almost three years later, after moving in the owner asked if the new building could then obtain USGBC certification. They asked because all of their competitors' buildings were then getting certification. At that point it was unfortunately too late, but had they been open to the idea at the beginning, it would not have been a problem for the project to achieve that goal. Recently, we had potential owners asking for our past history of overall building energy performance and green building certifications at the Request for Qualifications stage.

We would like to underscore the power of institutional commitment as one of the more important factors for achieving a sustainable solution. In order for a team of people to move in a positive, forward direction, there must be a solid level of commitment in that direction. That commitment must then be expressed to the professionals hired to deliver the project. Expressing the commitment is the key for those mission-driven values to be carried out in the design and construction solution. If that commitment waivers to the point of opening up internal factions, it becomes challenging for the design and construction teams to deliver the best solution.

We have seen project leadership on the owner side change mid-project (even in the midst of construction) only to completely derail the established sustainability goals and expectations the team started with. All the benefits from the clarity established in the vision, principle, and goals dialogue disappear when owner-side commitments break down.

Project Team Passion

For achieving high levels of success, we must consider project team passion. It is the nature of human beings to perform exceptionally well at something if they are interested at their core. Teams will be able to reach higher degrees of sustainability if they are champions of sustainable design and proactive about implementing it.

Owners should not handicap themselves by selecting a team that is developing sustainable solutions just to be compliant with owner expectations. The USGBC LEED program has been a great market-changing tool, but it is only a guideline and a starting place. An inexperienced team that is using a green building rating system tool or trying to incorporate sustainable methodologies only because it is a requirement of the project will find an arduous path ahead of them. If they passionately want to achieve better solutions, that passion can partially compensate for lack of experience.

Every owner should seek a project team that has the desire and ability to find creative solutions, which might be outside the realm of a green building rating system. It is mainly through innovation that sustainable design and construction solutions will continue to grow. A passionate team combined with a committed owner who has clear goals could even take the project beyond the earliest expectations while still meeting budget and quality constraints.

Facilitating Integration in Process

After a design team is put together, expectations are clear, the owner is committed and everyone is passionate about what can be achieved, the design process can start. As the team works hard to achieve a sustainable building, continued dialogue is a must. A good tool for continued dialogue is team workshops. The number of workshops depends on the project type, project schedule, and available fee.

Keep in mind that developing ideas in the early stages of design is relatively inexpensive compared to other costs of building. In our experience, by the end of the schematic design phase, only 20–25% of the design fees have been spent, but about 70–80% of environmental impact and operating costs have been determined. These early ideas can be tested for outcomes and thus allow necessary changes to take place early before a lot of intellectual and financial capital is already spent. Changing design decisions in the early phases is much more effective than after the whole team has entered construction documents or, even worse, has made changes when the project has been partially built.

You should have whole team workshops in each of the early phases: predesign, schematic design, and design development. The workshops are most effective if they span over two or three days, but they need to be established based on the size, complexity, and fee allowable in the project. As the team moves into the latter phases of the project, such as construction documents or construction, it is important to still work together as a team. Collaboration in these phases, though, can happen in smaller groups and on an as-needed basis as long as information from those sessions is shared in a timely manner with the rest of the team.

Design Phase Workshops

A trademark of integrated design teams is the workshop, a time when the entire team physically gets together to work on aspects of the project. Each phase of the design process will likely have a different number of workshops, and each project will have conditions that suggest fewer or more workshops overall.

Predesign

In predesign, the first workshop should happen at or near the project site. The first day should encompass a site tour, a tour of any existing facility the owner is using, and a dialogue focused on the owner's vision, principles, and goals. Realize that the dialogue could take anywhere from a whole day to three days depending on project size. An individual building can be done in a day—a master plan takes longer. Let's continue with a building example.

The second and third day of the first predesign workshop can be spent with the entire stakeholder group reconfirming the decisions made the day before, leading to an understanding of the program, the site, the building type, and climate. Other project requirements like code compliance, zoning regulations, and the regulatory planning process should be described. Next, the team can start developing big-picture options for some of the main project systems. Early thoughts and diagrams for structural, mechanical, electrical, plumbing, envelope and skin systems, building location, site development, constraints, and opportunities can be presented.

It is best if the predesign workshop information is captured by the architect and put in a deliverable for reference throughout the project. Each team member contributes his or her expertise to the document. Prior to distribution back to the project team, the owner should review and approve the document. Each team member is required to understand the contents prior to proceeding. With the established baseline, teams can move into schematic design workshops.

Schematic Design

During the first schematic design workshops, the project team develops several concepts for the overall design of the building and site. The number of concepts depends on the project, but three or four are not unreasonable. The team will have a few weeks for the experts to test each of these concepts from a high-level view for performance, cost, and environmental impact. Analysis should not be overly complicated, but rely on experience and simple simulations and order-of-magnitude calculations. The results should be compared to the targets developed during goal setting for suggested direction.

In a second schematic design workshop, the project team will review the results and optimize the concepts. Some of the better-performing strategies from one concept could be integrated into another. The team should take the best parts and pieces and revisit the concepts. These can be refined into no more than two schemes to analyze again before settling on one concept.

Architectural beauty and grace notwithstanding, the winning concept should have the greatest operational performance and lowest environmental impacts while meeting the stipulated budget. Based on the full complement of information, the project team can put together a report that includes a summary of decisions made to date, the site and building design, a program confirmation, environmental impact report, project schedule, and cost estimate. The report should also include options that could be considered for bringing the project costs in line with the budget or added if more financial resources become available. Before moving to the next phase, the owner should review and approve the single design solution and confirm the project budget.

Design Development

As the project continues into the design development phase, workshops will focus on refinement of the overall design. Architectural, structural, mechanical, electrical, and plumbing systems will be further integrated and reviewed for their effect on construction schedule, first and long-term operating costs, performance, and environmental impacts.

Water Runoff

We were on a team developing a manufacturing and warehouse project in an area where stormwater runoff was a key issue. One of the project goals was to reduce stormwater runoff below city requirements. Early in schematic design, the strategy involved using an intensive green roof, which allows for large plants. At the same time, the team was targeting a steel structural system, which best met the owner's needs for aesthetics, cleanliness, durability, and speed of erection. How did these choices integrate together in detail?

Due to the weight of the intensive green roof, more structural support was needed, but that would have increased costs and limited the spanning distance, which would have required more steel columns than was desired in the space. The team found that they could still achieve the same level in reduction of stormwater runoff by talking with the civil engineer and the landscape designer. Together they decided to use an extensive green roof, one only 3–6 inches deep, and keep the structural system light and cost effective. Site strategies for runoff reduction like pervious paving and bioswales can be implemented to make up the difference between the intensive and extensive green roofs. Without the holistic view brought by the team of architect, owner, structural engineer, civil engineer, and landscape architect, the solution could not have been reached.

There are many situations like the one described in the sidebar "Water Runoff" where early design strategies and the ways they integrate with each other need refining to achieve the project goals. Working together at the same table enables these solutions to come to light more effectively than waiting for them to be discovered during a review period.

Construction Delivery Method

As the design and construction industry starts to successfully re-embrace some of the strategies and practices of past generations along with new technologies, there is some debate as to what the best delivery method is for true triple-bottom-line performance. Is it the time-tested method of design-bid-build, guaranteed maximum price, or design-build? In this section we will explore some examples from the heartland region by which you will see that none of the methods are automatically better than the others.

Design-Bid-Build

Design-bid-build is a process of documentation that has been utilized by architects for decades. Design-bid-build keeps the contractor from any interaction or participation with the owner or project team during the design phases. As the name suggests, the architect and consultants design the project and then send it to a group of contractors who competitively bid on the job. The owner weighs the bids against the project budget and reputation of the contractor to make a final selection. After the project is awarded, the contractor is brought on to the team to begin construction.

The design-bid-build process was originally created to aid the owner in getting the best price available from the contractor and as a means of cutting costs. Over time and with additional complexities in the building industry, design-bid-build has created some adverse conditions between design and construction teams. The contractor is not engaged early in design phases to share expert opinions on constructability, and the design team is left to guess at what the best details will be to convey the design intent of the project. Design teams without an experienced, well-connected cost estimator also struggle to design within budget.

On paper, design-bid-build as a process doesn't set itself up well for the integration associated with truly sustainable solutions. However, high-performance green buildings like the Lewis and Clark State Office Building in Jefferson City, Missouri, exemplify how a team can partner to overcome the shortcomings of the design-bid-build process.

Designed by BNIM Architects, the 120,000-sq.-ft. USGBC LEED-NC Platinum–certified office building cost only $151/sq. ft. The project was commissioned by the Missouri Department of Natural Resources (MoDNR) for its offices and reflects their mission to protect and restore Missouri's natural resources. The project team was challenged to design an office building that would set new standards for sustainability without increasing costs, focusing on energy efficiency, healthy workplace, and stewardship of resources (Figure 3.5). Each decision solved multiple design problems in a highly integrated design. Strong partnering that started in design phases and continued with the addition of the contractor after bid resulted in the Platinum certification, beyond the owner's original goal and still within MoDNR's standard preset budget.

Image © Assassi | Courtesy of BNIM Architects

Figure 3.5 Lewis and Clark Office Building

Several factors contributed to the success of the project:

Integrated design To accomplish a Platinum rating with a modest budget and no contractor participation during design, a high level of collaboration among the design team was necessary to balance economic and environmental aspects of the project.

Partnering A high level of enthusiasm and partnering between the owner, tenant, and designers—sustained by charettes and community outreach—was critical to promote a *can-do* spirit. This spirit inspired the eager construction team, who were driven to gain additional points for the project by outperforming some original goals set in their absence. The construction team had never done a *green* building before and has since been recognized by a national award for their partnering on the project.

Design The building's form, orientation, envelope, and systems were integrated to maximize energy performance and optimize daylight, views, and thermal comfort throughout the workplace. The design is 60% more energy-efficient than a baseline building. Operable windows throughout each space decrease dependency on mechanical ventilation systems. An under-floor plenum allows occupant-control over thermal comfort. Building materials with low volatile organic compounds (VOCs) were used, such as carpets, paints, sealants, and adhesives.

Resource use Eighty-five percent of materials from a former structure were diverted from landfill. Seventy-five percent of new building materials came from within a 500-mile radius. Collaborating with the Missouri Department of Corrections' Vocational Enterprises program, the design team redesigned the state's standard systems furniture to be compatible with Greenguard Environmental Institute standards. The combined efforts transformed the program's practices for future projects. Restorative site planning treats all stormwater runoff via bioswales, level spreaders, and native planting. A 50,000-gallon cistern captures rainwater for reuse. Waterless urinals and low-flow fixtures further minimize potable water usage, saving 405,000 gallons of water in the first 13 months.

Negotiated Guaranteed Maximum Price

In a negotiated guaranteed maximum price (GMP) delivery method, the goal is to limit the construction price of the building by setting a top end price for the building to be constructed. This makes owners comfortable that they will get a project delivered for no more than a set amount, unless of course there are changes that are not in the documents on which the price was guaranteed. In the GMP scenario, the owner still separately hires the designers and contractor, but the contractor can be engaged early on in the design process, thereby providing the desired opportunities for collaboration and team commitment.

A superb example of the GMP construction delivery method is the Heifer International Center in Little Rock, Arkansas. Developed as the first phase of a 22-acre development on an EPA-classified brownfield east of downtown Little Rock, the 94,000-sq.-ft. office building recently won a 2007 American Institute of Architects (AIA) Committee on the Environment Top Ten Award and a prestigious National 2008 AIA Honor Award. Completed in 2006, the project is also USGBC LEED-NC Platinum Certified. The project team included Elements, a consulting division of BNIM Architects, as the Sustainable Design Consultant to the Architect of Record, Polk Stanley Rowland Curzon Porter Architects. Figure 3.6 shows the completed project, which excluding the cost of land cost $190/sq. ft. Much of the team's success can be contributed to the commitment of the owner.

Figure 3.6 Heifer International Center, Little Rock Arkansas

In 2003, after going through a good portion of the early design scope, Elements was brought in at the owner's request to share knowledge with the existing design team about sustainable design and facilitate achievement of Heifer's green design goals. Our work started with a series of eco-workshops centered on the mission of Heifer. During the workshops, the entire project team further developed the goals of Heifer's internal

Green Team, setting high expectations for the design. With new knowledge and resources available, the entire project team turned into champions, led by the owner's commitment to pursue their sustainability mission.

A specific example of owner commitment is the approach taken by the owner to recycle or salvage 97% (by weight) of the 13 existing buildings and associated paving on site. Heifer first removed all the hazardous components, and then salvaged what they wanted from the buildings, including bricks for reuse. Next, Heifer offered the remaining materials to their employees to harvest building components, followed by local contractors, then the community. After all of these efforts, the buildings mostly consisted of the masonry walls, concrete floors, steel structure, a few nonrecyclable walls, and roofing materials. After removing the unsalvageable materials and recycling the steel, the project team worked within the community to find a new deconstruction company that would grind the remaining concrete and masonry materials on site. The grindings were then used for fill on site and the excess sold to another construction site.

Another example is how Heifer's commitment to water drove integrated team thinking and collaboration. During the eco-workshops, Heifer expressed their commitment to water, by stating that of all the countries they worked in, the United States treated water most carelessly and the project should be an example of respecting water as a resource. The team took Heifer's mission-driven value and created a project where no water leaves the site except blackwater from the toilets.

The unparalleled respect for water starts with a permeable paving system in the parking lot encouraging stormwater infiltration. Excess water goes into natively planted bioswales for filtration, and eventually gets stored in a retention pond. The retention pond gravity feeds a constructed wetland that surrounds the building and snakes through the property creating a new habitat area. Ducks and other wildlife moved into the wetland a few months after the project was completed. Rainwater from the 30,000-sq ft. roof is collected in a five-story 42,000-gallon water tower. That water supplements a separate gray water storage tank fed from lavatories and condensate from outside air units. Together the storage tanks supply water for toilets and the cooling tower, which account for 90% of the project's water needs.

Design-Build

The design-build delivery method has gained a lot of popularity in recent years. In effect, design-build partners the designer and builder under one contract to the building owner. In the other two examples given earlier, the design team and the contractor were separate entities. Using the design-build method, both designer and contractor do not need to be the same company but the goal is to create a more unified team.

A shining example of success via design-build is the Sunset Drive Office Building, Olathe, Kansas ($178/sq. ft.). Built by McCownGordon Construction for Johnson

County, Kansas, the 127,000-sq. ft., design-build office building houses seven Johnson County departments. Upon completion in 2006, the project received a USGBC LEED-NC Gold certification (Figure 3.7). The project approach included using an integrated team that brought the contractor, designers, consultants, and subcontractors to the table during the initial development stages. The team's integrated approach allowed for on-the-spot analysis of design ideas by the contractor and subcontractors building it. The integrated process offered cost and constructability analysis at an early stage to help minimize redesign and also find creative ways to offset some of the more expensive components of the project.

Figure 3.7 Sunset Drive Office Building

An example of the team approach was the integration of the mechanical, electrical, and plumbing (MEP) subcontractors with the MEP engineers during the design. Together they evaluated equipment and controls to maximize efficiency but maintain budgets. Another example was the steel contractor saving the project significant material costs by recommending a change to the structural grid spacing. The financial savings on steel allowed for investment in more efficient MEP systems. With the early subcontractor involvement and buy-in on the process, the outcome was much better and made achieving LEED credits for recycled materials, locally manufactured, and on-site recycling much easier to achieve.

Is One Construction Delivery Method the Best?

As you can see from our examples, the delivery method is not as important to the project outcome as project team collaboration, institutional commitment, and project team passion. Each of the projects we described was delivered by a different method at reasonable first costs. Each obtained high levels of environmental performance, including all being 50% more energy efficient than the baseline energy code.

There is even a new delivery method that could lend itself to becoming the best option of all: lean construction (`http://www.leanconstruction.org`). Lean construction is a production management–based approach to project delivery. In the lean construction method, the architect, contractor, and owner are all contracted together, not separately. Some key aspects of lean construction are as follows:

- The facility and its delivery process are designed together to better reveal and support customer purposes.
- The work is structured throughout the process to maximize value and to reduce waste at the project delivery level.
- The efforts to manage and improve performance are aimed at improving total project performance because that goal is more important than reducing the cost or increasing the speed of any activity.

Moving Forward

Your next project will be here soon! Start working on the important things now: secure stakeholder commitment at all levels of the organization, pick a passionate project team (experienced if you can), and invite all design and construction disciplines to the table as soon as the delivery method allows. Whatever your approach, be sure that you dream big, collaborate, and have fun!

Methodology For Sustainable Solutions

4

I would feel more optimistic about a bright future for man if he spent less time proving that he can outwit Nature and more time tasting her sweetness and respecting her seniority.

—E. B. White

Now that we have explored the concepts behind sustainability and how they can affect a team, we need to investigate how the concepts affect design. We will describe an order of operations that will help any design team achieve a more sustainable result. By thinking about specific issues at the correct time in the project process, you can minimize negative impacts and keep both first cost and operation costs low. Once you understand how to create sustainable solutions through design, you can integrate the power of BIM.

Order of Operations

As discussed in Chapter 1, developing sustainable solutions requires an expansion of traditional thinking. It is necessary to include more input parameters and consider a longer period of time while making decisions during the design process. Often as designers, we are asked by peers, clients, or other professionals to break down the process for sustainable design into simple steps that are easier to follow. This is our *order of operations*, and it is derived from the following common methodology for reducing the energy consumption of buildings:

1. Understanding climate
2. Reducing loads
3. Using free energy
4. Using efficient systems

We've expanded on the thinking behind the energy consumption methodology and through our work have developed the following order of operations, which you can take advantage of through the design process. We will show you how to apply our order of operations to the design of a building's energy use, water use, material use, and site:

1. Understanding climate, culture, and place
2. Understanding the building type
3. Reducing the resource consumption need
4. Using free/local resources and natural systems
5. Using efficient manmade systems
6. Applying renewable energy generation systems
7. Offsetting remaining negative impacts

Understanding Climate, Culture, and Place

If understanding climate, culture, and place sounds like an important *no-brainer* thing to do, you are right and likely ahead of the game. However, think of all the buildings that have been designed and built over the past 30 years that have not applied this basic concept.

Understanding climate is one of the first challenges for any team achieving a successful design. A simple way to understand how designers have forgotten about climate is to picture the example of a glass office tower. Figure 4.1 shows some of the similarities in design of glass office towers in Chicago and Houston. Both cities have drastically different climates but similar office towers. Many of the major cities in America have a glass office tower, from Miami (which has approximately 4,300 cooling degree days) to Anchorage (which has approximately 10,600 heating degree days). What we have been saying as designers, builders, and owners is, "Let's put this building here and use whatever energy is necessary to keep the occupants comfortable with a mechanical system." If designers had considered the climate in which they were developing, a different solution would have likely arisen.

The culture of people in each respective area is also different. Should every office worker in America have the same indoor environment? Regarding a sense of place, in some building types we have quickly moved toward every building looking the same. Take, for example, the American strip mall or big box store; they are designed to look the same regardless of city, from the exterior to the interior layout.

Images courtesy of Brad Nies and Filo Castore

Figure 4.1 Skyline: Chicago and Houston

There are also built environments in which some want to replicate the look of a faraway place in a new location, which usually requires getting building materials from that faraway place. One example is a North American client or designer who has an affinity for Italian marble.

Understanding Climate

It does not take a lot of effort to capture the basic scientific understanding of climate in a place. Making that understanding intuitive will take time and practice, but the data required for the foundation of good design decisions is readily available. As part of our firm's practice and workflow, we gather scientific data and develop a climatology chart based on that data for every place in which we work (Figure 4.2). The chart includes basic information on sun, wind, moisture, temperature, a psychometric chart, and flora and fauna for the given locale.

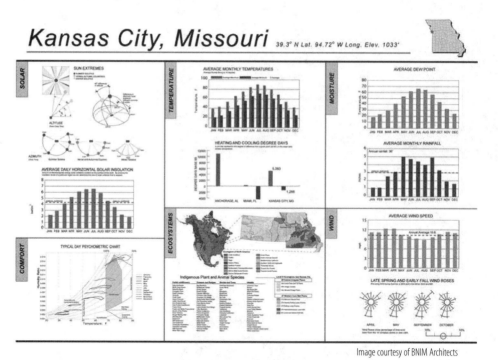

Image courtesy of BNIM Architects

Figure 4.2 An example of a climatology chart

We will explain how to gather and use climate information in the following sections.

Location

All of the climate information needed is related to the project site's position on the earth, so the first thing a team should do is learn the latitude and longitude of the project site. This seems rather basic, but it is an important step, which makes finding the rest of the climate information much easier. Because you are using a BIM tool, you can get this information by selecting your project location in the Project Location dialog box. Alternatively, you can get location information from maps, other software, or websites, including those that supply other data that we will describe later.

Knowing the latitude and longitude can quickly tell the project team when the seasons are during the year. You can also determine how far off the project location is from solar (true) south. Solar south is the direction toward the geographical South Pole from a given point. Solar south can differ from magnetic south depending on the location's geophysical space on the globe. The difference between the two is called *magnetic declination*. To maximize opportunities for using the sun for passive heating, energy, and daylight, the building should have a long east-west axis and face solar south. In general terms, you want to keep the long façade of the building within 15 ± degrees of solar south.

Also, you can use the latitude for a back of envelope calculation on the correct angle for use of fixed-tilt photovoltaic (PV) panels. For best performance on an annual basis, PV panels are normally placed equal to the angle of latitude because this maximizes the sun's perpendicular exposure to the PV panels across the year. Kansas City is located at 39 degrees latitude; PV panels on a project in Kansas City are best placed at a 39-degree tilt from the horizontal ground plane.

Sun

Sun information includes two primary items: the basic sun angles for that area, and the insolation data for that area. The insolation amount decreases the farther one moves from the equator. Azimuth and altitude are the two measurements of the sun's position in relationship to a given location on earth. Azimuth is the horizontal component of the sun's position expressed in angles from true south. A positive number describes the position as east of south, and a negative number describes a position as west of south. Altitude is the position of the sun in elevation expressed in angles from the horizontal plane of the project location. It is important to note that we recommend you gather this information in *clock time* as opposed to *solar time*. Clock time accounts for the position of the sun relative to that area's observance of daylight saving time (DST). Clock time is more beneficial because building operation schedules are geared toward uses figured on clock hours, not solar hours. The most recognizable difference is the noontime position of the sun. Many designers expect the sun to be perfectly perpendicular to a building oriented true south at noontime. This is not the case during DST as the clock is one hour ahead of the sun; the sun would be closer to perpendicular to this true south–oriented building at 1 P.M. Figure 4.3 shows some of these conditions.

Sun angles can be gathered from several sources. One of these sources is the manually operated Pilkington Sun Angle Calculator, originally developed by Libby-Owens-Ford, and now offered by the Society of Building Science Educators (SBSE). There are also web-based tools such as SunAngle offered by Sustainable By Design (http://www.susdesign.com/sunangle/).

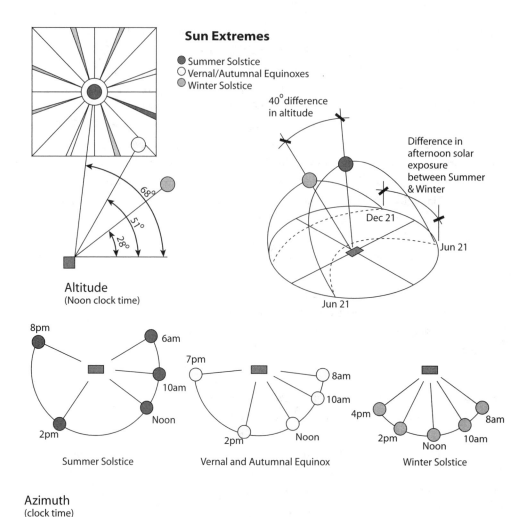

Sun Extremes

● Summer Solstice
○ Vernal/Autumnal Equinoxes
● Winter Solstice

40° difference in altitude

Difference in afternoon solar exposure between Summer & Winter

Dec 21

Jun 21

Jun 21

68°
51°
28°

Altitude
(Noon clock time)

Summer Solstice

8pm
6am
10am
2pm
Noon

Vernal and Autumnal Equinox

7pm
8am
10am
2pm
Noon

Winter Solstice

4pm
8am
2pm
10am
Noon

Azimuth
(clock time)

Image courtesy of BNIM Architects

Figure 4.3 Basic sun angle information for Kansas City, MO

You can use the basic altitude and azimuth angles for several things during your conceptual and schematic design phases. First, combining the sun angles with the information gathered early about the location of solar south, you can orient your building properly. You can also properly choose the best locations for glazing based on solar access, as well as develop any necessary external shading devices to help minimize solar heat gain and undesirable direct solar penetration. The basic altitude and azimuth angles allow you to determine the basic external shade depth and whether the shades are best placed horizontally, vertically, or a combination of both. Not all project sites or building programs allow for the most optimal orientation. In these situations, it is best to review each façade for the potential needs of external shading.

Also keep in mind that these are the basic angles sliced in section. The actual sun angle shining on a building is a compound relation between the azimuth and altitude angle. These basic angles work great for early design decisions and intuitive learning. More refined compound angles should be used for final design refinement and detailing. Thankfully, most design software allows you to visually review the compound angles on the fly, including most BIM tools (Figure 4.4).

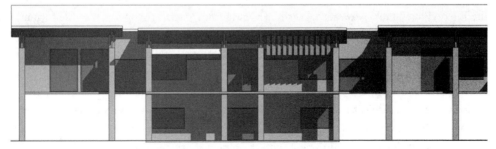

Figure 4.4 View of external shading devices sized in Autodesk Revit Architecture

By knowing the insolation levels of a particular region, you can determine the size of solar collectors that are required for both hot water heating and electricity generation. The number is measured in kilowatt hours per square meter per day, or kWh/m²/day. In Figure 4.5 you can see that the best time to capture energy from the sun in Kansas City is from March through September.

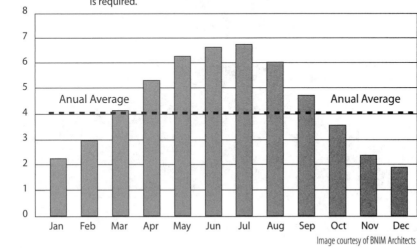

Average Daily Horizon Solar Insolation

Amount of electromagnetic energy (solar radiation) incident on the surface of the earth. By knowing the insolation levels of a particular region, we can determine the size of solar collector that is required.

Image courtesy of BNIM Architects

Figure 4.5 Insolation data for Kansas City

Temperature and Dewpoint

The next important set of information is temperature data. You should gather the average maximum, average, and average minimum temperatures on a monthly basis. Temperature data is readily available through weather data files supplied for most energy simulation software packages. Free downloadable tools like Climate Consultant (`http://www.aud.ucla.edu/energy-design-tools`) allow you to easily view compiled climate data without having to learn or own an energy simulation program. Climate Consultant is a graphical interface that visually displays climate data using files compiled in the EnergyPlus (`http://www.eere.energy.gov/buildings/energyplus/`) weather file format. Prior to the accessibility that Climate Consultant provides (and for areas where weather data has not been provided in the EnergyPlus format), you can gather temperature data on the Web from sites such as Weatherbase (`http://www.weatherbase.com`).

After gathering the temperature data at a glance, you can identify potential time periods where the project might be able to use natural ventilation. Cross-check these time periods with the moisture information, which will be discussed later in this section. Also design external shades in conjunction with the temperature and comfort data from the climatology chart. Optimal design for external shading should block out the unwanted heat during the cooling season and let in desirable solar gain during the heating season without producing discomfort from glare. In Figure 4.6, note the average diurnal swing—the difference between the average maximum and average minimum temperatures. The diurnal swing can identify possibilities for night cooling.

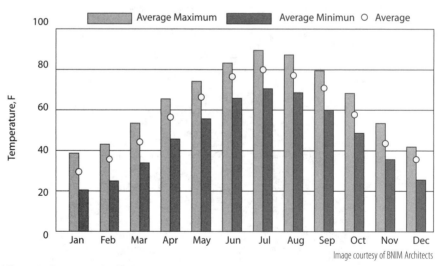

Figure 4.6 Temperature data for Kansas City

Based on temperature data, cities in the United States are benchmarked by heating and cooling degree days to identify the potential need for heating and cooling in the building. A *degree day* represents the difference between the mean daily temperature and the control temperature, which is usually 65 degrees Fahrenheit (F). For example, if the mean temperature for a given day was 85F, this equals 20 cooling degree days (CDD). A mean temperature of 45 equals 20 heating degree days (HDD). At a glance, this tells you whether the climate is primarily heating or cooling dominated. Figure 4.7 compares the cities that we work in to some of the worst cases in both categories for the United States.

Moisture data is something that goes hand and hand with temperature data because it is these two together that determine overall comfort. To capture the relationship between temperature and moisture, you need to gather monthly average dew point temperatures. Dew point temperatures are available through the same sources that you get the temperature data. High average dew point temperatures suggest potential for human discomfort if they are close to the average temperature. When dew point and temperature are close in value, this is commonly expressed as a high relative humidity. High temperatures tell our body to cool by sweating, and high relative humidity inhibits evaporation of sweat. These combined conditions of high temperature and high dew point create human discomfort.

Heating and Cooling Degree Days

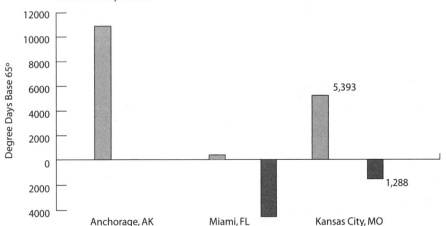

Image courtesy of BNIM Architects

Figure 4.7 Heating and cooling degree day data for Kansas City

Rainfall

Another moisture data set you need to gather is average monthly rainfall (Figure 4.8). You can use the previous mentioned sources—energy simulation software weather files or websites like Weatherbase—to collect rainfall data.

Rainfall numbers are used for simulating and understanding several scenarios. Most notably you can determine how much rain falls on the site in a given period.

With this known quantity of rainwater, you can figure how much runoff potential has either created or mitigated based on your choices for surfaces in the design of elements, such as roofs, walkways, driveways, and landscaping. You can determine how much water can be captured for reuse for features like toilet flushing, irrigation, or a water feature like a fountain or water garden.

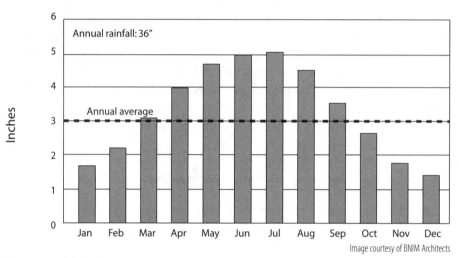

Figure 4.8 Rainfall data for Kansas City

Psychometric Chart

The easiest way to look at which heating and cooling strategies are viable for a given climate is by referring to a psychometric chart, another data set that is included in our climatology chart. By definition, a psychometric chart is a graph of the physical properties of moist air at a constant pressure. Among other things, it maps out three of the data sets talked about previously on one chart: temperature, dew point, and relative humidity.

Instead of mapping the individual data sets out on your own, there are tools that can do this for you. Many of them can use the energy simulation software weather file data sets. One that we mentioned earlier was Climate Consultant. Another is Weather Maker, developed by National Renewable Energy Laboratory (http://www.nrel.gov). Weather Maker is provided as part of Energy-10, an energy analysis package offered by the Sustainable Buildings Industry Council (SBIC), and uses the Energy-10 weather file format.

In the heart of the psychometric chart is the *comfort zone* (Figure 4.9)—the area where humans traditionally feel comfortable. You can overlay typical heating and cooling strategies as zones on this chart so at a glance you can see how much time and during which period of the year a particular strategy will work effectively. The greater number of data points that land within the comfort zone, the less mechanical heating, cooling, and humidity control will be required.

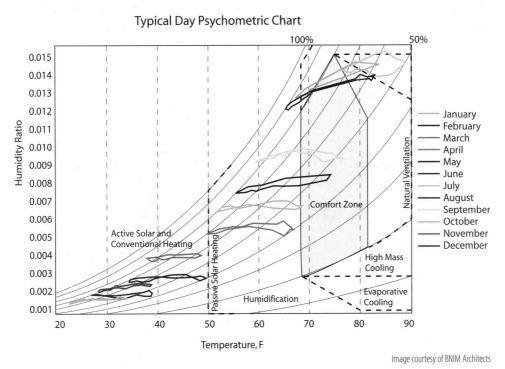

Figure 4.9 Psychometric chart for Kansas City

Wind

You should also gather wind data, including speed, direction, and duration, if available. Depending on the project location, this might be the most challenging data to find. Most weather information comes from weather stations at major airports, which works well if your project site happens to be near one. Each of the data sets that we've discussed so far typically does not vary significantly from the nearby airport data. Given that, the data that can vary the most from specific site to specific site is wind.

Use the wind data you can find as close to your site as possible for early decision making. While websites like Weatherbase feature wind speed, the data set does not include direction or time. The Energy-10 weather file that the Weather Maker tool uses also only provides wind speed. However, the EnergyPlus weather file format allows Climate Consultant to show speed, direction, and duration. We have gotten the direction and duration in various ways over the years, such as contacting regional universities or using the Climate Atlas of the United States, developed by the National Climatic Data Center in Asheville, North Carolina. If the initial data is favorable for inclusion of wind-based strategies, it is advisable to have a wind anemometer with data logger set up on the project site for gathering specific site information.

For wind, you should gather average speed on a monthly and annual basis (Figure 4.10). Also, look at wind direction for months that could be conducive for natural ventilation. The wind direction and speed for months where the temperature and humidity suggest natural ventilation as a cooling strategy is important so that you can optimize the window openings relational to the prevailing breezes.

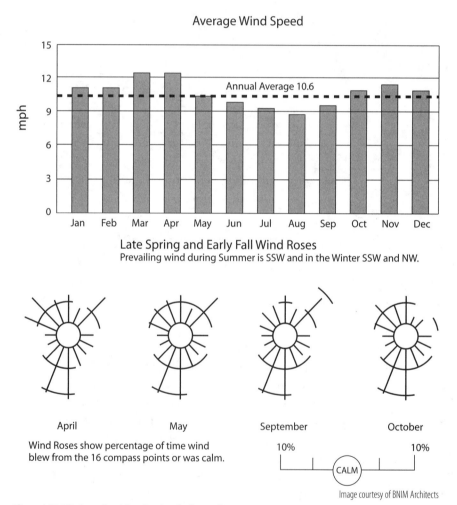

Figure 4.10 Wind speed and direction data for Kansas City

Flora and Fauna

Information on indigenous flora and fauna is the second most challenging piece of data to gather, at least in a format that can be used or referenced quickly. Within our own practice, we prefer to start with information from the EPA's Ecoregion Level IV data. This data is available at http://www.epa.gov/wed/pages/ecoregions/level_iv.htm (Figure 4.11).

This chart can provide a start to some of the indigenous flora and fauna in an area and capture the main types of ecology around your project site. You must fill in the rest using reference books or experts, which can be integrated as part of your project team. At early stages, when you develop your climatology chart try to list wildlife, trees and shrubs, grasses and sedges, and forbs and wildflowers.

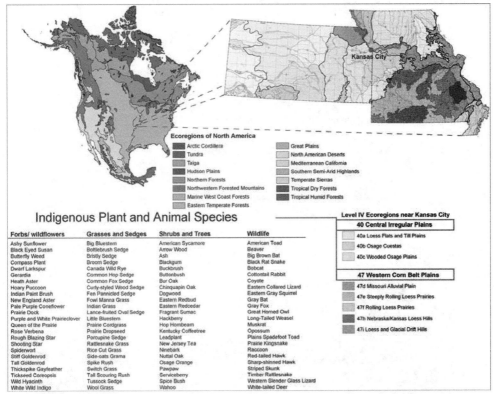

Image courtesy of BNIM Architects

Figure 4.11 Ecoregion data for Kansas City

Understanding Culture

Culture needs to be understood at two levels: the culture of the community and the culture of the client's organization. If you are not from the environment and location in which you are designing, it can be challenging to truly get a handle on the local culture. The only real solution for this is spending time in the community interacting with its members. Understanding the culture of an area becomes even more important if you are working on a large-scale master plan or community-supported building. Part of our approach to understanding culture at both scales includes our highly collaborative process and teaming with local project partners.

Culture of Community

When working at the community scale, we like to have open dialogues as early as possible with all stakeholders. This includes everyone who lives in, works in, or leads the community. All are allowed a voice and chances to express it. Community members educate us on what they feel is most valuable and precious to them, what makes them unique, and what they need, want, and fear most about the project.

Greensburg, Kansas

Recently several of our BNIM colleagues have been volunteering time in support of rebuilding Greensburg, Kansas. Eighty-five percent of the town of Greensburg, approximately 1,450 people, was completely wiped out on May 4, 2007, by an F5 tornado.

Image courtesy of BNIM Architects

The town spent quite a bit of time in a community effort with professionals across the region, state, and country, developing a vision for how to rebuild as a *sustainable* town.

As part of the rebuilding effort, the previous three schools (K–5, 6–8, and 9–12) were going to be combined into one school campus. Much debate was centered on whether the new campus should be in town or outside of town. The argument for locating the school out of town was related to a long-standing and acrimonious debate about school consolidation between towns. The logic was that a consolidated school would have to be understood to be in neutral territory. Students involved in the workshop understood that this would mean isolating education from the life of the town.

Greensburg, Kansas *(continued)*

Image courtesy of BNIM Architects

They felt that pupils from other towns would far prefer, as they would, an educational experience that was more integrated with the life of a place.

In the end the students spoke up in front of everyone and made a compelling case for having the new campus in town. They clearly expressed impatience with the older generation's old jealousies and infighting and urged them to place the interests of the quality of the educational experience first. It was stated that regardless of whether the campus was in or out of town, it must be a good school to learn in. However, being in town provided them with several benefits, including being close to a library and giving older kids the ability to go off campus for lunch. Off campus lunch also supports other businesses in the community, and in the end with the athletic facilities, the new campus would also become an entertainment center.

The students voted for the integrated holistic approach. The school board fully supported this decision and was instrumental in making the project happen in its new location, in town. If the students had not had the opportunity to voice their ideas, it could have turned out for the worse.

Culture of an Organization

When working at the building scale, the project team needs to understand the culture of the organization. The list can be quite lengthy, but here are some basics:

- What is the history of the organization?
- What is the overall vision for the organization's future?
- How is the company structured?
- What is the internal demographic of the employee base?
- What is the overall commitment to sustainable thinking?
- What and/or who is going to be the key driver in decision making?

Understanding culture will lay the foundation for developing a vision, principles, goals, and a clear decision-making process for the project that the team and owner can use for making tough decisions through the course of the project. Most of these items can be conveyed through simple dialogue with the organization's project leader, but expanded dialogue with a wider spread of organizational stakeholders can allow a better understanding.

However the understanding of an organization's culture is accomplished, when the time comes to develop the vision, principles, goals, and decision-making process, we encourage stakeholder participation from the lowest level to the highest. This can include the owner, building occupants, maintenance staff, the contractor, consultants, and others. It is important to garner this type of participation so that all the team members start with the same understanding. Knowing where each person is accountable for some portion of the project at the start is important. The design team will get an education from the client about the organization and its needs. The client hopefully gets an education from the design team about what is possible. Including everyone early in the visioning process gives everyone ownership over the direction of the project and leads to a more team-based workflow.

From our experience, many business owners are looking to create a healthier workplace that attracts and retains the best employees. One of the best ways to accomplish this is by developing a workplace that allows access to natural daylight and views to the outside for more staff members. For some organizations, this might contradict the culture established by the existing office space; it might require a change in office location and type. For example, to meet the goals for daylight and views there will likely be fewer closed offices and those remaining closed offices will be interior, not on the perimeter, unless they allow daylight and views through. By talking with staff members and executives of the organizations about the challenges (such as recognizing organizational hierarchy, and privacy) as well as showing examples of the latest office space trends and explaining the benefits of the new layout, you can ensure that the cultural change can be worked through at every stakeholder level.

Understanding Place

Every place is unique and has its own sense of character—or at least it did prior to you developing it. Joking aside, the methods by which we've developed our land into towns, cities, and metropolises define and redefine that place. Developing and incorporating the various design styles that have emerged over the years, our built environment defines where and who we are.

By many appearances, the suburban parts of America are trying to destroy this fundamental act of nature with the never-ending "just add water" houses with strip malls located every 10–15 minutes apart. Even some of the major core redevelopment plans are replicated from past success in another city simply supplanted in the new locale. If you stop to look around and understand the character of a place before designing, you can eliminate the trend of architecture as object and support the existing public realm or, in some cases, support the remaining natural splendor.

It might help if you think of each building as part of a family that relates to one another but each type has its own role in a functioning system. Some buildings are monuments, some are for public events, some are for business, some are for the community, some are for education, and so forth. Each one working within the overall fabric and correctly representing its role can add to the vitality and complexity that makes a place that place and the wonderful spaces in-between, some of which are best left natural.

Recently we worked as part of an interdisciplinary team on a university master plan development. The team was charged with setting sustainability goals, creating guidelines, and conceptualizing the development of 8 million square feet of buildings and associated infrastructure over 30 years on a site of approximately 980 acres. Key components of the existing site included an original old-growth forest, second-growth forest, two streams, a rail line, a landfill, a chemical dumpsite, an existing municipal facility, and a recently closed airport. Adjacent land included undeveloped property, neighborhoods, a public school, university maintenance buildings, and arterial roadways. The process involved months of study of these conditions and stakeholder dialogue with more than 75 individuals who represented the community and the university, including individual schools, facilities, planning, maintenance and operations, energy services, vice chancellors, trustees, and others.

As a result of learning about the place, its neighbors, and the culture of the community that used them, the concept design for the development was sited on only 250 of those acres with a concentration on the previously impacted property and near the main artery. This allowed protection of existing natural systems, restoration of damaged systems, and concentration of development that would support a transit-oriented solution.

Understanding the Building Type

Once you grasp the fundamentals of climate, culture, and place, you can move on to the actual building. Many designers understand the overarching difference between building types but sometimes forget to incorporate this into the details. For the most part, designers have done a good job at making houses look like houses, schools like schools, offices like offices, and so forth. However, they've not been as forthright with how each building type responds to the climate around it.

The second-largest challenge to a successful design is understanding how a particular building type responds to its surrounding climate. We believe some of this forgotten understanding is a result of the industry's transition over the last half of the twentieth century to relying on codified uniform standards across multiple climate zones and the manufacturers tying product warranties to these standards. Failing to comprehend the relationship between building type and climate at the beginning can often result in misapplied technologies and higher costs.

For example, to identify the most appropriate resource-efficient strategies you must understand the building you are going to apply those strategies to. What is the most basic strategy for saving energy for a home in Kansas City? Hopefully most of you answered a quality building envelope. A review of the following energy use graphs (Figures 4.12 through 4.14) from a simulation of a typical home in the Kansas City region shows between 45–50% of the energy load is from heating and cooling, with about 90% of the heating load and over 60% of the cooling load coming from conduction. Conduction is the transfer of heat through matter—in this case the transfer of heat through materials making up the envelope of the building. For example, heat will move quicker through a metal stud than it will move through insulation.

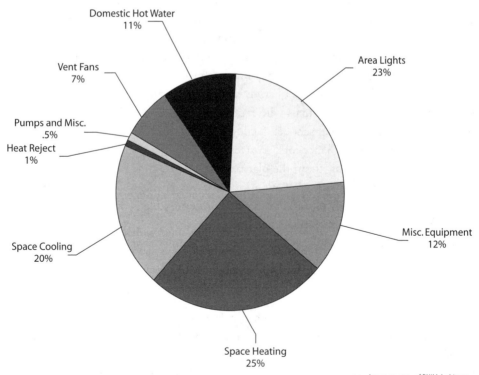

Figure 4.12 Energy consumption chart for a Kansas City residence

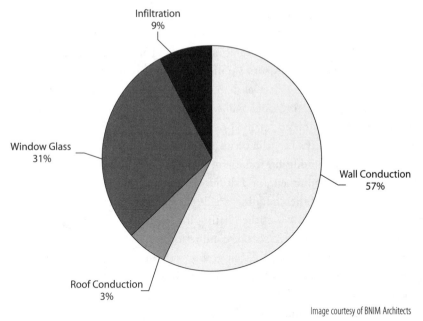

Image courtesy of BNIM Architects

Figure 4.13 Heating load chart for a Kansas City residence

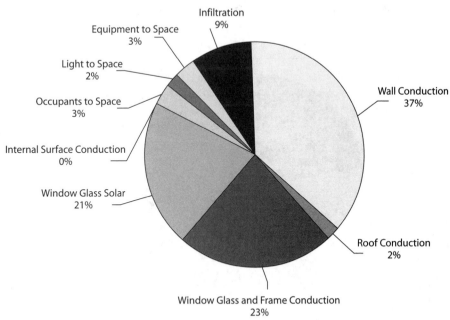

Image courtesy of BNIM Architects

Figure 4.14 Cooling load chart for a Kansas City residence

A home is a relatively small building with few occupants and a lot of exterior envelope per square foot of floor. Due to this makeup, the home reacts more to changes in its external environment than its internal environment. On an annual basis, Kansas City experiences very cold, dry winters and hot, humid summers. Therefore, if you want to keep a Kansas City home at a set temperature and humidity, you'll need a high value of thermal resistance in the roofs, walls, and windows.

Should the same approach taken for the house be applied to a 200,000-square-foot office building in Kansas City? No, the office building is a much bigger building with an entirely different use. In addition to having a lower skin-to-floor area ratio, it has more internal users, more equipment, and different operating times. The combined heating and cooling loads in the office building are likely to be between 35% and 40% of the total energy load, while 50–60% of the heating load is from conduction and only about 30–40% of the cooling load is from conduction.

You still need good thermal resistance, but going to the same level as you would on a house doesn't make sense. Look at other ways to reduce energy load for the office building type, such as percentage of glazing, external shading, daylighting, automated lighting controls, and efficient equipment. On the same percentage basis, the cooling load from equipment in an office building is six times that of the load in the house and the cooling load required from occupants is three times that of a typical residence. Some typical Kansas City office building energy loads are shown in Figures 4.15 through 4.17.

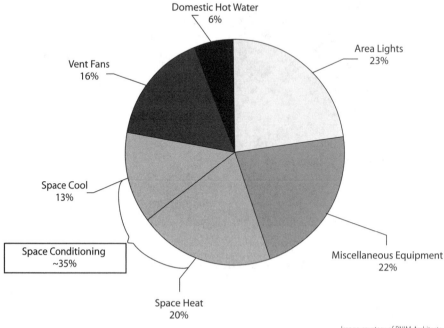

Figure 4.15 Energy consumption chart for a Kansas City office building

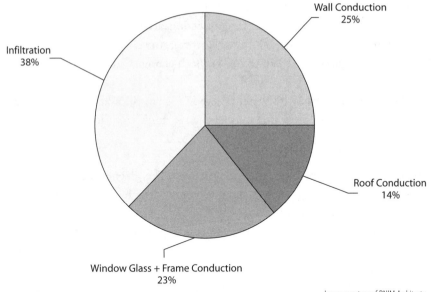

Image courtesy of BNIM Architects

Figure 4.16 Heating load chart for a Kansas City office building

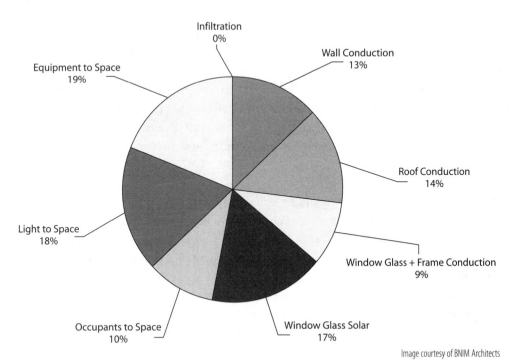

Image courtesy of BNIM Architects

Figure 4.17 Cooling load chart for a Kansas City office building

What if each of these buildings was relocated from Kansas City to Seattle? The design drivers would change. For example, the conduction-driven heating load of the office building would be a little higher, 60–70%. However, the cooling load driven by conduction would drop to between 10% and 20%. Both changes are due to the difference in climate.

Similar exercises can be run with water. The point is you should understand the building's need for resources and how those needs change in different locations.

Reducing the Resource Consumption Need

In the green building industry, there is a common saying: "The greenest building is the one that is never built." From those championing use of existing building stock you might hear, "The greenest building is the one that is already built." Both statements are targeting the same objective. If it is not absolutely necessary, don't create it.

Space

When a project team is starting programming for a project or beginning designs based on a client-provided program, the first question they should ask is, "Does the client need this space?" This question should be asked at the whole project scale and the individual room scale until things are sized as appropriately as possible. Financially creating space has first costs associated with construction and long-term cost associated with operations and maintenance. Space has upstream environmental impacts from manufacturing and construction as well as downstream environmental impacts related to maintenance and disposal or recycling. The "Do we need this?" line of questioning is sustainable both environmentally and economically for the resources of materials, energy, and water. Once the required space need has been defined, it is time to turn to reducing the required resources to build and operate the project.

Materials

What resources or materials will you be using? How can you use as few as possible or use the ones you must have the most effectively? We believe that every material, BTU, and gallon of water used should have a purpose in a project, and it is even better if they have more than one. Every element and component in a project can be shown in a number of ways.

Using the building structure as a finish surface can be done with concrete floors and carefully installed metal decks. Both of these materials have the potential to assist in extending daylight into the building. The concrete can easily be painted to add reflectance, and the metal deck has its own natural reflectance. So, with either of those solutions you have an integrated system, which is the solution our company utilized in the University of Texas Health Science Center at Houston School of Nursing (UTHSCH SON).

Anita B. Gorman Conservation Discovery Center

Let's consider the tongue and groove wood decking used in the Anita B. Gorman Conservation Discovery Center. The decking is used both as the roof deck and is left exposed below as an attractive interior ceiling finish, removing the need for another material to act as the ceiling. Not having a second ceiling material can also reduce the overall height of the building since the clearance tolerances for running the matrix of ductwork, grilles, and lights above a ceiling are now eliminated.

Image © Assassi | Courtesy of BNIM Architects

When it comes to using concrete, we have to talk about the content of Portland cement. Portland cement has one of the highest embodied energies of all building products. While Portland cement is only about 10–12% of a common ready-mix concrete mix, it is accountable for at least 85% of the embodied energy of concrete, according to the Portland Cement Association's report "Life Cycle Inventory of Portland Cement Concrete."

Embodied energy refers to all the energy required for the creation of that material or product, from harvest to delivery to use. Common stages of material manufacture are raw material extraction, manufacture, assembly, transport, and installation. Concrete has many benefits, including its durability and high mass, the fact that its surface can be an attractive finish, its recyclability, and the fact that it can be made locally. Lucky for us there is a way to reduce its embodied energy.

University of Texas Health Science Center at Houston School of Nursing

UTHSCH SON, designed by BNIM Architects in collaboration with Lake/Flato Architects, contains high fly ash concrete for the structure. The project replaced 48% of the Portland cement in the concrete mix with fly ash. Common use of fly ash is 25%. Fly ash is a by-product material of coal-fired power plants, and in concrete mixes it acts very much like Portland cement. By using such a high content, the project team reduced almost half the need of a hard-to-harvest building material and in that process saved 1,808 tons of carbon dioxide from being emitted.

Image courtesy of Hester + Hardaway Photographers

Energy

From an energy perspective you can reduce a building's need in many ways. We have listed the 12 most common energy efficiency measures:

- Building orientation
- Building massing
- Optimized envelope
- Optimized glazing
- Optimized shading
- Daylight dimming
- Optimized lighting
- Efficient equipment
- Passive solar

- Thermal mass
- Natural ventilation
- Optimized mechanical systems

For now we will concentrate on the first seven. A truly great thing about the first seven listed energy load reduction strategies is how they can be combined for a collective better solution. For example, as you now know, you would use proper building orientation, facing solar south. Along with that, the building mass should be elongated east-west to maximize the benefits of that southern exposure. By selecting a proper glazing percentage, location, and type of glass on this south wall, you can harvest usable daylight, allowing you to include daylight dimmers around the south perimeter of the building. You could further enhance the daylight penetration and reduce the solar conduction load with the use of external shading devices and internal lightshelves. Because the building is receiving most of its lighting needs from the sun, you can reduce the number of overhead electric lights and provide high-efficiency task lights. All of these strategies put together greatly reduce a building's need for cooling.

Each of these steps can be made easier by orienting your building properly in the first place, which keeps the first cost of each strategy low and the long-term benefits high. Each of the strategies integrated in the previous paragraph has a cumulative effect on reducing the need for cooling energy, whereas individually they each might only have a small impact. As part of the design process, set goals for each strategy for various levels of achievement, as shown in Figure 4.18.

Design Criteria/Characteristics		Market	LEED Certified	LEED Silver	LEED Gold	LEED Platinum	Living Building
Total Site Area	(sf)	56,000	56,000	56,000	56,000	56,000	56,000
Building Form	Dimensions (ft)	120' (N-S) x ?' (E-W)	120' (N-S) x ?' (E-W)	80' (N-S) x ?' (E-W)	60' (N-S) x ?' (E-W)	40' (N-S) x ?' (E-W)	40' (N-S) x ?' (E-W)
	Area (ft²)	90,000	90,000	90,000	90,000	90,000	90,000
	Stories	Office: 2 floors; Garage: 3 levels	Office: 2 floors; Garage: 3 levels	Office: 3 floors; Garage: 3 levels	Office: 3 floors; Garage: 3 levels	Office: 3 floors; Garage: 3 levels	Office: 3 floors; Garage: 3 levels
	Orientation	-	-	-	Solar-based	Solar-based	Solar-based
Occupancy	People	300	300	300	300	300	300
Glazing %	North	60	50	40	40	40	40
	South	60	50	40	40	40	40
	East	60	50	30	25	20	20
	West	60	50	30	25	20	20
	Skylight	-	-	-	-	-	-
Glazing Characteristics		U / SC / VLT	U / SC / VLT	U / SC / VLT	U / SC / VLT	U / SC / VLT	U / SC / VLT
	North	0.42 / 0.6 / 0.71	0.32 / 0.46 / 0.64	0.29 / 0.43 / 0.7	0.29 / 0.43 / 0.7	0.16 / 0.35 / 0.6	0.16 / 0.35 / 0.6
	South	0.42 / 0.6 / 0.71	0.32 / 0.46 / 0.64	0.29 / 0.43 / 0.7	0.29 / 0.43 / 0.7	0.16 / 0.35 / 0.6	0.16 / 0.35 / 0.6
	East	0.42 / 0.6 / 0.71	0.32 / 0.46 / 0.64	0.31 / 0.4 / 0.47	0.31 / 0.4 / 0.47	0.16 / 0.31 / 0.6	0.16 / 0.31 / 0.6
	West	0.42 / 0.6 / 0.71	0.32 / 0.46 / 0.64	0.31 / 0.4 / 0.47	0.31 / 0.4 / 0.47	0.16 / 0.31 / 0.6	0.16 / 0.31 / 0.6
	Skylight						
	Daylight and views	Limited access to Daylight and views	Daylight and views at common areas	Daylight and views at common areas	Ambient daylight for general lighting	Daylight for visual tasks	Daylight for visual tasks
	Insulation, operability	Double-glazed, fixed	Double-glazed, fixed	Double-glazed, operable	Double-glazed, operable	Triple-glazed, operable w/ controls	Triple-glazed, operable w/ controls
	Light Shelves	No	No	No	Yes	Yes	Yes
% Glazing Shaded during the months: X thru X	North	0	0	0	50	100	100
	South	0	0	100	100	100	100
	East	0	0	30	50	100	100
	West	0	0	30	50	100	100
	Exterior Shade	No	No	South	South, East & West	South	South
	Vertical Screen	No	No	No	No	East & West	East & West
	Vertical Fin	No	No	No	No	North	North
Thermal Properties	Wall R-value	R8	R13	R20	R25	R33	R33
	Roof R-value	R20	R30	R30	R33	R40	R40
	Floor R-value	R19	R19	R19	R23	R27	R27
	Mass	no	no	no	yes	yes / high mass	yes / high mass
Temperature Range	Cooling/RH	72	72	74	76	78	78
(Degrees Fahrenheit)	Heating/RH	72	68	68	68	68	68
Percentage closed office		60%	50%	40%	30%	20%	10%

Image courtesy of BNIM Architects

Figure 4.18 Energy performance matrix

Energy needs can be reduced by simple policy decisions as well. Consider the benefits of changing the most often used set point temperatures of 71 degrees for heating and 73 degrees for cooling to reduce the load of the heating and cooling system. You can cut the overall energy need significantly by operating at 70 degrees for heating and at 76 degrees during the cooling season. Unlike the material reduction strategies mentioned at the beginning, you can quickly simulate energy reduction strategies, both policy and design. Figure 4.19 is a chart with results from simulating the potential energy savings by changing the set point temperature for a five-story, 50,000-sq.-ft. office building in three different climate zones.

CHAPTER 4: METHODOLOGY FOR SUSTAINABLE SOLUTIONS

ENERGY(MBTU/Year)	BASELINE	CASE 1		CASE 2		
Boston, MA		Heating/Cooling setpoint				
	71/73	70/76	70/78	70/74	68/76	66/78
Lights	600.6	600.6	600.6	600.6	600.6	600.6
Misc. Equipment	549.2	549.2	549.2	549.2	549.2	549.2
Heating	1483.2	1309.5	1262.1	1403.9	1106.6	921
Cooling	331.8	266.3	223.9	312.8	257.3	221.1
Pumping	213.6	194.7	189.8	204.6	164.9	138.8
Ventilation Fans	363.8	330.8	318.2	349.4	309.9	282.6
Domestic Hot Water	68.5	68.5	68.5	68.5	68.5	68.5
Total MBTU/Year	3610.7	3319.6	3212.3	3489	3057	2781.8
Percent energy reduction vs. baseline	0%	8%	11%	3%	15%	23%
Eugene, OR		Heating/Cooling setpoint				
	71/73	70/76	70/78	70/74	68/76	66/78
Lights	600.6	600.6	600.6	600.6	600.6	600.6
Misc. Equipment	549.2	549.2	549.2	549.2	549.2	549.2
Heating	1059.2	907.4	854.9	999.4	699.6	521.9
Cooling	297	230.4	191.3	271.7	226.3	191
Pumping	41.9	42.8	45	41.9	34.2	31.2
Ventilation Fans	317.4	295.2	284.7	309.2	272.1	249.8
Domestic Hot Water	67	67	67	67	67	67
Total MBTU/Year	2932.3	2692.6	2592.7	2839	2449	2210.7
Percent energy reduction vs. baseline	0%	8%	12%	3%	16%	25%
Kansas City, MO		Heating/Cooling setpoint				
	71/73	70/76	70/78	70/74	68/76	66/78
Lights	600.6	600.6	600.6	600.6	600.6	600.6
Misc. Equipment	549.2	549.2	549.2	549.2	549.2	549.2
Heating	1302.4	1162.4	1122.1	1235.3	989.1	829.5
Cooling	813.1	697	636.2	772.6	683	608.2
Pumping	143.6	143	144	143	120.6	103.5
Ventilation Fans	371.1	337.7	325.5	357.3	322.6	299.1
Domestic Hot Water	65.1	65.1	65.1	65.1	65.1	65.1
Total MBTU/Year	3845.1	3555	3442.7	3723.1	3330.2	3055.2
Percent energy reduction vs. baseline	0%	8%	10%	3%	13%	21%
Average percent energy reduction vs. baseline	Baseline	8%	11%	3%	15%	23%

Image courtesy of BNIM Architects

Figure 4.19 Temperature set point reduction simulation

Water

While energy conservation and efficiency gets a lot of press with the bulk of the world focused on reducing greenhouse gases, reducing the built environment's need for water could be an even more important effort. For too long we've regularly used drinkable water for flushing our waste and watering our expansive residential and commercial monoculture turf grass lawns. These are the two primary areas where we can reduce the built environment's need for water.

C.K. Choi Center for Asian Research

The University of British Columbia–Vancouver (UBC) hired BNIM Architects to advance the state of the art in sustainable design and construction on the UBC campus by working with the administration; their consultants, led by Matsuzaki Wright Architects; and all stakeholders to set exemplary goals and to serve the local team as a consultant to facilitate the creation of a benchmark facility.

The C.K. Choi Center for Asian Research was completed in 1996 and is a 2000 American Institute of Architects Committee on the Environment (AIA COTE) Top Ten award-winning project. In addition to setting new standards for energy and resource efficiency, saving an important remnant of old-growth forest, and the many building materials that were salvaged from a building being demolished across the street, the building did not need a sewer connection. Not needing a sewer connection was accomplished by the use of composting toilets on each floor and incorporating a constructed wetland.

Image courtesy of www.michaelsherman.ca

First let's look at reducing the amount of clean drinkable water for flushing toilets. There are many options for toilets now that flush with much less than the standard 1.6 gallons per flush (GPF) units that have been the maximum allowed for 15 years now. And let's not forget the many existing buildings that still have the grandfathered 3.5 GPF units, flushing a full 220% more than the currently allowed standard. Furthermore, do we really need drinking water to flush our waste? Especially more water per flush than we need to drink on a daily basis? No, we do not. Not only does this reduce the amount of water we need, it also eliminates all the associated supply piping!

Urinals have a similar option for water-free units. Just like a normal urinal, they are connected to standard waste piping connected to whatever treatment system is selected. Water-free urinals have been used everywhere, from park restrooms, to restaurants, to corporate offices, to the 259 units inside Rose Bowl Stadium in Pasadena, California, and finally even the Taj Mahal, India (Figure 4.20).

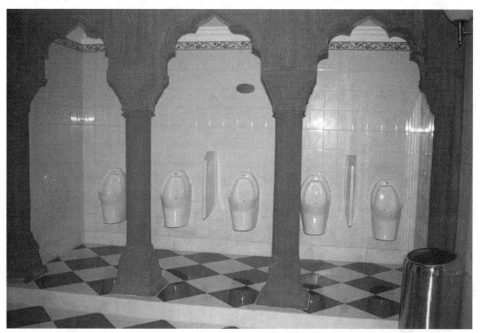

Figure 4.20 Falcon Waterfree urinals, Taj Mahal, India

Designers can help eliminate the use of clean, drinkable water for irrigation. Something we believe should be a must for reducing the overall project water need is use of indigenous landscaping materials in lieu of the *drug-dependent rugs* we know as turf grass. Landscape materials for projects should be native to the area similar to what is shown in Figure 4.21. One of the benefits this brings is they can survive on the average and seasonal rainfalls for that climate area, allowing you to eliminate the extensive irrigation systems used to keep the turf grass green and growing so someone can mow it each week. We can reduce the need for water and capture a greenhouse gas reduction strategy at the same time!

Figure 4.21 Iowa Association of Municipal Utilities, Ankeny, Iowa showing native plantings

Using Free/Local Resources and Natural Systems

It has been said many times that nothing comes for free, but Mother Nature provides three things at no cost: wind, rain, and sun. You only have to pay for the systems to collect these resources. Although it is ultimately true that each of these is unpredictable on a daily basis, scientists have tracked weather patterns enough to reasonably predict the availability on a monthly and annual basis. We captured these predicted values while overcoming our first challenge: understanding climate, culture, and place.

Earlier in "Reduce the Resource Need," we introduced the concept of embodied energy in building materials. This energy can be reduced through your material selections. By selecting products from the region, or using salvaged materials, the energy to transport those materials to the site is lessened.

Wind

Let's talk about using wind first as it can be the most challenging to use of the three free resources. Wind can be used primarily for two things: energy generation and natural ventilation cooling, both used in lieu of off-site energy resources. At this stage in the process, we are more interested in the potential for natural ventilation cooling, one of the 12 most common energy-efficiency measures listed earlier.

Prior to the development of mechanical ventilation systems, all buildings relied on natural ventilation. Natural ventilation cooling uses the natural forces of wind and buoyancy to deliver fresh air into buildings. These two types of natural ventilation for buildings are referred to as *wind driven ventilation* and *stack ventilation*. To deliver the most efficient design for natural ventilation, a building should implement both types. Figure 4.22 shows operable windows, the most common type of natural ventilation.

Image courtesy of BNIM Architects

Figure 4.22 Image of operable windows

In favorable climates and buildings types, natural ventilation cooling can reduce energy use, improve indoor environmental quality (fresh air and less mechanical system noise), and reduce operating costs. If designed and executed properly, a system that uses wind combined with the natural convention flows of a stack ventilation system requires significantly less energy compared to a conventional cooling system. At most, it might need a little fan energy to assist when the breezes are not strong enough.

Integrating the use of natural ventilation relies on smart decisions for many portions of the building design, including:

- Building location on site and proper orientation
- Building mass and dimensions
- Window types, locations and operation
- Integration of stack inducing elements (open stairs, chimneys)
- Efficient envelope construction (conductance and infiltration)
- External elements (shading devices and vegetation)
- Flexible temperature ranges for comfort

Let's start optimizing our design by looking at our psychometric chart. Quickly we can see when the exterior conditions are in the natural ventilation cooling range. Looking at our wind charts we can see the direction and speed of the wind during those same time periods. A basic move for facilitating natural ventilation for the design would be to organize the windows of the building to capture those breezes. Typical building design relies on rules of thumb for design of these elements to harness the power of wind for the purpose of natural ventilation. When more detail is required, we can use a computational fluid dynamics model to predict the details of natural airflow. These detailed computer simulations are labor intensive, the software is expensive, and it requires a specialist. However, this can be justified where accurate understanding of airflow is important.

The climate zone sometimes limits trying to use the free natural cooling effect of wind for a project; other times we are limited by the building type, and other times by policy. As alluded to earlier, natural ventilation cooling cannot be used in all climates and becomes more challenging with indoor load-driven buildings. For example, in Kansas City, it can only be used for about 10% of the year; the bulk of that is from May to September but for only 25% of that time period.

Another tricky thing regarding the use of natural ventilation is that the quality of the air outside is not better in all cases. For example, when we looked at using a natural ventilation cooling mode for part of the year for the Heifer International Headquarters in Little Rock, Arkansas, we found out from the user group and the local team that the optimal time period coincided with the heavy oak pollen season. Pollen is not something we would want to pull into an office building through open windows. Even when working with areas and buildings that are amenable to using natural ventilation, sometimes you will run into a policy problem. Who is going to close and open the windows at the right time?

Rainwater

Rainwater is a free resource that can be beneficial in every climate zone. Using rainwater reduces the need for municipally provided potable water, especially for non-potable water needs. To use rainwater, you have to collect, filter, store, and convey it to the end use. This is referred to as rainwater harvesting. A comprehensive guide to rainwater harvesting is The Texas Guide to Rainwater Harvesting, developed by the Center for Maximum Potential Building Systems, http://www.cmpbs.org.

Real-life Life Applications of Collecting Rainwater

The UTHSCH SON collects 826,140 gallons of rainwater each year. That water is used for toilet flushing and irrigation. The storage component for the rainwater harvesting system is located right out front for everyone to see and experience.

Image courtesy of Hester + Hardaway Photographers

At the Lewis and Clark State Office Building in Jefferson City, Missouri, a 50,000-gallon cistern located in the basement stores rainwater collected from the roof. The collected water is used for toilet flushing and irrigation.

Rainwater can be collected from the roof, parking lot, or site runoff. You can store it in barrels or cisterns, located on the roof, at grade, hidden away in the sublevels of the building or under the parking lot. Rainwater can be used for many things, such as irrigation of site landscaping, development of water features on site, water for industrial processes, flushing toilets, chiller water, geothermal heat sinks, or even for potable uses. Each level of use has an increasing requirement for filtration and cleaning.

Using the rainfall data gathered in the phase of understanding climate, culture, and place together with design decisions to this point, you can easily figure how much rainwater is available to the project. Adding to this the knowledge of the project's water need, you can adequately size the storage system. Depending on the loads that you decide to feed with the rainwater harvested, you must also design the filtration and cleaning system. Because the systems grow in cost, complexity, and energy use with each level of filtration and quality, you should feed the lower lower-quality, non-potable needs first, such as irrigation and toilet flushing. In most situations it is unlikely that a rainwater harvesting system designed to create potable water can compete financially with a municipal potable water system.

Use of a rainwater harvesting system also reduces water runoff from the developed area. It is possible for a project due to size or building type to still have more rainwater arriving on site than it can reuse. For the past several decades, people have been happily just piping this water away with high embodied energy man-made structures like concrete pipes and, in some cases, pumping systems to another location so somebody else can deal with it. This standard practice causes erosion and flooding problems downstream in quantities and rates that are too challenging for natural systems to handle.

Therefore, when we create a situation where we are creating runoff from a site, localized natural systems should be used to handle both the quantity and quality of the water prior to letting it leave the site. Strategies for this include green roofs, pervious paving, bioswales, rain gardens, and constructed wetlands. Each of these strategies can add a bit of elegance to the building grounds as well (Figures 4.23a-d).

Sun

The most powerful of Mother Nature's resources is the sun. The sun provides us three key resources; light, heat, and power. During this step, we are interested in maximizing the use of the sun's light and heat in lieu of using energy from the municipal grid for those purposes. Use of natural daylight is appropriate for almost every building that has spaces requiring light. Use of the sun as a heating source is limited to the appropriate building type and climate zone.

Image courtesy of Brad Nies

Figure 4.23a Pervious paving, Missouri Botanical Gardens

Image courtesy of BNIM Architects

Figure 4.23b Rain Garden, Kansas City

Image courtesy of BNIM Architects

Figure 4.23c Bioswales at Anita B. Gorma Conservation Discovery Center, Kansas City

Image © Assassi | Courtesy of BNIM Architects

Figure 4.23d Constructed wetland at Anita B. Gorman Conservation Discovery Center, Kansas City

There are few buildings that don't have spaces where light is required. Two basic options for lighting a space are use of natural light and use of artificial light. Integrating the use of natural daylight for primary interior illumination of buildings is called *daylighting*. Natural daylight is the highest quality and most efficient light source available today and is comes free of charge. All artificial lighting options require a physical fixture (material resources) and electrical energy. Some of those systems even produce heat, which contributes to the cooling load of a building. These are the things you can reduce or eliminate by using natural light first.

In the previous chapter we ran through a scenario that described strategies for reducing the cooling load of an office building. The strategies used in that scenario also increased the amount of daylight used in the project. Solutions for properly integrating a daylight strategy vary with climate and building type. Figure 4.24 shows a simple massing model used to explore daylighting.

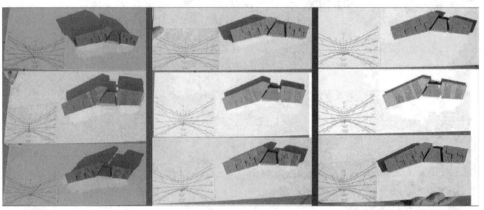

Image courtesy of BNIM Architects

Figure 4.24 Image of the Lewis and Clark State Office Building in Jefferson City, MO, Chipboard model

When working on daylight strategies, try to keep in mind the following design strategies:

1. Orient the building to face solar south.

In the Northern Hemisphere, the sun spends most of its time in the southern portion of the sky. By choosing this orientation, not only have you created a situation where you have more time to capture free light and heat, you have also provided the most effective way to control how much of each is captured and when.

An open office workplace environment placed in Houston will have the same desire for a uniform lighting condition with high contrast at the desk surface as one in Des Moines, Iowa. However, the building in Des Moines could benefit from some solar heat gain over the course of the year, whereas the building in Houston would want to eliminate as much solar heat gain as possible.

2. Determine where to put the glazing and how much is required to create a day-lighting solution.

Sunlight is bright, regardless of what direction it is coming from. In the morning and evening, the sun is low in the sky and challenging to control, which is why good sustainable design would put a relatively small percentage of glazing on the east and west sides of a building. The north side of the building rarely sees sunlight except in the early morning and late afternoon during the summer, allowing more glazing to be put on that façade.

In the open office environment, you know that usable light is needed on the desk surface. Because the sun brings light from above, glass located above desk height is most appropriate for this. In fact, the higher the window head height, the deeper light can penetrate into the space. Any glazing below the desk surface is not contributing to usable light but only to the heat gain. Furthermore, considering that occupants are usually sitting down at their desks for the majority of the workday and glass has poor thermal conduction resistance, having a large portion of the glass below the work surface is probably not a smart decision.

Each façade deserves a detailed look at the balance between the percentage of glass used to provide daylight penetration and the thermal conductance resistance of the exterior wall for comfort in relation to the activity going on within the immediate adjacent space. A lobby space, for example, can handle more fluctuation because its occupants are transient and can easily maneuver to a preferred location. The decision of how much glass and where cannot be divorced from type of glass and external shading.

A glazing unit has three important factors to consider:

- U-value: a measure of the rate of heat transfer through a material
- Visible light transmittance (VLT)
- Solar heat gain coefficient (SHGC)

Each of these variables has an impact on the occupant's comfort and the design's ability to harvest daylight. It is likely that the values for VLT and SHGC will be different on each façade.

Until the recent strides in specularly selective glazing, a glazing unit with a better SHGC meant it had a lower VLT, or a heavier window tint, which reduced that unit's ability to harvest daylight.

3. Another method to achieve the same result without expensive glazing is to use external shading.

For example, if you shade the southern glass you can capture that shading benefit and in turn use a glass with a lower SHGC and higher VLT. The shade will do two things:

- Reduce heat gain

- Control unwanted glare inside the building

The designer must understand how the sun moves because designing a fixed external shade allows it to only work during certain times of the year. If shades are not active, users should have internal shades to adjust the light to their individual needs. External shades can be beneficial to tricking the building to the right orientation if due to site constraints the best orientation is not possible. Figures 4.25a and 4.25b show some external sun shading devices on the east and west facades.

Figure 4.25a East side of UTHSCH School of Nursing

Figure 4.25b West side of UTHSCH School of Nursing

By adding a glazing unit above the external sunshade, you could reflect the light off the shade up into the building, bouncing it off the ceiling or floor above as a light source. The light can be further extended into the building by combining this strategy with an internal lightshelf. According to the LBNL "Guide to Daylighting," it is possible to project light 1.5 to 2 times the head height of the window into the building.

The idea is to get an even spread of usable natural light into the building without creating heat gain or discomfort from glare. A good quantity of usable light would allow you to put in daylight dimming controls on the electric lighting. These controls allow the lights to gradually dim as the natural light increases and decreases. Advances have been made so that this dimming is continual and our eyes don't notice the change because the light levels are being kept at a constant as determined for the activity of the space.

The benefits of using natural light are not limited to reduced cooling and electrical loads. Use of fully integrated daylighting systems can enhance the visual acuity, comfort, and beauty of a space as well as increase human health and productivity. These benefits are largely connected to the natural light itself and the visual connection to the outdoors that is inherent to capturing daylight.

Materials

The AEC industry is only starting to embrace an understanding of what it takes to acquire building materials. In the previous step "Reducing the Resource Need," we introduced the concept of embodied energy while describing how to eliminate the need for some materials.

Our first step in the order of operations covered the need to understand place. Now at this step the two ideas, place and reducing resource needs, tie together as you start selecting more materials for your project. When choosing materials for your project, remember your commitment to place. Part of the reason people are drawn to a city or town that embraces regionalism is simply the way it looks. One of the reasons a development looks the way it does is due to the use of regionally available materials; designers and builders created part of the sense of place through materiality.

If you recall, part of the embodied energy of a building material includes transportation. Today building materials and products are shipped worldwide by ship, air, train, and truck, requiring a lot of fossil fuel resources that create harmful emissions. Factories work night and day to supply the project with what we choose, no matter how far and at nearly a moment's notice. You can significantly reduce this negative climate impact by choosing materials closer to the project site. At the same time, you can have a positive impact on the local economy by putting people to work in the community.

One type of local material you should not overlook is salvaged materials. This is becoming a growing industry across the country. There are reclaimed timber operations that travel around the country taking down old barns and other buildings and re-milling the wood for reuse in a variety of applications like flooring, tables, cabinets, and structural members. Some demolition contractors are also starting to shift towards deconstruction, creating their own smorgasbord of salvaged building components. Habitat for Humanity, as one example, has built a business out of salvaged materials with their Habitat Restore retail outlets (http://www.habitat.org/env/restores.aspx).

The wood decking at the Anita B. Gorman Conservation Discovery Center described earlier was created from beams salvaged from a nearby 100 year-old warehouse that was being demolished. The scraps from creating the wood decking were turned into an end-grain block floor for a classroom at the Discovery Center (see Figure 4.26).

We believe strongly in selecting as many materials from within the region as possible. Benefits include a better connection to the place, better economics for the local surrounding community and, in most cases, a smaller environmental footprint. We will cover more details about local materials in Chapter 6: Sustainable BIM Building Systems, in the Sustainable Materials section.

Figure 4.26 Salvaged wood for the Discovery Center

Using Efficient Man-made Systems

At this point you have reduced the project's need for resources as much as possible and passively gotten all you can from Mother Nature. It is unlikely that every building's needs could be met by natural systems. The gaps between what can be acquired naturally and what must be provided by man-made systems will be larger in some regions depending on the building type and climate. However, because of the steps already taken, the gap is significantly smaller than the traditional need for man-made systems developed over the past three decades. To fill in the remaining building resource needs, we designers need to look at our own inventions.

Mechanical Systems

First things first: get the right-sized mechanical system. Due to excessive on-off cycling, oversizing of systems can raise purchase cost, increase energy use, and shorten product life. This is especially true for heating and cooling systems.

Because you've done such a good job of minimizing the project's needs, it is not possible to rely on "Well, the last project needed that much" to establish equipment size. When selecting the mechanical systems, we recommend using computer simulations for a look into what the project really needs rather than relying on what system was used on the previous building of this size by the engineer. For example, in designing an office building you could have done such a great job that your cooling density is significantly better than a market-like expectation of 240 sq. ft./ton but more like 800 sq. ft./ton. Once you know the size or amount of equipment necessary, you will need to select the most efficient version combined with proper use of control systems.

As we described before, space conditioning, lighting, and equipment are some the biggest needs of the built environment. Each of these systems is made with varying degrees of efficiency. Loosely described, efficiency is the ratio of what you get to what it took to get it. For example, how much energy did it take to generate the cooling for your building, the hot water, the lights, or for you to run the computer, copier, dishwasher, television, and so forth, compared to what you got in return? Wouldn't it be nice to get more for less?

You must consider many things regarding the efficiency of air cooling and heating, all of which cannot be covered in this book. One of the more popular technologies that is getting a lot of use and press these days is Underfloor Air Distribution (UFAD). UFAD takes advantage of the raised floor systems made popular in computer rooms and data centers (Figure 4.27). Floors can now range in height from two inches to four feet, allowing lots of equipment from data cables to ductwork to be run underneath. UFAD systems have been used in everything from schools, to condos, to office buildings, and even casinos.

Image courtesy of BNIM Architects

Figure 4.27 Image of a UFAD installation

One of the latest uses includes using the underfloor area as a supply air plenum. Air delivered via this method has several great advantages. From an indoor air quality perspective, the supply air is no longer delivered from above through the hot, dirty return air. From an energy efficiency perspective, delivering air where you need it, closer to the occupants, allows several gains. First, because it doesn't have to blow fast and hard through the hot return air, you don't need as much fan energy. The air can come out slowly and stratify as it warms and gets removed via the returns above. Second, you can deliver the cool air at warmer temperatures—10 degrees warmer in fact than what a traditionally overhead distribution system requires, saving lots of cooling energy and allowing for more outside air to be used during the appropriate time frames.

When it comes to selecting the actual mechanical unit, standard packaged systems have published rating systems for efficiency. For a packaged commercial air-conditioning system, you can look at the published Energy Efficiency Ratio (EER). According to the Air-Conditioning and Refrigeration Institute (ARI), EER is the cooling capacity of the unit divided by its electrical input at a peak rating condition of 80 degrees indoors and 95 degrees F outdoors. If a team wanted to consider the overall unit efficiency under partial loaded conditions and varying temperatures, they would look at the Integrated Part Load Value (IPLV). It is possible to make the efficiencies higher. Instead of a factory-made packaged unit, the engineer can design a split system combining minor assemblies of more efficient pieces. Also, the EER and IPLV ratings are for air-cooled equipment. Water-cooled equipment is generally considered to be even more efficient (Figure 4.28), but you must take into account the energy needed to buy the cooling tower and pumps.

Image courtesy of Brad Nies

Figure 4.28 Water-cooled heat pumps

Heat pumps have two values to consider: their EER for the cooling mode and their Coefficient of Performance (COP) during the heating mode. COP is the heating capacity (in Btu/h) at standard heating conditions divided by its electrical input. Compared to standard electrical resistance heat, which has a COP of 1, air side heat pumps have a COP of 2 to 4 and ground- or water-based sourced heat pumps have a COP of 3 to 5. Again, the higher the COP value, the more efficient the unit.

When looking at a boiler or furnace, pay attention to the thermal efficiency. These technologies are converting heat from a source to a different medium—for example, heat from burning natural gas to water. A furnace that is 80% efficient essentially loses the remaining 20% of energy used as heat to the area surrounding it. With these systems, it is good to point out that the most efficient might not be the most cost effective. We've noted earlier that electric resistance heat is near or at 100% efficient. In many locations around the United States, natural gas is cheaper than electricity per thermal unit. If your electricity comes from a coal-fired power plant, the natural gas is also a cleaner-burning fuel. For these reasons, a gas-operated unit might be preferred and lifecycle cost should be calculated. Either way, you are still better off selecting a 90% efficient gas furnace over an 80% unit (Figure 4.29).

Image courtesy of Brad Nies

Figure 4.29 Boilers in an office building

In our discussion of boilers and furnaces, we mentioned the idea of lost energy. Project teams can take the energy efficiency of building systems even further than the efficiency of an individual unit by integrating the systems. It is possible to capture some lost heat and use it for other purposes. Perhaps the engineer could exhaust the boiler to a heat exchanger that the water return pipes flow through during the heating season, preheating the return water prior to it running through the boiler again. The same process can be applied to the air systems. This creates higher total system efficiency.

Plumbing

With regard to water heating, people have stored water for a long time in a tank and continually keep it hot for use in sinks, showers, and other fixtures around the building the minute it was called upon. As you know from washing your hands or starting a shower, you sometimes have to wait for this hot water as the water in the supply pipe has cooled off. This describes a very inefficient system, which is rapidly being replaced with on-demand water heating units. These units heat the water as it flows through when it is requested, reducing the need to try to keep an entire tank at a given temperature. The on-demand systems are small enough to be located nearby the hot water fixture, thereby also making them an efficient in regards to water use.

As described earlier, the two largest uses of water in a typical building are flushing toilets and irrigation. While we described pathways to eliminate both, you might not be able to eliminate that use and there are remaining water uses that can also employ efficient fixtures. If you were unable to get water-free toilets and urinals, you still have options for water efficiency. Toilets and urinals are rated with the term gallons per flush (GPF). Today you can get dual flush (1.6/0.8), low-flow (1.2 GPF), or ultra low-flow (0.8 GPF) toilets. Urinals have just as many varieties. The standard is 1.0 GPF, but you can get a 0.5 GPF, or an even a 0.125 GPF.

What is it you do after you use the toilet? You wash your hands. Using a metered or an infrared sensor operated faucet can save about 75% of the water as compared to a standard lavatory faucet fixture. An advantage to sensor operated is that it is completely touchless; however, either a battery-powered or hardwired power source is required to operate the sensor.

What about the irrigation system? Sometimes an owner will not be comfortable having no control over the look of the grounds and will demand the ability to water when necessary. When put in this situation, use a high-efficiency drip irrigation system that can deliver water 50% more efficiently or better than a traditional system. Moisture sensors are also recommended. How many times have you seen a sprinkler system running during a rainstorm?

The two remaining parts of a building that require efficient systems are lighting and equipment.

Electric Lighting

Since daylighting has been properly integrated, what is needed now is efficient light fixtures together with control systems. Commercial light fixtures have three main components that affect their efficiency: the fixture, the ballast, and the light. The design of the fixture, its reflectors, diffusers, and the types of lamps it can use affect the throw of the fixture shown in the lighting distribution curve. The ballast provides the necessary starting voltage to turn on the lamp, while limiting and regulating the lamp current during operation. Ballasts are rated with a Ballast Efficiency Factor, which is a ratio related to specific ballast and lamp combination; as before, the higher the number, the greater efficiency. Then there is the lamp itself, which is measured by efficacy.

We are accustomed to selecting bulbs based on wattage: the traditional 25-, 40-, 60-, 75-, and 100-watt incandescent bulbs. This is misleading because a good portion of the power used in an incandescent lamp actual goes to heat, not light. What is of interest is the amount of light that you get from that source for a given amount of power. The total amount of light from a bulb is measured in lumens. Efficacy is measured in lumens per watt comparing light output to energy consumption. Select your lights with the highest efficacy for the desired situation. Table 4.1 explains the typical efficacy ranges of electric light sources.

▶ Table 4.1 Typical Efficacy Ranges of Electric Light Sources

Light Source	Typical System Efficacy Range in lm/W*
Incandescent	10–18
Halogen incandescent	15–20
Compact fluorescent (CFL)	35–60
Linear fluorescent (T8, T5)	50–100
Metal halide	50–90

* Varies depending on wattage and lamp type.
Source: US Department of Energy, Building Technologies Program

Efficient Equipment

Efficiency for remaining types of equipment used in buildings—such as computers, monitors, appliances, copiers, printers, and so forth—can easily be judged. The U.S. Department of Energy runs the Energy Star program together with the U.S. Environmental Protection Agency. Energy Star offers businesses and consumers energy-efficient solutions, making it easy to save money while protecting the environment for future generations.

Energy Star is simple to use. On the Energy Star website at http://www.energystar.gov, you can find over 50 categories of products that are eligible for the Energy Star program. Each category has a free downloadable list of products that meet the program requirements and a statement of how much more efficient those are than standard equipment. Some product categories even have a cost savings calculator. It is one thing to own the equipment, but another to implement some of the savings features, like power management. LBNL found that using all power management features in office equipment reduces the power consumption of that equipment up to 24%. One of the most common things we find when reviewing an owner's equipment in an existing space is the continued use of traditional computer screens or Cathode Ray Tube (CRTs) displays. There are savings to be had by replacing them with LCD (Liquid Crystal Display) screens. LCDs use significantly less energy and put off less heat, and they have less glare than the traditional CRT screen. This equals not only energy savings but also better comfort for the users.

While efficient equipment usually has a higher first cost, it will pay off over a period of time. For many of us in the United States, energy for power is relatively inexpensive, so choosing the efficient system is sometimes challenging. The good news for you, the reader, is that you've reduced all of the project loads to this point; therefore, the project needs a smaller unit than it would have otherwise. That means the first cost premium for efficient equipment could be at zero additional cost due to the smaller size of the unit needed because of all the sustainable strategies you've implemented.

Applying Renewable Energy Generation Systems

Renewable energy is energy from sources other than fossil fuels. As opposed to the finite resources that make up fossil fuels, renewable energy sources are constantly replenished and will never run out. Now that you have made the building efficient and collected as much free energy as possible, you can supply the energy needs with renewable energy.

At this point you should have an elegantly designed building that requires as little energy as possible to operate. So what is the best way to supply that necessary energy? Renewable energy sources. Currently, only 2% of the electricity in the United States is generated from nonhydro renewable resources, according to the EPA (http://www.epa.gov/cleanenergy/energy-and-you/how-clean.html). Figure 4.30 shows the distribution of fuel mixes for our energy sources.

There are seven recognized renewable energy sources:

• Solar

• Wind

• Biomass

• Hydrogen

• Geothermal

• Ocean

• Hydropower

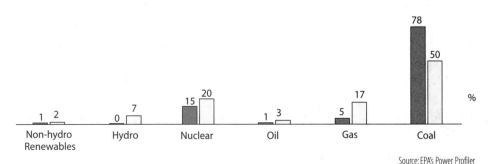

Figure 4.30 Energy generation fuel mix percentages for Kansas City and the Nation

Some of them work well at both large and small scales. Some cities are already mostly powered by renewable sources, like Seattle, Washington, which is 49% hydro. Kansas City, on the other hand, is 78% coal and only 1% renewable. We believe that power should be located on site to minimize energy loss due to distribution, so we will focus on site-based renewable energy.

Why wait until this point to apply them? First of all, it takes resources to create systems that harness energy from renewable sources and not all of them are considered benign. It is widely agreed, though, that they are cleaner than any fossil-fuel based system and arguably safer than a nuclear-based power system. Less energy need also means less power generation required, which saves material resources and limits remaining potential negative environmental impacts from energy production.

Each renewable system is not available for every location. Wind speeds for reasonable power generation start at around 12 mph. Kansas, for example, has great wind power potential, whereas Arizona has almost none. Wind resource maps are available per state from the Energy Efficiency and Renewable Energy website (http://www.eere.energy.gov/windandhydro/windpoweringamerica/wind_maps.asp). Regardless of what the maps say, it is recommended that you measure the wind on your site before you purchase a turbine. When it comes to generating power from photovoltaics (PV), Arizona has the upper hand. Arizona has almost twice the potential for solar electric power than Kansas on an annual basis. Examples of wind turbines and PV panels are shown in Figure 4.31a-c.

Figure 4.31a Amorphus PV array at Anita B. Gorman Conservation Discovery Center

Figure 4.31b Crystalline PV array at Anita B. Gorman Conservation Discovery Center

Figure 4.31c Small scale wind turbines at EcoWORKS, developed by Zimmer Real Estate Services and design by Gastinger Walker Harden Architects

A final reason why you should wait until now to employ these renewable energy-generating technologies is cost. If you compare the cost of using energy available from the municipal grid to using on-site renewable energy, renewable energy can be significantly more expensive depending on your location. In Kansas, where there are no state incentives or rebates from the utility, it might take 35 years to pay for a photovoltaic system on a residence. In California, because of the high utility rates, along with the state- and utility-based rebates, that same system can pay for itself in just 10 years. Commercial utility rates have been known to be half of the residential rates, doubling each of those paybacks. So the less you need to generate, the more cost effective your system is.

If an onsite renewable system is still too expensive for the project, we recommend considering the purchase of renewable energy certificates (RECs) for the energy that must be taken from the grid. RECs are additional fees an owner pays to sponsor putting renewable energy on the grid. They are paid per annual kWh of use in the range of one to two cents per kWh. The fee is paid to a certificate broker who subsidized the development of the renewable power station. When purchasing RECs, make sure the certificates are part of a third party–verified system like the Green-E Certified program required by the USGBC LEED system. Purchasing RECs is close to a carbon offset but not quite.

Offsetting Your Negative Impacts

You are almost finished! The remaining task is to offset your remaining environmental impacts, the bulk of which is in the embodied energy of the design effort, the materials selected, and the embodied energy of the eventual project construction. All of this embodied energy can be equated to a carbon dioxide unit equivalent, which you can then offset by supporting programs that compensate for or reduce emissions. The goal is to achieve a neutral (net zero) result, negating the impact of designing and constructing the facility. It wouldn't hurt to have the owner agree to offset any remaining negative impacts from operations as well. BNIM Architects has been offsetting the impact of the firm's operations since 2005.

A number of organizations offer carbon offsets for purchase. However, they are not all created equal. Offsets linked to renewable energy and energy efficiency projects are more permanent than those that involve planting trees to sequester (absorb) carbon. The reason boils down to permanence. Eventually the trees will die, will be destroyed through natural disaster, or will be harvested, releasing all or some of the carbon back into the atmosphere (Figure 4.32).

Image courtesy of Brad Nies

Figure 4.32 A second-growth forest on Bainbridge Island, Washington

An international system has been developed to ensure key environmental criteria are accounted for in providing and purchasing offsets called the Gold Standard (see http://www.cdmgoldstandard.org). Offsets that meet these criteria carry its special label. Since energy efficiency and renewable energy projects encourage moving beyond or limiting fossil fuel use and considerably decrease environmental risks, they are the only offset measures to qualify for the Gold Standard (Figure 4.33).

Image courtesy of Lyndall Blake, Kansas City Power & Light

Figure 4.33 Spearville wind farm

Social indicators are also reviewed as part of qualifying for the Gold Standard to ensure the offset project furthers sustainable development goals in the country where the project is based. Furthermore, Gold Standard projects must meet very high additive criteria to ensure that they contribute to the adoption of new sustainable energy projects, rather than simply funding existing projects. As with all exceptional programs, Gold Standard projects must be independently verified by a third party to ensure integrity.

After completing the seven steps in the order of operations, you will have created one of the most sustainable buildings possible. If you did them all perfectly, the building is truly sustainable. The next thing to discuss is what it takes to complete these exercises: an architect cannot do this on his or her own, and certainly not without a willing owner. Let's not forget someone has to construct the project, and then yet another group of people have to operate and maintain it. Let's next look at how to develop capacity to achieve a sustainable building through an integrated team of professionals.

Sustainable BIM: Building Form

5

Get the habit of analysis—analysis will in time enable synthesis to become your habit of mind.

—Frank Lloyd Wright

In this chapter, you'll learn how to use some of the sustainable design concepts that we discussed in previous chapters with BIM models. We will look at some real-world applications and examples of design strategies and show how you can apply them by using today's BIM technology. In this chapter, we'll discuss building orientation, building massing, and daylighting.

Getting Started

Before we delve into discussing any specific workflows involving BIM and sustainable design, it is important to recognize that many strategies are both cumulative and interdependent. Adding some strategies on top of others can have a compounding benefit; stopping too early may have only increased first cost with little long-term benefit. The same is true regarding interdependence. Take the example of building orientation, glazing, and daylighting. Rotating your building in the proper direction, using the right glass in the correct amount and location, and integrating sun shading into the project to optimize the use of natural light all build on each other. The amount of usable daylight that you might capture will be greatly reduced with highly reflective glass or if the building faces the wrong orientation. The appropriateness of any of these individual strategies and the benefits are dependent on building type and climate.

Figure 5.1 shows the cumulative effects different energy efficiency measures can have on a building. The first cost for the building is the line with diamonds starting at the lower left, while the annual operating cost is the line with squares starting at the upper left. For this project, the energy efficiency measures were applied in order of the greatest individual impact first. As you can see, the first cost increases dramatically with the addition of the first few energy efficiency measures.

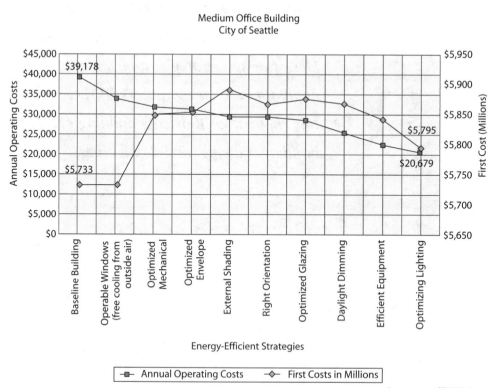

Figure 5.1 Graphing the cumulative effects of energy-efficient strategies

However, as you increase the energy efficiency of the design by adding some of the lesser individual measures, not only does the annual operating cost begin to drop but so does the first cost of the project. The reason for the drop in costs is simple: these strategies are dependent on each other. When the right strategies are combined, the expensive first cost and operating cost systems or technologies get smaller because the required load is reduced. A more efficient system will have lower operating costs but generally it is likely to have a higher first cost. If your building has a better envelope, you will retain more of your heating and cooling and therefore need a smaller HVAC system. The project only pays for the envelope once; however, it pays for the inefficient or wasteful HVAC system every time it is used.

BIM has characteristics similar to a building's systems. All of the components in a model have a parametric relationship to each other.

Adding a door to a wall adds an opening while also removing wall material *and* adding another door to your door schedule.

Understanding and capitalizing on these interrelationships typically takes numerous iterations that span multiple projects. Optimizing the integrated strategies and technologies for a high-performance, sustainable design requires a continual look at understanding how they work together to deliver the best potential. That is where BIM comes in, which gives you the ability to iterate and analyze faster than in a more traditional process.

We are going to set some basic guidelines for the analysis that we will be exploring in this chapter and the next. We plan to highlight a series of simple design concepts that will help guide a project toward a more sustainably driven outcome. These concepts are as follows:

- Building orientation
- Building massing
- Daylighting
- Water harvesting
- Energy modeling
- Renewable energy
- Materials

We are also going to demonstrate these concepts using a real-life scenario of a 46,000-sq.-ft. open office building type set in Kansas City, Missouri, on a nonurban site. Figure 5.2 shows a perspective of the BIM.

In all the topics that we are going to discuss, we plan to follow the order of operations that we discussed in the previous chapter, touching on each of the topics in turn. We plan to discuss the desired outcome for a sustainable building and how to achieve that with the use of today's BIM.

Image courtesy of BNIM Architects

Figure 5.2 Perspective of the sample project

A note about the accuracy of your findings: the BIM model will only be as accurate as the quality of the information that goes into it. In order for you to successfully pull information out of a BIM model, it must first be put in there accurately. Although that might seem obvious, it is always good practice to cross-check your information with some critical thinking. If the numbers look unrealistic, take a minute to check them.

Bad Modeling Has Bad Effects Downstream

Like poor ecology, poor BIM modeling can have a negative impact downstream on team members and project stakeholders. As an example, we were called in to help on a project that was the victim of some poor modeling. A contractor had been given a model by another architect and had used it for take-offs for cost estimating. The architectural firm (this was their first project using BIM) had unwittingly not connected the walls to the floors in the model, so the walls hovered three feet above the floor surfaces all throughout the model. Because they had not looked at the model in 3D, they didn't catch the mistake until after the model was delivered to the contractor. The contractor in turn did not check the accuracy of the estimate, instead trusting the accuracy of the architect.

You can only imagine everyone's surprise when the actual construction costs came in much higher than the estimate because the first three feet of almost every wall in the project was not taken into account.

Throughout all of these concepts, we are going to be using a variety of tools that revolve around a BIM model. Some of the tools will require a heavier use of BIM than others, but all of them will utilize the model geometry you've created as part of your design.

As you move between some of these tools and applications, you need to be concerned about interoperability, or how well the applications talk to one another. For example, if you are using one application for your BIM model and have to move that information to another application for energy modeling, make sure that you are choosing compatible programs. Not every application is interoperable with all of the others.

In this vein, there is a growing industry standard called Industry Foundation Classes (IFC) that has been created as an open source, nonplatform-specific means of communication between BIM applications and analysis packages. Most BIM packages on the market can export to an IFC file type.

Building Orientation

Building orientation in sustainable design is defined as the way a building is placed on its site relative to the path of the sun. How a building addresses the sun and how the glazing openings are defined can have a large effect on the energy efficiency of the building systems and the comfort of the occupants. Because proper orientation sets up the building for optimization of solar-based passive strategies and sometimes wind based, it naturally creates lower energy solutions for lighting, heating, and cooling. Orientation has no direct impact on reducing water use or increasing water capture.

Building orientation is something that should happen in the beginning stages of the building design. At predesign, you should know the geospatial location of the project, where solar south is, and the direction of the prevailing breezes.

Orientation is the foundation for keeping energy loads low, and it should not be deviated from in later phases. While proper orientation in and of itself normally creates a smaller single-digit percentage energy efficiency gain, as shown in the case of Figure 5.3, it sets up the other strategies for greatest success. There are many successful designs that do not have correct orientation, however negative impacts from incorrect orientation compound energy inefficiency and either drive additional first costs to control unwanted heat gain and glare from the sun or create long-term user discomfort.

Note that while we have focused on the energy efficiency and comfort aspects of correct orientation, there is an energy supply benefit too. To maximize the benefit of a solar hot-water system or photovoltaic electric system, the panels should face solar south. The systems themselves can be expensive. Make it easier on yourself by providing integrated locations on the building for placement of these systems without extra structural components and optimize their output with proper orientation.

Now that we have explored the importance of building orientation, let's look at ways to incorporate this into the early stages of the design process. We plan to focus on a repeated pattern of design investigation for this concept as well as the others in this chapter and the next. Although this pattern is by no means prescriptive, these are the necessary steps to identify, understand, and solve some of the core ideas behind sustainable design using BIM in the workflow. Each section will discuss the impacts on climate, culture, and place. Once you have a good grasp of the localized issues, we'll investigate reducing the needs of the project.

Orientation	Rotations from true South	Orientation	
		Energy Use KBtu/sf-year	Annual Operating Cost Savings (over base case)
⬚	90^0 W	61.9	Base Case
◇	45^0 W	62.1	0%
▱	15^0 W	60.9	0.9%
▭	0^0	61.2	0.7%
▱	15^0 E	60.7	1.3%
◇	30^0 E	61.5	0.7%
◇	45^0 E	61.7	0.5%

Image courtesy of BNIM Architects

Figure 5.3 Simulated percentage of energy efficiency gained for different orientations of five-story, 50,000-sq.-ft. office building in Seattle

The next step is to set specific project goals. With those in place, we'll move to a BIM-based solution and finally analyze the results to see how they impact the design. At times, it will be necessary to repeat these steps as often as necessary to achieve our goal of a sustainable design.

Understanding the Impacts of Climate

Climate's impact on building orientation stems from the ability to use passive design strategies such as heating, cooling, and lighting.

In a hot climate, employ shading strategies to keep the building cool and eliminate direct sun penetration. The first step to this is orienting the building so that shading becomes easier to do, requiring fewer materials and less cost. In a cold climate, you would want to encourage sun penetration to reduce heating loads and absorb solar radiation. Again, facing the sun will set the project up for the easiest and most cost-effective solution. In either climate, you want to use daylight for your primary lighting source. All of these strategies are typically done by orienting the longer façade of the building to face the sun; north of the equator it should face south (Figure 5.4), and south of the equator it would face north.

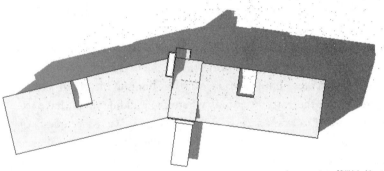

Figure 5.4 Proper building orientation

In a climate that has opportunities for using natural ventilation, the building openings should be oriented to capture the prevailing breezes, which will reduce the need for mechanical cooling equipment and/or fan assistance to draw in cool air (Figure 5.5). Remember that for certain cultures, specific buildings (for example, religious buildings) must have special spaces that face a certain direction. This influences building orientation and may or may not conflict with the other passive strategies.

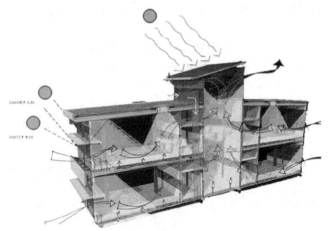

Figure 5.5 Using natural ventilation with proper orientation

There are two levels at which place affects a project: at the macro level, the location of the project relative to the rest of the planet and at the micro level, where the project sits on its site. Place from the larger view impacts building orientation because of the earth's declination. With the idea being to face solar south, not magnetic south, as you move across a climate zone, the best angle for orientation shifts a few degrees. For example Kansas City, Missouri, is in the same climate zone as Washington, D.C. Solar south in Kansas City is 2.43 degrees east of magnetic south, and Washington, D.C., is 10.43 degrees west.

In the micro world of an individual building site, place also has an impact related to solar access, views from and to the project, and the overall organization of the built fabric. Not all urban sites allow solar access, thus limiting the potential for use of this free resource. Also, there are situations where the building might have to face the wrong orientation due to street access or a desired view. We as occupants of buildings want to have great views to the outdoors, and sometimes that view does not coincide with the optimum orientation for capturing daylight, using shading or the capturing prevailing breezes. In those situations, the design team will have to *trick* the building into thinking it is oriented properly by extensive use of external shading and internal light shelves, and optimizing the percentage of glazing on each façade.

Reducing Resource Need

Each building type reacts to its climate in a different manner. Some are dominated by the external load and others by internal loads. An office building and a science lab are both internal load–dominated buildings. An office building, though, can have its internal load greatly reduced by correct orientation. In our example at the beginning of the chapter, we talked about how the combination of orientation, external shading, and daylight dimming can create a significant reduction in energy use, such as the 20% reduction shown in Figure 5.6. The science lab, on the other hand, has much of its load created by the equipment, so the savings from those orientation-based strategies will be significantly smaller. When designing an extreme case like a lab, a hospital, or a computing center, the need to orient the building properly will be of less importance. However, it is still usually one of the most inexpensive yet most effective means of reaching a truly sustainable design.

Orientation	Rotations from true South	Orientation		Orientation + shading		Orientation + shading + daylighting	
		Energy Use KBtu/sf-year	Annual Operating Cost Savings (over base case)	Energy Use KBtu/sf-year	Annual Operating Cost Savings (over base case)	Energy Use KBtu/sf-year	Annual Operating Cost Savings (over base case)
	90° W	61.9	Base Case	57.1	6.39%	54.4	15.24%
	45° W	62.1	0%	56.5	6.84%	53.8	15.7%
	15° W	60.9	0.9%	56.6	6.89%	52.3	18.27%
	0°	61.2	0.7%	56.7	6.84%	52.3	18.27%
	15° E	60.7	1.3%	55.7	7.90%	51.7	18.89%
	30° E	61.5	0.7%	56.3	7.30%	52.1	18.33%
	45° E	61.7	0.5%	56.3	7.15%	52.2	18.03%

Image courtesy of BNIM Architects

Figure 5.6 Simulated cumulative effects of proper orientation on other strategies for a five-story, 50,000-sq.-ft. office building in Seattle

A house will represent the other extreme because it is externally load dominated. Taking advantage of orientation will offer a greater impact over the whole design and life of the project.

There are a number of ways to reduce the need for mechanical and electrical systems with proper building orientation. Proper orientation has the following benefits:

- Allows the greatest opportunity to use natural daylight and less electric lighting systems.

- Allows for the most effective incorporation of electric lighting controls.

- Allows for less complicated external shading devices.

- Allows for integration of renewable energy systems like PV panels by having them facing solar south. They can be integrated as shading devices or even skin systems.

Setting Project Goals

After you understand the design problems regarding proper orientation, setting project goals is the next step. Because proper building orientation is going to be site specific, it's important to set realistic goals based on the project conditions. If you are in an urban site, it might not be possible to achieve the ideal building orientation (as it might be on a nonurban site), but you can still set a project goal of proper orientation for maximizing the benefits of other strategies that you will implement later as the design evolves.

Proper building orientation should be one of the first questions you ask of your design team. If proper orientation is possible, it becomes a lot easier and more effective to implement a number of other sustainable strategies. If possible within the constraints of your site and program, set the long side of the project to face solar south, as shown in Figure 5.7.

Image courtesy of BNIM Architects

Figure 5.7 A properly oriented building

Using BIM for Building Orientation: Finding Solar South

After you establish your project goal of proper orientation, you need to apply that to your model. This will be a simple thing to do within the BIM environment, and you can easily see the effects of a properly orientated building. As we noted earlier, proper orientation is key to optimizing many of the other strategies. Most BIM software packages assume south is *down* on the screen. This can also occur when the building is reoriented to be perpendicular to the sheet, rather than facing a given direction. While this is fine for documentation, it falls far short of our needs for proper orientation and can actually result in improper sun shading. To compensate for the difference between "sheet south" versus solar south during analysis, you must determine how far from solar south the project is and adjust the model environment to suit. Although a couple degrees might not have a noticeable impact, 10 or 15 degrees will.

To make this adjustment, you must do two things. First, find the degree of declination, or the angle from south that you need to make your adjustment to solar south, and then orient the project to face that angle. For the purposes of orientation, treat screen south like magnetic south. You need two tools to do this: your basic design in BIM and the Internet.

To find solar south in BIM, first establish your location. You will see this come up again and again in a number of the methods that we utilize. A sense of place and the impact of a specific location on design cannot be overemphasized. In your BIM application, there is a way to set project location that will provide you with the actual longitude and latitude of the project. In Autodesk's Revit Architecture, the dialog box looks like Figure 5.8; open it by selecting Settings > Manage Place and Locations.

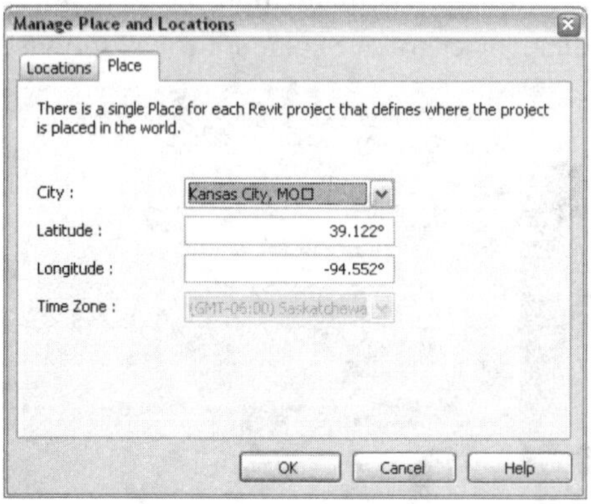

Figure 5.8 Locating the project

Setting your location in your BIM application will establish the latitude and longitude for you based on the city and state within which your project will be built.

Using these numbers, you can visit the National Geophysical Data Center's (NGDC) website at www.ngdc.noaa.gov/seg/geomag/jsp/Declination.jsp. This site will calculate the declination from magnetic north based on longitude and latitude (Figure 5.9).

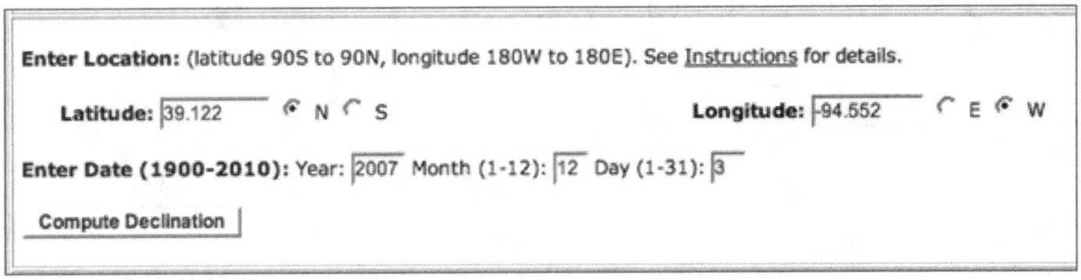

Enter Location: (latitude 90S to 90N, longitude 180W to 180E). See Instructions for details.

Latitude: 39.122   ○ N ○ S   **Longitude:** -94.552   ○ E ○ W

Enter Date (1900-2010): Year: 2007 Month (1-12): 12 Day (1-31): 3

Compute Declination

Figure 5.9 Calculating declination

Clicking Compute Declination will give you your declination as of the current day and year (Figure 5.10). For our project based on Kansas City, it is roughly 2.5 degrees east of south. Alternatively, if you have an electronic survey with a north arrow oriented to true north or based on a geodetic coordinate system (not magnetic north), you can import this as a background into your BIM model. You can then use this imported survey as a basis to figure your angle of declination.

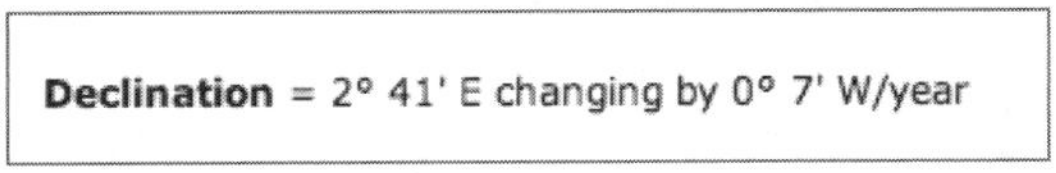

Declination = 2° 41' E changing by 0° 7' W/year

Figure 5.10 The project declination

Now all that is left is to rotate your project to the proper angle. Specific BIM applications can vary, but some let you set true north and project north as two separate angles. This is primarily so your drawings can be oriented properly in the sheet set while you can simultaneously glean proper sun shading and solar orientation from the model.

Making this change is a simple matter of setting true north within the BIM environment; basically rotating the project. The following figures show two examples of building orientation.

Figure 5.11 shows the two plans in comparison. The one on the left is at magnetic south while the plan on the right shows solar south taken into account. The second set of images (Figure 5.12) shows the same conditions in elevation. Note the significant changes in shadows during the same time of day. This will dramatically affect the quality of light within the spaces. It only stands to reason that as the shading is impacted, so is the heat gain, daylighting, and other environmental design strategies within the project. Making sure that you have proper building orientation sets the stage for many of the other sustainable strategies.

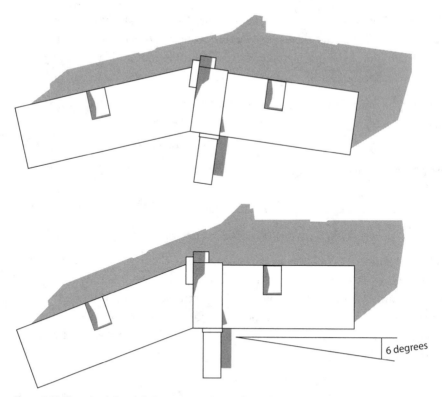

6 degrees

Figure 5.11 The project before and after proper rotation to solar south

Figure 5.12 Elevations before and after proper orientation

Building Massing

Second to proper orientation, proper building massing is key to a healthy, sustainable building. Proper massing allows good access to daylight for all the building occupants while still creating an efficient building envelope optimized for thermal efficiency and comfort.

Building types have great flexibility when it comes to building mass, but within each specific type certain proportions have become acceptable or the norm—some for aesthetic reasons and others for efficiency of leasing. Office buildings, for example, come in many different shapes and sizes. Some are tall and skinny, some are short and wide, some are tall and wide, and others are short and skinny. There could be an optimal mass for each building type, but even if there were, would we want them all to look that way? That being the case, it is important to understand the ideal situations based on building type and location so as you design, you can adapt the building form accordingly, with the knowledge that it is not always possible to fit the ideal massing condition. Factors like site restraints, economics, programmatic needs, and aesthetics can also be form-driving elements in design.

The primary reason for proper building massing is simple. By choosing the right mass for the building type and climate, you are reducing the building's overall energy needs. This then allows you to spend project funds on more efficient equipment, which makes purchasing on-site renewable systems more palatable.

Using Building Type and Orientation Together

Some projects, like a university lab building, have building types embedded within them. Inside a lab building are the lab type, the classroom type, and the office type. Separating these types in different masses allows for several efficiencies. BNIM Architects took this approach with the Fayez S. Sarofim Research Building at the University of Texas Health Science Center at Houston.

Building orientation allows optimum penetration and control of natural light in relationship to the differing programmatic elements of flexible laboratory space, support laboratories, office, and common areas. Sectional organization allowed the design team to optimize the spatial characteristics of different program elements. By separating office and lab elements, the environmental control system is able to capture and reuse energy that would normally be wasted. The design parti clearly separates the lab type and the office type, allowing sustainable design strategies specific to each type while enabling these types to operate synergistically.

(continued)

Using Building Type and Orientation Together *(continued)*

The following three images show the program elements, shading strategies for the different building types, and how daylighting, massing, and shading strategies can all be implemented in a final building solution:

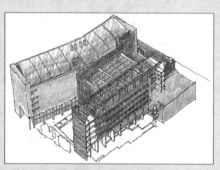

Massing diagram of programmatic Spaces

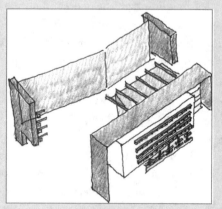

Diagram of shading and daylighting strategies

The final built condition

Images © Assassi | Courtesy of BNIM Architects

Understanding the Impact of Climate, Culture, and Place

Climate, culture, and place have a number of impacts on the building's massing strategies and how they impact the sustainable opportunities:

- Climate's impact on building mass affects the ability to use passive design strategies for heating, cooling, and lighting.

- If a building is going to rely heavily on daylighting, it will likely have a narrow footprint, or perhaps a large atrium to bring light down into the interior space, or it might have clerestories, or a shed roof optimized for either north or south light collection.

- A building that is going to rely on natural ventilation will need a *chimney* component whether it is a formal chimney or a tall common space like a hallway or lobby that draws air through the building via natural convention flows.

- Passive heating suggests a narrow footprint with south-facing glazing to capture the solar radiation during the day.

- Climate also affects building mass in the ability to collect rainwater. For a building in a climate where it rains little, you might want a larger roof to extend its rainwater collection capacity. This same roof can also be used as a whole building shade because the dry climate can also be hot.

For all of these conditions, the building mass will be organized a bit differently in specific climate zones for each of these passive strategies. For example, a given building placed in Iowa and Texas could both use daylighting strategies. However, on an annual basis you would be more interested in passive heating in Iowa and passive cooling in Texas because of their climate zones.

Organizational culture can impact building mass; for example, if the mission of the client includes wanting the occupants to have great connections to the outdoors, the building footprint might not be very deep. This would extend a level of transparency through the building connecting the inside and outside visually and allow use of natural daylight. This might also suggest that the building should be low to the ground so that the occupants can easily get to the outside. If a building's occupants need to stay removed from direct sunlight, as is the condition in some labs, the building mass might respond with large overhangs to block direct sunlight or include an adjacent daylit atrium to give a feeling of volume and openness. This notion of organizational culture suggests that we need to also consider the microculture of the building's occupants in addition to the surrounding culture and climate of the area the building is in.

Place also has an impact on building mass. A building located in an urban area is more likely to have multiple floors on a portion of a city block than a suburban building, which typically has more land available. In the same manner, urban projects usually have structured parking associated with them whereas suburban greenfield projects (buildings built on undeveloped land) have sprawling asphalt parking lots.

In several ways, building massing can also relate to the context of the site. Figure 5.13 shows the sketch of a building that has been oriented properly to take advantage of the climate conditions and has its massing designed to contextually work with the site. Some of the design elements that can help a building mass relate to site are as follows:

- A building in a sensitive ecological environment might be organized on stilts so that it touches the ground lightly so as not to disturb the ground and also allow habitat to travel uninhibited through the built area.

- A given site might also be adjacent to a sensitive ecosystem, like the edge of a forest or stream, and as such, the building mass might be more vertical because of it.

- A building mass might need to be kept low because the surrounding ecology or neighboring properties have solar access rights.

Notwithstanding all of these possible constraints, the building mass should be consistent with its surroundings.

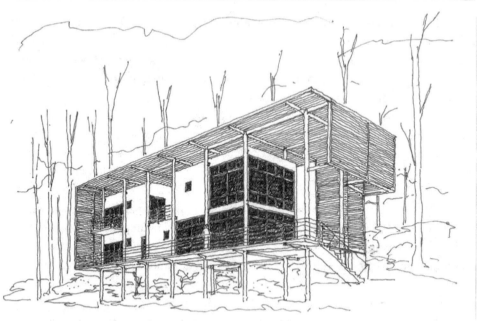

Figure 5.13 Sketch of an off-the-grid home optimized for climate, culture, and place

Reducing Resource Need

Buildings themselves react to the climate in different ways. As described earlier, the office building is internal load dominated whereas the single family home is dominated by the exterior environment. Playing into these strengths and weaknesses can significantly reduce your resource consumption and save you money. If you consider an office building in Kansas City, traditionally it is a cooling load–dominated building in need of some perimeter heating during winter months. This pattern is largely driven by the traditional large footprints and limited exterior skin that are commonly found in speculative office developments.

Using BIM for Building Massing

In our example of the office building, at this stage of the project we need to explore some massing opportunities. Because we have a suburban greenfield site, we are not constrained by typical urban conditions and are free to explore some different building forms.

First, we need to establish a baseline building mass and volume in our BIM application to compare the pros and cons of the other building shapes that we are going to explore. We need to start with the typical *big box* speculative office building shape that is so commonly seen in any office park around the country. This will help us establish a benchmark.

All of the building forms we want to explore need to have the same basic values. They each need to have the same amount of occupiable space to make the comparison equal, the same number of users, the same operating schedule, and the same lighting, HVAC, and envelope systems. We can derive much of this from the ASHRAE Standard 90.1 document (http://www.ashrae.org). As we change form and shape, other things, such as the building volume and the amount of exterior wall, will change. Both of these values will also have an impact on the building cost and the heating and cooling loads of the building.

To ensure some consistency within our comparison, we have set some parametric parameters in our BIM model. For our big box office building, we've locked a ratio and set the square footage to be equal to the client's program area (Figure 5.14). In Figure 5.15, we can see the parametric values we've established to maintain this square footage and proportion.

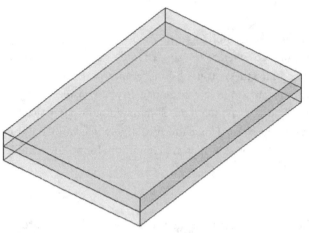

Figure 5.14 Big box design: a two-story structure with a 3:2 ratio

Figure 5.15 Parametric values to maintain building form based on size

Now that we've established our baseline, we can look at a couple of other building forms. Ideally, to get the best daylight into an interior space we'd like to keep the building width approximately 60′. So, operating under this constraint, it will change the parameters of our building to reflect what Figure 5.16 shows. Figure 5.17 again shows the values.

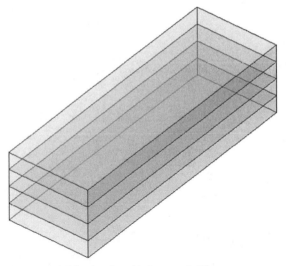

Figure 5.16 Building form for a thin, four-story building

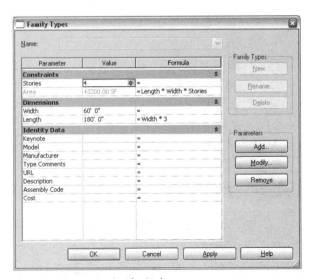

Figure 5.17 Parametric values for this form

    This shape has the required benefit of natural daylight in all the spaces, but it exceeds a three-story height, which, in our case, makes the building more expensive due to additional code requirements for a four-story structure. In another analysis, we want to look at another two-story option to keep the building low but still give us good access to daylight. For this, we'll look at a C-shaped option as in Figure 5.18. Figure 5.19 shows similar parametric values.

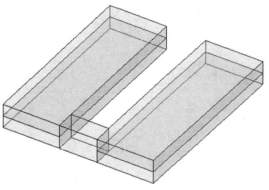

Figure 5.18 C-shaped building form

Figure 5.19 Parametric values for the C-shaped building

You can see how by keeping the same building floor area, we can have a number of different schemes that allow us some flexibility for a better solution. As described earlier, part of developing sustainable solutions includes correctly balancing economic factors. We also need to consider overall cost and as we have changed the building shape, we have impacted the first cost by increasing the area of exterior wall.

To gauge how well some of the schemes are at allowing us to approach the most sustainable solutions, we need to simulate some of the design strategies on all of the schemes. By making a few more assumptions, like HVAC system, glazing properties, exterior wall properties, and operating schedules that are common across the schemes, we can compare the effectiveness of optimizing some of our design strategies for energy efficiency and low operating costs. The quickest way to set that up is to export the three simple BIM models to an energy-analysis software program so we can run and analyze the simulations. (Details of exporting to different energy analysis tools are covered in Chapter 6.)

Analyzing Building Form

Now that we have a few design iterations, we need to figure out what the best approach is for this particular building, site, and client. With an energy analysis package, we can run a few simple energy simulations, based on which we can compare the annual energy costs in each building type. Data in the graph shown in Figure 5.20 comes from the simulations. Each design scheme has the same parameters for HVAC system, exterior glazing percentage, glazing type, exterior wall type, and operating schedule. We begin with a baseline energy use per square foot on the left bar (for each building shape). By cumulatively adding an improved building envelope (second bar) and glazing (third bar), and adding automatic daylight dimmers for the lighting (third bar), you can see how quickly the annual energy use drops and therefore the costs to own and operate the building drop. As shown by the results of the simulations, the big box building can only be optimized by 12%; however, the narrow and tall building can gain 20% savings on its energy costs while the C-shaped building gains a total of 22%. This savings is a significant amount in the lifecycle cost evaluation of project costs.

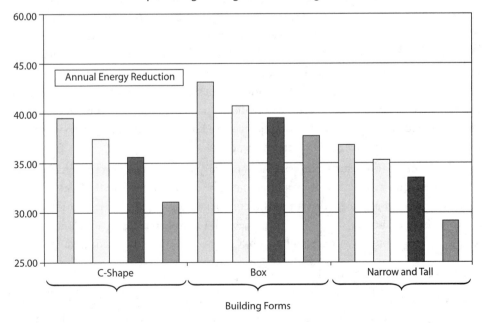

Image courtesy of BNIM Architects

Figure 5.20 Analyzing the building forms

This large reduction in energy use can then be applied to reduce the size mechanical system and begin to offset some of the costs incurred by adding more building envelope. By continuing to adjust and reanalyze the building form, we can create the shape that not only performs the best and is visually appealing, but that also creates the best environment for its inhabitants. Better spaces categorized by visual and temperature comfort and connections to nature provide productivity benefits for the building users. Because employees are often the most expensive portion of any organization's cash outflow, the cost of these improvements is often minor.

Optimizing the Building Envelope

As we manipulate the building form, we also must be conscious of the skin that wraps it. The quality, permeability, conduction resistance, amount of glazing, and other factors will combine to determine the comfort and efficiency of the building mass and systems. To grasp how these factors will impact the building design, we need to know how to optimize the envelope based on many of the same parameters we have discussed previously. We accomplish this by considering climate, place, and the properties of the envelope materials.

Understanding the Impacts of Climate and Place

Climate affects the walls and glazing from a heating, cooling, and daylight integration standpoint. Different climate zones require different resistance between the indoor and outdoor environment whether it is simply conduction or conduction and air infiltration. Glazing recommendations will vary from climate to climate on particular façades as will the recommended percentage of glass on each of those façades. This means that based on the climate and cardinal direction of any given façade, we want to pay careful attention to the amount of glazing we put into the design. For example, in our location in the Midwest, the east and west sun can be harsh on the interior environment early in the morning and late in the day. To counteract these conditions, we minimize the percentage of wall area to open area on those façades.

Recommendations for wall resistance also vary from climate to climate. For buildings over three stories, recommendations can be found in the ASHRAE Standard 90.1. At the residential scale, you can find recommendations at the DOE's Building America website at http://www.eere.energy.gov/buildings/building_america, among other places. Local building codes will also have stipulated their own requirements.

Understanding Envelope Energy Use

There are two main issues related to creating the most appropriate envelope design for optimized energy use. First is the amount of operational energy saved. Second is the level of comfort provided by choosing the correct materials for the climate and building type. To demonstrate the impact of choosing the right materials in a building's skin, let's look at two of the most commonly used elements: insulation and glazing.

Insulation

In the example of building insulation, many products are available on the market that are superior based on performance, or because they use or reuse resources more wisely than competitive products. Insulation comes in many flavors: batt, rigid, loose fill, foamed in place, or spray-in. Batts can be made of fiberglass, mineral wool, or cotton; rigid insulations are foams; loose fills are cellulose, vermiculite, or perlite; and spray-ins are foam based. Each of these has a different R-value per inch (insulation value) ranging from 2.2 to 8, which corresponds directly to the potential savings in operating energy and resulting human comfort. Within those products categories, you can find different environmental characteristics. Batt insulation can be made from fiberglass with different amounts of recycled content, or entirely from recycled cotton blue jeans. Rigid foam insulation can be made from different types of foam; extruded polystyrene, expanded polystyrene, polyisocyanurate, or fiberglass, each having a different embodied energy and availability.

Glazing

When selecting glazing, it is important to review four key energy efficiency values of the gazing unit:

U-value A measure of heat gain or heat loss through glass due to the differences between indoor and outdoor temperatures. It is the reciprocal of the R-value. The lower the U-value, the less heat is transmitted through the glazing unit.

SHGC (Solar Heat Gain Coefficient) The fraction of directly transmitted and absorbed solar radiation that enters into the building's interior—the higher the SHGC, the higher the solar heat gain.

VLT (Visual Light Transmittance) The percentage of visible light that is transmitted through the glass.

LSG (Light to Solar Gain Ratio) Defined as a ratio equal to the Visible Light Transmittance (VLT) divided by the Solar Heat Gain Coefficient (LSG = VLT / SHGC). In its Federal Technology Alert publication, the Department of Energy's Federal Emergency Management Program views an LSG of 1.25 or greater to be Green Glazing, otherwise known as Spectrally Selective Glazing.

Regional Insulation

A few years ago on a large office building project, we ran into problems getting the rigid foam that we specified for the roof because there was not enough material left in the entire U.S. market to meet the need for our building. Since then the product has been discontinued. As this trend continues, good renewable resource bio-based systems and recycled material systems will become invaluable. Some manufacturers like Owens Corning have started putting information on their website and issuing product literature stating the recycled content and manufacturing location so a designer can clearly see the environmental impact while selecting a primary building component like insulation. Newer spray in foam products are shifting away from petroleum-based foams to bio-based foams, supplying extremely high R-value per inch from a renewable organic product. The insulation manufacture locations that the following figure shows are within a 500-mile radius distribution circle:

Insulation manufacturing plants with 500 mile radius circles

Depending on the climate and building type, you will need different values for your glazing. In many cases it is appropriate to have different values on the different façades. If building occupants are sitting near the windows, a project team would be wise to pick a glass with a low U-value. You can find expected U-values for the traditional climate zones based on percentage of glass in the ASHRAE 90.1 manual. When designing for daylighting, the windows above the lightshelf would likely have a higher VLT than the windows below. It is possible when external shades are well designed to use a unit with high VLT and low SHGC because the external shade blocks the undesired solar heat gain. Recent advances in glass have developed units with great properties in all areas. One example of this is the Solarban 70XL, with a VLT of 63%, U-value of .27, SHGC of .27, and LSG of 2.33, according to the manufacturer's data sheet. Figure 5.21 illustrates how we have set goals for glazing properties to increase performance during a project in California. By setting goals for various levels of LEED, we can begin to see how these goals affect various aspects of sustainable design.

Design Criteria/Characteristics		Market	LEED Certified	LEED Silver	LEED Gold	LEED Platinum	Living Building
Total Site Area	(sf)	56,000	56,000	56,000	56,000	56,000	56,000
Building Form	Dimensions (ft)	120' (N-S) x 7' (E-W)	120' (N-S) x 7' (E-W)	80' (N-S) x 7' (E-W)	60' (N-S) x 7' (E-W)	40' (N-S) x 7' (E-W)	40' (N-S) x 7' (E-W)
	Area (ft²)	90,000	90,000	90,000	90,000	90,000	90,000
	Stories	Office: 2 floors; Garage: 3 levels	Office: 2 floors; Garage: 3 levels	Office: 3 floors; Garage: 3 levels	Office: 3 floors; Garage: 3 levels	Office: 3 floors; Garage: 3 levels	Office: 3 floors; Garage: 3 levels
	Orientation	-	-	-	Solar-based	Solar-based	Solar-based
Occupancy	People	300	300	300	300	300	300
Glazing %	North	60	50	40	40	40	40
	South	60	50	40	40	40	40
	East	60	50	30	25	20	20
	West	60	50	30	25	20	20
	Skylight	-	-	-	-	-	-

Glazing Characteristics		U	SC	VLT	U	SC	VLT	U	SC	VLT	U	SC	VLT	U	SC	VLT	U	SC	VLT
	North	0.42	0.6	0.71	0.32	0.46	0.64	0.29	0.43	0.7	0.29	0.43	0.7	0.16	0.35	0.6	0.16	0.35	0.6
	South	0.42	0.6	0.71	0.32	0.46	0.64	0.29	0.43	0.7	0.29	0.43	0.7	0.16	0.35	0.6	0.16	0.35	0.6
	East	0.42	0.6	0.71	0.32	0.46	0.64	0.31	0.4	0.47	0.31	0.4	0.47	0.16	0.31	0.6	0.16	0.31	0.6
	West	0.42	0.6	0.71	0.32	0.46	0.64	0.31	0.4	0.47	0.31	0.4	0.47	0.16	0.31	0.6	0.16	0.31	0.6
	Skylight	-	-	-	-	-	-	-	-	-	-	-	-	-	-	-	-	-	-

		Market	LEED Certified	LEED Silver	LEED Gold	LEED Platinum	Living Building
	Daylight and views	Limited access to Daylight and views	Daylight and views at common areas	Daylight and views at common areas	Ambient daylight for general lighting	Daylight for visual tasks	Daylight for visual tasks
	Insulation, operability	Double-glazed, fixed	Double-glazed, fixed	Double-glazed, operable	Double-glazed, operable	Triple-glazed, operable w/ controls	Triple-glazed, operable w/ controls
	Light Shelves	No	No	No	Yes	Yes	Yes
% Glazing Shaded during the months: X thru X	North	0	0	0	50	100	100
	South	0	0	100	100	100	100
	East	0	0	30	50	100	100
	West	0	0	30	50	100	100
	Exterior Shade	No	No	South	South, East & West	South	South
	Vertical Screen	No	No	No	No	East & West	East & West
	Vertical Fin	No	No	No	No	North	North

Image courtesy of BNIM Architects

Figure 5.21 Different glazing goals for varied levels of performance

Daylighting

Daylighting is the use of natural light for primary interior illumination. This reduces your need for artificial light within the space, thus reducing internal heat gain and energy use. Natural light is the highest-quality and most efficient light source available today—and the source is free.

An effective daylighting design relies heavily on proper building orientation, massing, and envelope design topics we have already discussed. The proper combination of these strategies allows you to optimize your building's use of natural resources and minimize your dependency on artificial lighting. A fully integrated daylighting system can enhance the visual acuity, comfort, and beauty of a space while controlling external heat gain and glare (see Figure 5.22).

Here are some common terms associated with daylighting:

- A foot-candle, which is a measure of light intensity. A foot-candle is defined as the amount of light received by 1 square foot of a surface that is 1 foot from a point source of light equivalent to one candle of a certain type. Depending on the sky conditions, daylight can produce anywhere from 2,000 to 10,000 foot-candles.

- Illuminance, which is the luminous flux per unit area on an intercepting surface at any given point, expressed in foot-candles. Commonly described as the amount of light on a surface.

Figure 5.22 A daylight atrium

- Luminance, which is the luminous intensity of a surface in a given direction per unit of projected area, expressed in foot-candles. Commonly described as the amount of light leaving a surface.

- Visual acuity, which is a measure of the ability to distinguish fine details.

- Glare, which is the sensation produced by luminance within the visual field that is sufficiently greater than the luminance to which the eyes have adapted to cause annoyance, discomfort, or visibility difficulty.

Figure 5.23 demonstrates the use of daylight in a modern lab space.

Image © Assassi | Courtesy of BNIM Architects

Figure 5.23 Correct daylighting enhances the quality of a space.

Not only does natural daylight help light our interior spaces, but it also supplies us with a connection to the outdoors. Providing occupants with natural light and ties to the outside has been proven in a number of cases to have a positive effect on human health and productivity. Studies on daylighting from 1992 through 2003 have shown that buildings with good daylighting design have positive effects on their occupants; these effects include increased productivity levels, low absentee rates, better grades, retail sale increases, improved dental records, and healthier occupants. Details of the studies are below:

"Study into the Effects of Light on Children of Elementary School Age: A Case of Daylight Robbery" (1992) by Hathaway, Hargreaves, Thompson and Novitsky, Policy and Planning Branch, Planning and Information services Division, Alberta Education, compared children attending elementary schools with full-spectrum light versus those with normal lighting conditions and found:

- Students in full-spectrum light were healthier and attended school approximately 3.5 more days/year

- Libraries with superior light were significantly quieter
- Full-spectrum lighting provided for more positive moods
- Students who received additional vitamin D from full-spectrum light had nine times less dental decay than students in schools with average light conditions.

"Student Performance in Daylit Schools" (1996) by Michael H. Nicklas and Gary Bailey, Innovative Design analyzed performance of children attending three new daylit schools in Johnson County North Carolina, compared to old and new non-daylit schools in the same county and found:

- Students attending daylit schools outperformed those in nondaylit schools by 5% in the short term.
- Over the long term, students in daylit schools outperformed those in nondaylit schools by 14%.

"Daylighting in Schools: An Investigation into the Relationship Between Daylighting and Human Performance" (1999) by Heschong Mahone Group studied the effects of daylighting on human performance through school districts in Orange County California, Seattle, Washington and Fort Collins, Colorado and found:

- 15–26% better progression in math and reading related tests in one year in California.
- 7–18% higher test scores, in Seattle and Fort Collins.

"Windows and Classrooms: A Study of Student Performance and the Indoor Environment" (2003) by Heschong Mahone Group investigated whether daylight and other aspects of the indoor environment effect student learning and found:

- Ample and pleasant views support better learning outcomes.
- Glare negatively affects student learning.
- Direct sun penetration into classrooms through unshaded east or south windows has a negative impact due to glare and thermal discomfort.
- Lack of occupant control of light through windows has a negative effect on learning.

"Skylighting and Retail Sales: An Investigation into the Relationship Between Daylighting and Human Performance" (1999) by Heschong Mahone Group studied the effects of daylighting on human performance for a chain retailer who had a mix of daylit and non-daylit stores and found:

- Skylit stores had 40% higher sales.
- If non-daylit stores added skylights, gross sales would increase by 11%.

"Windows and Offices: A Study of Office Worker Performance and the Indoor Environment" (2003) by Heschong Mahone Group reported on the contributions of windows and daylight to improved worker performance and found:

- Call center employees with better views processed calls 6–12% faster.

- Office workers with better views performed 10–25% better on tests of mental function and memory.
- Employee self-reports of better health conditions strongly related to those with better views.
- High-cubicle partitions equated to slower performance.
- Glare potential from view windows decreased performance by 15–21%.

Figure 5.24 shows daylighting in an office environment. A good use of daylight combined with other sustainable design strategies can raise the productivity rate of employees by at least 1% or more. Although this is a seemingly small number, it is equivalent to over 20 hours of production time a year per employee. If thought of on the scale of a major school or company, this small percentage can mean significant savings.

Image courtesy of Mike Sinclair

Figure 5.24 Daylighting in an office space

To ensure these positive results, a design team should consider specific factors when they create a daylit designed space:

Consider eye adaptation to light. Eyes are involuntary muscles and react automatically to differences in light levels. Minimizing high contrast in the visual plane provides even light levels and less strain on the eye muscles.

Orient the building on an east-west axis. South sun is the easiest to control.

Choose the right glazing. Each façade has a unique condition to solve.

Provide tall windows on perimeter walls. Doing so allows greater natural light penetration.

Provide external shading devices. This reduces direct light penetration and undesirable heat gain.

Provide light shelves. You can project light up to two times the window head height into the building.

Consider light reflectance values when choosing materials. Ensure appropriate reflectance on surfaces.

Arrange interior spaces to optimize the use of daylighting. This reduces or relocates walled perimeter offices.

Use automated lighting controls. Lighting controls include motion or occupancy sensors, automated dimmers, timers, internal blinds, and automated external shading devices.

Use appropriate light levels. Use light levels appropriate for tasks performed in the space.

Now that you've seen the impact and importance of daylighting in home, work, and school situations, you can begin to see how you can incorporate that information into your design. Before we look at the impacts of daylight inside a building, it's important to consider how available (or, at times, abundant) daylight is to a particular location. Based on the availability of daylight and how you want to address the lighting, this can allow you to integrate new features into your designs (Figure 5.25).

Figure 5.25 Integrated external shading devices on a building façade

Understanding the Impacts of Climate, Culture, and Place

The ability to use daylight in your design is directly related to climate and place. Certain climates have more sunny days than other climates. This is just a fact of nature. Seattle, Washington, has on an annual average a 43% possibility of sunshine, with only 71 clear days. Phoenix, Arizona, on the other hand, has an annual average of 86% possibility of sunshine with 211 clear days. Cloudy days can be good for daylighting, too, because the clouds bounce the ambient light around, bringing it in at more angles, but less harshly. Cloudy days create more of an even light solution, although at a lower light level.

The temperature is related to the number of sunny days. Although you would have more of an opportunity to bring in lots of natural light to a building in Phoenix, you must be extra careful not to add unwanted heat to the building.

The building's location and what makes up the immediate surroundings have an effect on your ability to use daylight in your design. If your project site is quite open, you could have great access. If you are in a dense urban area, the challenge will be greater. In other situations, your site might be oriented the wrong way, in which case you might be spending time and effort trying to "trick" the building into capturing daylight or working hard to create a solution for keeping unwanted glare out.

Setting Project Goals

The most common goal related to daylighting design is the ratio of interior to exterior illuminance or daylight factor. This is what the USGBC LEED Indoor Environmental Quality (IEQ) Credit 8.1 is based on. In LEED-NC version 2.2, a couple of additional options are available, including demonstrating the availability of 25 foot-candles of daylight in 75% of regularly occupied areas at the workplane level (30 inches above the floor) at noon on the equinox using computer simulation, or demonstration of the same through measurements on site (on a 10′ grid).

In an office space, this means that 50% of the required lighting is supplied by natural light. The Illuminating Engineering Society of North America has published illuminance guidelines based on the task being performed (Figure 5.26).

The project goal for percentage of daylight in a space will influence several things, such as the type of glazing, the depth of the building, the location of atriums if in a wide building, the percentage of glass on a façade, the size and location of the window apertures, location and material of shading devices, the layout of interior spaces, the interior materials and finishes, and so forth.

Type of Activity	Foot-candles	Reference work plane
Public spaces with dark surroundings	2-5	General lighting throughout spaces
Simple orientation for short temporary visits	5-20	
Working spaces where visual tasks are only occasionally performed	10-20	Illuminance on task
Performance of visual tasks of high contrast or larger size	20-50	
Performance of visual tasks of medium contrast or average size	50-100	
Performance of visual tasks of low contrast or very small size	100-200	
Performance of visual tasks of low contrast and very small size over a prolonged period	200-500	Illuminance on task, obtained by a combination of general and local supplementary lighting
Performance of very prolonged and exacting visual tasks	500-1000	
Performance of very special visual tasks of extremely low contrast and small size	1000-2000	

Source: From the IESNA Lighting Handbook

Figure 5.26 Daylight needed for tasks

In the section "Optimizing the Building Envelope" earlier in this chapter, we reviewed glazing unit properties. Now let's look at building width. In the case of an office, we believe an ideal building width for daylighting is around 60′, with windows on both the north and south sides and an open office plan (Figure 5.27). Light fixtures along the perimeter can be controlled with continuous dimmers set to keep the light levels at the desired level for office tasks. Rooms near the center of the building can be the enclosed private areas or areas that are not regularly occupied, as they will not quite get any usable daylight. With low partitions, most of the people in this plan should have a view to the outside.

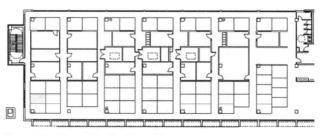

Figure 5.27 60′ as the ideal building width

For the Heifer International Center, the project team set a goal of keeping the building 65′ wide to maximize opportunities for both daylight and views (Figure 5.28). Client-driven policies and programmatic requirements unfortunately kept enclosed offices along the perimeter, but the clients did, however, agree to make the inner wall fully glazed. Had the perimeter offices not been fully enclosed, the daylight would have traveled further into the space.

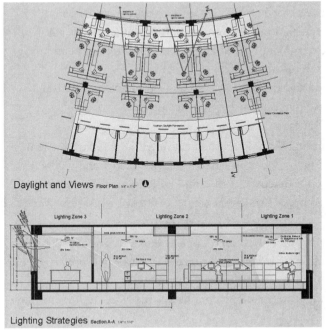

Figure 5.28 Daylighting concept for the Heifer International Center plan

Using BIM for Daylighting

After you've established the goals for setting natural daylight and views into your space, you can begin using the BIM model. Before we jump into the model, let's first discuss the tools that you will need to perform this analysis. To do daylighting, you will need:

- The BIM model
- A daylighting simulation package

In our example, we will be using the BIM model primarily for geometry generation. Geometry reuse can be a tremendous timesaver based on the complexity of the project and the unnecessary redundancy of re-creating model geometry in a variety of applications. We will go into a higher-level analysis of this problem when we discuss energy simulation in the next chapter. However, suffice it to say that the less time you spend remodeling a building design simply to test and quantify the availability of natural light, the more time you will have to spend designing solutions.

At this point, let's discuss daylight simulation software packages currently available. There are a number of applications in a wide range of prices. The most accurate tools developed to date have been based on the Radiance engine, written primarily by Greg Ward at Lawrence Berkeley National Laboratory (LBNL). Radiance is still maintained by LBNL; it is a free, government-funded application so it doesn't benefit from development funds as do other applications.

A number of packages on the market use the Radiance engine as a basis and supply a front-end user interface that allows designers to use the engine readily. A few of these applications are as follows:

Integrated Environmental Solutions Virtual Environment Integrated Environmental Solutions Virtual Environment (http://www.iesve.com) can run energy and daylight analysis as well as import model geometry directly from a BIM model. The package is robust but can also be rather complex for newer users.

Daysim Daysim (http://irc.nrc-cnrc.gc.ca/ie/lighting/daylight/daysim_e.html) is a free application created by the National Resource Council Canada as a Canadian-government sponsored daylighting tool. This tool utilizes the newer and preferred Perez all-weather sky model to run its calculations. It is also compatible with files created in Ecotect (an energy-modeling application) and in Autodesk's 3ds Max. It does not, however, produce 3D images but just data.

Autodesk's 3ds Max Daylighting in this application is a new feature in what used to be primarily a rendering application (http://www.autodesk.com/3dsmax). This tool has a simple interface for running daylighting applications and a high level of interoperability with other Autodesk BIM applications, such as Revit Architecture. Not only will 3ds Max transfer model geometry between BIM and analysis, but it will also transfer materials, surface reflectivity, and electric light fixtures and photometric data.

Each of these applications also employs TMY2 data. TMY2 data sets include hourly solar radiation values over the course of a year. These data sets are geographically based. To read the TMY2 User's Manual, visit http://rredc.nrel.gov/solar/old_data/nsrdb/tmy2/. By using one of these tools, you can take your BIM model geometry and extract it for daylighting analysis. Make sure that you have the design at a stage that reflects the level of accuracy you want from your daylighting analysis. At a minimum, you want to have the major reflective internal surfaces, such as the walls and ceilings, and the right window apertures with the correct glazing. Figure 5.29 is one of 16 different clerestory/skylight configurations that we studied quickly in the concept design phase for an office building based on simple volumes.

Figure 5.29 Daylighting study of a two-story open office space

If you are using external shading devices or internal lightshelves, include those in your model geometry as well. As the design progresses, you will want to include furniture, or shapes that represent furniture. In any situation you can change one item's variable or the whole item incrementally to test what improvements to that portion of the design bring to the quality of the space.

Daylight analysis images are rendering the scientific quantification of light in a space; few are focused on visual rendering quality. See the comparison of a daylight simulation to a rendering in Figure 5.30. Daylight analysis simulations inform the designers about quantity of light, evenness of light, penetration of usable light, potential glare issues (Figure 5.31), and ideal locations for automated sensors.

Figure 5.30 Daylighting in a rendering

Image courtesy of BNIM Architects

Figure 5.31 Daylight simulation showing penetration and potential glare

The daylight light levels in a space are typically shown and measured in three ways: first as a light-level contour map (Figure 5.34), second as a grid of light levels across the image (Figure 5.32), and third as a false color image (Figure 5.33).

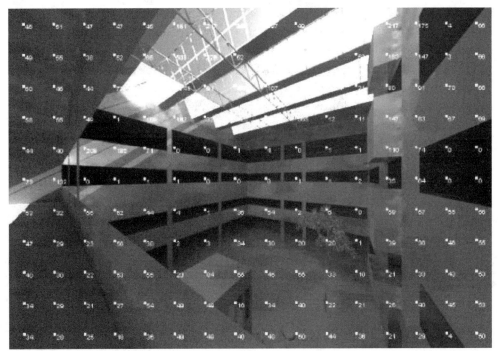

Image courtesy of BNIM Architects

Figure 5.32 A rendering with a grid of light levels overlaid

Image courtesy of BNIM Architects

Figure 5.33 A false color light study

Regardless of the output method you choose, what most teams are commonly looking for is the foot-candle level to comply with the Option 2—Daylight Simulation Model path for satisfying LEED IEQ Credit 8.1. Since Option 2 LEED-NC Version 2.2 requires 25 foot-candles of daylight in 75% of regularly occupied areas at the workplane level *at noon on the equinox*, with a clear sky, the simulation models should have the workplanes incorporated, as seen in Figure 5.34, and be run at that specific time.

Image courtesy of BNIM Architects

Figure 5.34 A model used for qualifying for the LEED daylighting credit

If you are thinking that a specific time period and sky condition seems rather limiting and not indicative of what could be happening during the whole year, you are in good company. The more sophisticated daylight simulation packages are starting to include more holistic analyses, such as *daylight autonomy*, defined as the amount of time during the year that a set light level is reached through the use of just daylight, and *useful daylight illuminance*, which looks at a range of acceptable light levels and removes the periods of time when it could be too dark or too bright.

Similarly, another calculation method allowed by IEQ 8.1 is called *glazing factor calculation*, which bases results on a simple mathematical calculation from inputting basic areas of the windows and floor, window height, window geometry, and the visible light transmittance of the glazing compared to a baseline. The glazing factor calculation method, while simple to communicate to design teams, does not take into account time and orientation, and overlooks the integration of shading and glare-control strategies.

Advancements in computing hardware and software afford you the ability to predict daylight accurately on an annual basis with stress on climate-based design. You should look more toward these methods, especially since continued advances in model transfer are cutting out a large chunk of your analysis time.

Sustainable BIM: Building Systems

To express is to drive.
And when you want to give something
  presence,
you have to consult nature.
And there is where Design comes in.

—*Louis Kahn*

In the previous chapter, we looked at sustainable concepts and methodologies that involve the building form and envelope. In this chapter, we'll focus our attention on the systems within the building and how to best explore concepts with the use of BIM. In this chapter, we discuss:

- *Water harvesting*
- *Energy modeling*
- *Using renewable energy*
- *Using sustainable materials*

Water Harvesting

Much of the focus of sustainable design is geared toward reducing energy use. However, depending on your region and location, water is one of our most critical and overlooked resources. The amount of water available is finite. There will never be more of it to use than we have available now. Seventy percent of the earth's surface is covered in water, but only 1% of that can be used for consumption. Of that 1%, the average person in the United States uses 53 gallons per day, and as our population continues to grow, so do our demands on our water.

Lake Mead and Georgia

There has been a recent population growth in the southwest. Lake Mead in Nevada above Hoover Dam is the main water supply for Arizona and parts of California and Nevada. That water comes from the Colorado River where there have been below average rains for the past few years and a large draw on the limited resources of the water reserves there. As of October 2007, the water levels have reached record lows. The current water level is 50 feet low, and it is predicted that without immediate water conservation, those levels can never be replenished. This water is responsible for irrigation for much of the farmlands in Southern California. Note that the white line in the following image represents the height of where the water level has been for decades.

This situation has prompted the city of Las Vegas to institute water conservation programs on a variety of levels. The Las Vegas valley has a 12-month water schedule for irrigating lawns and gardens, and it is no longer legal to wash your own car in your driveway due to the water it consumes. The city has also created a xeriscaping (using indigenous plants that do not need extra water for landscaping) rebate program where it will help offset the costs for residents to remove their water-dependent grass lawns and replace them with more climate-sensitive landscaping.

Source: U.S. Department of Parks and Recreation

Another example of water as a resource outside of the desert climate is the city of Atlanta. Most of Atlanta's water supply comes from Lake Lanier, which also feeds downstream to Alabama and Florida for crop irrigation. The city is in severe drought conditions that they expect to see only every 100 years. Currently, the lake is experiencing record lows and as of October 2007, the city has only a three-month water supply remaining.

In design, you typically only deal with the micro-level need for water at your project or building site. After understanding the impacts of your project water use on a more macro scale (regionally and globally), you can return to the project and look at how best to conserve that resource.

Understanding the Impacts of Climate

Understanding the impacts of climate can drastically affect the use of water in our daily lives. How we regard the use of water in our culture is drastically different than many cultures around the world. However, our use of water also affects the inhabitants of other countries and climates.

Both of the examples in the sidebar "Lake Mead and Georgia" are dramatic, and one could make the argument that if it is a 100-year condition that things will eventually stabilize. However, as we become more and more dependent on the limited resources we have available, we also become less and less able to deal with these types of situations. Also, 100 years ago we didn't have the demand for resources that we have today. If our need depends completely on a regular supply of water, we will severely struggle to recover from drought conditions when they do occur.

Reducing Water Need

Water-use reductions could be one of the most important things that we designers do. Currently, we have not realized the importance of reducing water need, but that is quickly changing. Other things that we can live without, such as oil, are currently getting more attention in the media, but water is a foundation for life and we must treat it as a precious resource. A variety of technologies have been developed, and more are developing to allow us to reduce our water demand but not sacrifice our lifestyles or safety. It is a simple matter of making sure every drop used has a purpose for life. Here are some simple strategies that can help you reduce a building's overall water need:

Elimination of water use The project team should ask itself, "What do we absolutely need water for?" The answer should be reviewed carefully. Of course you will need water for drinking and cleaning, but do you need water to flush urinals or toilets? Do you need water for your landscaping? The team should review the growing number of options for non-water-based systems. After the systems are selected, you can begin to make these systems as efficient as possible.

Selection of efficient equipment In Chapter 4 we covered several options for efficient equipment and systems. There are a number of efficient systems for the variety of water uses on the market. Many times, lower-efficiency units are purchased because they have a lower initial cost to the builder or owner. This cost difference is typically small compared to what you will spend in water bills over the lifetime of the unit. One first cost item that is often overlooked is the savings in initial tap fee.

Rainwater harvesting Rainwater can be reused with little energy and simple filtering systems for irrigation purposes. Going a bit further will allow the facility to reuse it for toilet flushing, of which in an ideal situation you would need little or none.

Graywater reuse If your project still needs water beyond what can be provided by rain, consider the next step: reusing graywater. Graywater is the water from your showers, sinks, drinking fountains, dishwasher, or laundry machines. A graywater system will likely be a bit more costly than a rainwater reuse system.

Treatment of water onsite For those who really want to close the water loop, a project can treat its own wastewater onsite. Several systems are available for this, such as the Eco-Machine from John Todd Ecological Design, Inc. (http://www.toddecological.com/ecomachines.html). Some installations of these systems are in the Omega Institute in Rhinebeck, New York, and the Anita Gorman Conservation Discovery Center in Kansas City, Missouri.

Commission Measure and verify that the systems chosen and installed in a facility are working properly and as efficiently as possible. Not only does this give owners confidence that they got what they paid for, it assures them that the components are running correctly and provides education on how to keep systems that way.

Operation and maintenance It shouldn't have to be said, but equipment must be cared for and maintained. Whether it is the most efficient device or not, you will have to care for it, from cleaning, inspection, and troubleshooting to partial replacement. If equipment isn't given proper maintenance, it will degrade ahead of replacement schedules and lead to additional waste.

Defining a Baseline and Setting Goals

The Energy Policy Act of 1992 sets flow rate standards for some water-based equipment, but baselines for irrigation water needs in most areas can only be set by regional conventional practices. The U.S. Green Building Council (USGBC) Leadership in Energy and Environmental Design (LEED) rating system Water Efficiency Credits 3.1 and 3.2 provide two credits for being 20% and 30%, respectively, more efficient than the EPA 1992 baseline case. LEED Water Efficiency Credits 1.1 and 1.2, provide credits for a 50% reduction in potable water use for irrigation or no potable water used for irrigation.

For many situations, all four of those credits are easily achievable. In December 2003, the Environmental Building News published data on credits achieved by the first 58 LEED-NC 2.0–certified projects; 90% achieved WE 1.1 (Water Efficiency credit), more than 75% WE 1.2, more than 60% WE 3.1, and more than 50% WE 3.2.

It can be valuable to set goals during the predesign or concept design stage of the project. For the Heifer International Center, a high-level project goal was to treat water as a valuable resource and let no water leave the site. This goal was achieved at every scale except for the blackwater. The team used a combination of integrated strategies, including waterless urinals, low-flow toilets, low-flow faucets, rainwater harvesting, graywater reuse, pervious paving, bioswales, and a constructed wetland.

Using BIM for Water Harvesting

Now that you have an idea of what the issues surrounding water conservation mean and we've established some methods to address the problems and set some project goals against an established baseline for water conservation, let's move into modeling a solution.

We have already established the project in the beginning of Chapter 5: an office building on a nonurban site in the Midwest. Before we jump into modeling a solution to analyze sustainable design decisions, let's begin by collecting the facts that we have available. Because water reclamation is not a feature currently available from within a BIM model, we are going to use the following three separate tools to gather and analyze our information:

- The BIM model of our project
- The Internet to look up rainfall data from reliable, documented resources
- A spreadsheet (in our case, Microsoft Excel)

You can perform the calculations by hand if you'd like, but a spreadsheet offers a way to verify the math and is readily accessible and understood by the project team. Google offers some free spreadsheet applications (http://docs.google.com) if you don't have a copy of Excel handy. For our own process, we like to automate things as much as possible to avoid both the time wasted transferring numbers from one application to another and the possibility of human error. For our workflow, we take the schedules created in the BIM model and export them to a TXT (text) file. These TXT files are then automatically imported into Excel using a macro that reanalyzes all of our calculations. Depending on your comfort with programming macros, you can work at a level that is accessible to you.

To calculate our rainfall amount in the BIM model, we need to identify some key project information. This data will help us design the project to best suit the specific region for the project.

Location

We already know the project location has been set in Kansas City, Missouri. By using the Internet, we can look up the annual rainfall for our location. In our case, we have chosen to use the data from the Kansas City International Airport. Our project is located at 39 degrees north by 94 degrees west. This information can be located in the following ways:

Parcel surveys Before any building project commences, a site survey is done that gives the longitude and latitude of the site.

Online As we will discuss in just a moment in the section on rainfall, a number of websites contain this information.

BIM Most BIM applications allow you to site your building, as we discussed in the last chapter. When we sited our building for solar studies, the application provided us our longitude and latitude. Figure 6.1 shows the dialog box where we chose our location.

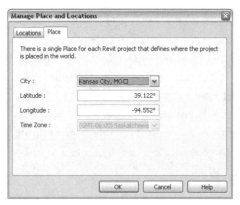

Figure 6.1 Setting location in BIM

Rainfall

Weather data can be found at a number of sites on the Internet, but for our use we have chosen the WorldClimate website at `http://www.worldclimate.com`. Another reliable source is `http://www.weatherbase.com`. This website allows you to do a quick search for your region based on the city name, and it also returns information about temperature, heating degree days, and cooling degree days. Figure 6.2 shows an excerpt from the website that shows our climate data.

Kansas City Intl. AP, Platte County, Missouri, USA

Average Maximum Temperature
24-hr Average Temperature
Average Minimum Temperature
Heating Degree Days
Cooling Degree Days
Average Rainfall
Average Rainfall

Figure 6.2 Climate data

By clicking the link for Average Rainfall, we are shown the information in Figure 6.3, which gives us our monthly and annual rainfall in inches and millimeters.

Average Rainfall

	Jan	Feb	Mar	Apr	May	Jun	Jul	Aug	Sep	Oct	Nov	Dec	Year
mm	29.7	31.6	66.8	87.7	138.3	102.0	114.9	98.5	119.8	82.9	55.5	42.6	971.4
Inches	1.2	1.2	2.6	3.5	5.4	4.0	4.5	3.9	4.7	3.3	2.2	1.7	38.2

Figure 6.3 Average rainfall

Site

By working with our landscape team, we need to understand what the irrigation needs will be for the project. By discussing the vegetation planned for the property, we can ascertain how often we will need to water and how much water will be required. Next, by meeting with our civil engineer, we can find out if there are any opportunities to collect and save water on the site in retention ponds. In this project, we have chosen to incorporate primarily native plantings, rain gardens, bioswales, and wetlands, thereby having minimized (but not negated) our needs for site irrigation.

Our landscape designer has supplied us with predicted water consumption averages for the course of the year (Figure 6.4). As you can see, our needs for water in the winter months are nonexistent while we have some demand for water in the hotter months of the year for the project's climate, namely July and August.

	Jan	Feb	Mar	Apr	May	Jun	Jul	Aug	Sep	Oct	Nov	Dec
Site Water Load (gallons)	0.0	411.0	914.0	1,424.0	2,297.0	2,679.0	3,246.0	2,876.0	1,690.0	741.0	353.0	0.0

Figure 6.4 Landscape water load

Early Collaboration with the Civil Engineer

Outside of the building needs, this is also a good opportunity to connect with the civil engineer on other issues surrounding the project, like the parking lot shown in the site plan below. By using pervious paving in the parking stalls and bioswales between parking rows, we can work to filter the pollutants from the surface water that falls on the site, keeping them from entering the groundwater or nearby surface streams. Bioswales can be a visually appealing and cost-effective way to deal with increased surface water created by the development in an ecological manner.

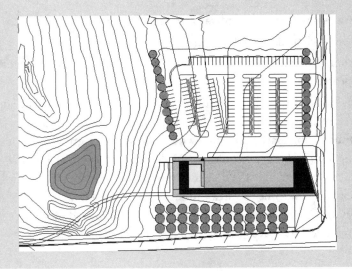

The BIM Model

As the final resource for our data search, we need to poll our BIM model. As we've said before, the data within the model is only as good as the data that we put into it. Make sure your information is accurate before you rely on the results of the analysis.

The information that we have collected so far with the exception of the site design is fairly static. Chances are our building location has been determined which sets most of the data we need to calculate rainfall. Our building design, however, can be flexible and dynamic. After you have been through the process of calculating water needs and conservation measures, it becomes quite easy to use this early on in the design process to help inform different design iterations.

We need to collect information from the BIM model to help us calculate how much rainwater we can capture from the available roof areas and our expected water demand from sinks, toilets, water fountains, and other building fixtures. Let's begin by figuring our roof area and seeing how much rainwater we can collect for reuse.

Roof Areas

Roof areas in a BIM model are fairly basic. What we need to figure out is the plan area of the roof as this will be the area we will have available to collect rain. This is a slightly different area than calculating for photovoltaics as we are not limited to the south-facing or horizontal roof areas. One important aspect is to make sure that we are only getting the area of the roofs from which we plan to collect water. This might eliminate certain roof types, as it might not be cost effective or desirable to collect water from every roof in the project. You will need to consider all of your roof surfaces to see how viable it will be to collect rainwater from them before using that area in your calculations. While all exposed roofs will catch the rain, it might not be easy (or worth it) to collect that rain from those roofs. Some of those types of roof areas could be:

- Entry canopies
- Green roofs (the rainwater will go toward irrigating the plant life)
- Occupied spaces such as terraces and decks
- Other small roofs where collection to a central location in the building might be unsightly or problematic

After we have the areas for rainwater collection established, we can create some boundaries to find the plan area of the roof. Figure 6.5 shows the calculated areas in gray. Properly constrained boundaries will follow the roof edge as it grows or shrinks as the design changes. This is different from simply calculating the plan area of the roof that you would have to do every time the design of the roof changes. Within a BIM model, you have the ability to define the area of the roof once with boundary lines (as they are called in Revit). These lines can by locked to the roof edge and they will dynamically adjust the calculated area with any changes to the roof design.

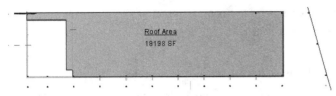

Figure 6.5 Roof plan

In our application, the heavy outline represents a line that is *locked* to the roof outline. In this way, as our building changes size and shape, our roof area will dynamically adjust. From the previous figure, we now know that we have 18,198 sq. ft. of roof area from which we can collect water. To get our rainwater collection potential, we perform the following calculation:

```
Roof Area x Monthly Rainfall x 0.8 = Monthly Rainwater Collection
```

The 0.8 multiplier assumes that we won't be able to collect *all* of the rain that falls onto the roof. We will lose some to evaporation, some will stay on the roof itself, and some will simply get lost in collection. Doing the quick math in a spreadsheet, or by hand, gives you the results in gallons per month, as Figure 6.6 shows.

	Jan	Feb	Mar	Apr	May	Jun	Jul	Aug	Sep	Oct	Nov	Dec
Rainwater Reuse from Roof	35,826.0	26,484.1	33,014.4	30,112.0	32,742.3	49,793.7	54,782.1	65,303.2	46,075.0	28,298.0	21,767.7	25,486.4

Figure 6.6 Rainwater reuse

Now, if we choose not to collect any of the graywater from within the building fixtures, we would have enough information to size our collection cisterns and use the rainwater for irrigation or flushing toilets. Because on this particular project we are going to try to maximize our water savings, the next thing we need to look at is our graywater collection potential.

Graywater

Graywater is defined as the wastewater from sinks, lavatories, laundry facilities, and water fountains. Graywater is different from blackwater, which is wastewater from toilets or sinks used for food preparation or disposal. Blackwater for this project can be handled off site at the municipal water treatment plant. In order to figure out how much graywater we have in the building to reclaim, we first need to look at our current design iteration and get a count on the number of fixtures we have in the building, what their uses are, and how much of the water we can collect from each of them.

We are going to set up our BIM model to do this counting and sorting of fixtures. By creating a simple plumbing schedule within the model (Figure 6.7), we can define the fields that we want to see reported. Again, these fields will be dynamically updated as we add or remove fixtures from the project as the design continues to progress. The fields that we want to collect are:

Fixture description What type of fixture is it?

Fixture count How many of each type do we have in the project?

Flow rate What is the flow rate or gallons per minute or gallons per flush (depending on the type) of each fixture? We can find this information in the specifications of each fixture type, or the specification can be written to only allow low-flow fixtures.

Graywater Is the water from the fixture going to be reclaimed for reuse? Because we are not treating the blackwater in the building, we can disregard any water flow from non-graywater-generating fixtures like toilets, urinals or mop sinks.

Plumbing Schedule			
Fixture Description	Count	Flow Rate	Graywater
Drinking Fountain-2D: Drinking Fountain-2D	6	1.5	☑
Lavatory-Single-2D: 26″ x 22″	5	2.5	☑
Sink Kitchen-Double: 42″ x 21″	1	2.5	☐
Sink Vanity-Round: 19″ x 19″	18	2.5	☑
Sink-Mop-2D: Sink-Mop-2D	3	1	☐
Toliet-Commercial-Wall-3D: 19″ Seat Height	25	1.6	☐
Urinal-Wall-3D: Urinal-Wall	4	1	☐

Figure 6.7 Plumbing schedule

Before we can do the next calculation, we need to get some additional information about the project and specifically about its occupants. The information we need to collect is as follows:

Number of occupants in the building This number is different than the code required maximum occupancy. This should be the owner's idea of how many people will be using the building in a given day.

Number of days of occupancy per month How many days per month is the building occupied?

Number of hours a day the facility is occupied Is it a 24/7 facility, or will it only be occupied during normal business hours?

For our project, let's set the number of occupants at an even 100. There are 60 male and 40 female occupants, and let's assume the building is only occupied during the workweek, so the average number of days the facility will be occupied in a given month is 22. We also need to set a number for how often people will use each of the fixtures:

• For men, we will assume two trips to the urinal and one to the toilet on average.

- For women, simply three uses of the toilet per day.

- It might seem like our data collection is beginning to get rather cumbersome and complex. The rainwater from the roof is beginning to look fairly easy right about now. This is why we recommended the use of a spreadsheet to help organize and collect these variables. After you have a spreadsheet set up to keep these numbers, you will find that few of them change between design iterations or from project to project. The numbers that will be the most dynamic will be the number of occupants and the number and type of fixtures.

Now that we have collected all the information we need about the building, the fixtures, and its future occupants, we can figure our building's overall water load, nonpotable water need, and graywater capture potential. The nonpotable water need will help us understand how much of the rainwater and graywater can be reused for the flushing of toilets, urinals, and site irrigation to help offset the overall building water load.

Overall Building Load

To determine how much water to save and reuse, we need to figure out what our current total demand is for the building. These calculations are fairly easy for us to make. Our spreadsheet applies the calculation shown below (Figure 6.8) to each fixture type in the building. Totaling all these results will give you the Total load for the building. This load should be equal for all the months of the year.

```
Total number of fixtures by type x Fixture Use x Flow Rate or GPM of
Fixture = Total load by fixture type
```

	Jan	Feb	Mar	Apr	May	Jun	Jul	Aug	Sep	Oct	Nov	Dec
Building Water Load (gallons)	28,688.0	28,688.0	28,688.0	28,688.0	28,688.0	28,688.0	28,688.0	28,688.0	28,688.0	28,688.0	28,688.0	28,688.0

Annual:
344,256.0

Figure 6.8 Overall building load

Building Nonpotable Water Need

This calculation is fairly straightforward, and we have all the information we need on hand. Because we already know how much water we need for irrigation, we only have to figure out how much is required for use in the toilets and the urinals:

```
Daily Use per Occupant x Gallons per Flush x
Number of Occupants = Daily Water Use
```

Doing this calculation for both toilets and urinals gives us the water use that Figure 6.9 shows. For our tool it is important to note that the number of males and females established earlier populates the Number of Occupants field. The formula in the spreadsheet accounts for the total of all female users using the toilet three times a day, plus one third of the male users using the toilet once a day as previously discussed. This is why the chart shows 60 occupants in the toilet row. Calculating our daily use for other fixtures is similar.

Flush Fixtures	Daily Use per Occupants	Flow Rate (Gallons per Flush)	No. of Occupants	Water Use
Toilets	3	1.6	60	224
Urinals	2	1.0	60	120

Figure 6.9 Water need

This gives us the daily use of the occupants for wastewater flushing: *344 gallons per day*. Now, we calculate the amount of nonpotable water needed per month:

```
Daily Water Use x Number of Occupied Days per Month = Monthly Graywater Load
```

Our building's nonpotable water load on any given month is *7,568 gallons*. This load, plus the monthly irrigation load, represents the total nonpotable water load for the project. If it is not a project goal to create potable water on site, this would be the load used when sizing your cisterns which we discuss in more detail at the end of this section.

Graywater Capture Potential

When calculating the amount of graywater that we can collect, we need to be cognizant of the source that we are collecting from. Each fixture in the building is going to return slightly different amounts of water based on its use. For instance, you can assume that most of the water in a drinking fountain makes it into the occupant rather than down the drain. Conversely, if you are using a lavatory to wash your hands, it is safe to assume that most of that water will end up down the drain.

Based on the type of fixtures that we have in the plumbing schedule we made in our BIM model, we only want to collect water from two of the sources: lavatories and drinking fountains. For the lavatories, we are going to assume we will get to collect 90% of the water used, and for the drinking fountains, 25%. Our formula for graywater capture potential will look like this formula and our calculated data should look like Figure 6.10:

```
Daily Use per Occupant x Flow Rate (gal/min) x
Duration x Number of Occupants x Percentage Collected =
Daily Graywater Return
```

Flow Fixtures	Daily Use per Occupant	Flow Rate (Gallons per Flush)	No. of Occupants	Water Use	Daily Graywater Return
Drinking Fountain-2D: Drinking Fountain-2D	3	1.5	100	135	34
Lavatory-Single-2D: 26" x 22"	3	2.5	100	375	338

Figure 6.10 Calculating graywater return

Our daily graywater return is *372 gallons*. We can now do a calculation similar to what we put together for nonpotable water need to find out how much graywater we can collect in a given month:

```
Daily Graywater Return x
Number of Occupied Days per Month =
Monthly Graywater Return
```

Our building's graywater return is *8,184 gallons* per month.

Analyzing Water Harvesting

Ideally, as we've been collecting this information, we have been assembling it in a way that can be quickly replicated and where we can easily test new iterations as the building design changes. We are finally at a stage where we can combine all of our information to figure the building's new load on our municipal water supply after we have used the rainwater we harvested and graywater that we collected from the building fixtures. From there, we can figure out how large a cistern we need in the building to properly store all the water that we have collected.

By combining all of the information that we have collected in all the previous calculations, we can figure our water savings on a monthly basis. The chart in Figure 6.11 shows our building load added to our site load (from above) to give us a monthly total of water we need for the project. Based on our loads, we are reclaiming more water than we need. This will allow us to treat some of our captured water for potable uses if desired.

	Jan	Feb	Mar	Apr	May	Jun	Jul	Aug	Sep	Oct	Nov	Dec
Water Load (gallons)	28,688.0	28,688.0	28,688.0	28,688.0	28,688.0	28,688.0	28,688.0	28,688.0	28,688.0	28,688.0	28,688.0	28,688.0
Building Water Load (gallons)	0.0	411.0	914.0	1,424.0	2,297.0	2,679.0	3,246.0	2,876.0	1,690.0	741.0	353.0	0.0
Total Monthly Water Usage (gallons)	26,688.0	29,099.0	29,602.0	30,112.0	30,985.0	31,367.0	31,934.0	31,564.0	30,378.0	29,429.0	29,041.0	28,688.0
Graywater Capture (gallons)	8,184.0	8,184.0	8,184.0	8,184.0	8,184.0	8,184.0	8,184.0	8,184.0	8,184.0	8,184.0	8,184.0	8,184.0
Rainwater Capture from Roof	10,430.4	11,881.5	22,130.5	30,656.2	48,886.7	40,270.3	40,088.9	32,107.4	42,084.3	30,202.7	20,860.7	14,874.6
Total Water Reuse Potential (Rainwater + Graywater) (gallons)	18,614.4	20,065.5	30,314.5	38,840.2	57,070.7	48,454.3	48,272.9	40,291.4	50,268.3	38,386.7	29,044.7	23,058.6
Remaining Water Load after Water Reuse (gallons)	10,073.6	9,033.5	-712.5	-8,728.2	-26,085.7	-17,087.3	-16,338.9	-8,727.4	-19,890.3	-8,957.7	-3.7	5,629.4

Annual:
Building Water Load (gallons)	344,256.0
Site Water Load (gallons)	16,631.0
Total Monthly Water Usage (gallons)	360,887.0
Graywater Capture (gallons)	98,208.0
Rainwater Capture from Roof	344,474.2
Total Water Reuse Potential (Rainwater + Graywater) (gallons)	442,682.2
Remaining Water Load after Water Reuse (gallons)	-81,795.2

Figure 6.11 Final water analysis

Below that line, in the next section we have entered our monthly graywater collection potential, plus what rainwater we can collect from the roof. This is followed by the total monthly water reuse potential in gallons.

The final row shows the total water still needed to purchase from the municipality. The negative numbers shown in this row constitute a water surplus in those months.

To reuse the rainwater and graywater that we collect, we will need a place to store it. The final step in our analysis is to size a cistern to hold the water that we need, returning the surplus to the water aquifer. It might not be desirable to collect *all* of the water on site as that would have negative impacts on those who are downstream of our facility (remembering we are all downstream from someone).

For your projects, once you've figured how much rainwater you collect, you will need a place to store the rainwater for later use. Sizing a cistern's system is a balancing act between the inflow and outflow rates. The size of the system needed to collect and store our graywater and rainwater is dependent on the climatic conditions. As a basic rule, we size the cistern system to meet three months of demand in dry climates and one month in wet climates.

Optimizing Water Harvesting

You might also be asking yourself why so much of this was done using a spreadsheet and not directly within the BIM model. There are two reasons for this.

First, there is currently no BIM application that allows this type of quick analysis, combining both climatic data and building systems.

Second, in the early stages of design, it can be desirable to make a series of quick changes to the building program to test various scenarios. Because this is an office building, how would our water demands be affected by smaller workstations? This would increase our density and thereby increase the number of occupants in the building. What would happen if our building became smaller? Or the amount of roof area we could collect water from? Doing all of this in a simple spreadsheet allows us some fast access to these kinds of questions.

In an ideal design scenario, we began this analysis early on in the design process, working directly with the owner, landscape architect, and civil engineer to best size the systems and cisterns for our water reuse. Now that you know how to calculate water savings, it can become a part of your early design stages in future projects.

Energy Modeling

Understanding a building's energy needs is paramount to helping the project become more sustainable. According to the U.S. Energy Information Administration, buildings in the United States account for 30% of the world's energy and 60% of the world's electricity, making the United States the primary consumer of energy in the world and the built form the largest consumer (Figure 6.12). That gives us a large burden to build responsibly and think about our choices before we implement them.

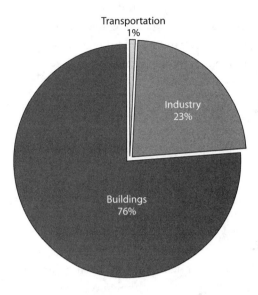

U.S. Electrical Energy Consumption

Source: U.S. Energy Information Administration

Figure 6.12 United States energy use

The energy needs of a building depend on a number of issues that are not simply related to leaving the lights on in a room that you are no longer using or turning down the heat or upping the air-conditioning. Many of the systems within a building revolve around the energy use. For instance, if you increase the windows on the south façade, you allow in more natural light and lower your need for electric illumination. However, without proper sunshading, you are also letting in additional solar heat gain with those larger windows, thus increasing your need for more air-conditioning and potentially negating the energy savings from lighting.

In exploring the use of energy in a building, all energy-related issues must be taken into account, and this is why we use energy simulation. These computer-based models use climatic data coupled with building loads, such as:

- The heating, ventilation, and air-conditioning system (HVAC)
- Solar heat gain
- The number of occupants and their activity levels
- Sunshading devices
- Daylight dimming
- Lighting levels
- And a number of other variables

The energy model combines these factors to predict the building's energy demands to help size the building's HVAC system and parameters of other components properly so we are not using a system larger than what we need and so we can understand the impact of our design on the global environment. By keeping the energy model updated with the current design, we can begin to understand how building massing, building envelope, window locations, building orientation, and other parameters affect energy demands.

We have already begun minimizing our energy use with proper building orientation, using a flexible building massing, and with the use of daylighting. Now, we can focus on the remaining energy needs of the building and work to help reduce those further.

Understanding the Impacts of Climate

Where we live and how we live in that environment impacts our energy needs. If we live in the southern United States, chances are we will need a cooler indoor environment for more of the year than if we lived farther north. Conversely, our winters are longer farther north, necessitating the need for heat and light. Personal preferences also take a toll on our energy demands. Do you leave the lighting or appliances on in a room you are no longer using? Do you keep your house or office warm or cool? There are some simple, passive approaches to energy savings that can easily be incorporated into a building design, such as:

- Using prevailing breezes for natural ventilation
- Protecting windows from sun with shading
- Utilizing daylighting strategies such as proper building orientation and sunshades
- Incorporating clerestories and light monitors instead of skylights
- Providing reasonable set points for temperature and humidity ranges

Reducing Energy Needs

Energy use reductions do not have to come at the cost of human comfort. It is more a matter of reducing the demand and conserving the energy we have instead of using it like an endless resource. Following are some simple strategies that can help to reduce a building's overall energy need:

Design for daylighting. Orienting the building properly, optimizing shading strategies, and using daylight dimming controls to optimize the use of natural light within a space saves on the electrical demands of a building.

Select efficient equipment. A number of efficient systems are available on the market. Select an efficient one and one that is correctly sized and not oversized. Many times, lower-efficiency units are purchased because they have a lower initial cost to the builder or owner. This cost difference is typically very small compared to what you will spend in energy bills over the lifetime of the unit.

Simulate energy performance during design. Creating an energy model helps to predict the demands a building and it systems will have. By setting goals and iterating the design of the project, you can find reductions in the energy loads.

These savings can be found in three primary areas:

- Lighting
- Heat/air-conditioning
- Power

By investigating your use of energy across these three areas, you can find opportunities to lower your demands. Some examples of those opportunities are:

- Better insulation strategies for the building envelope (exterior walls and roofs)
- More efficient heating and air-conditioning equipment
- More efficient light fixtures (T-5 and compact fluorescents)
- Energy-efficient computers, appliances, and equipment (EnergyStar, and so forth)
- Dimming and occupancy controls

Commission the project Measure and verify that the systems chosen and installed in a facility are working properly and as efficiently as possible. Not only does this give owners confidence that they got what they paid for, it assures them that the components are running correctly and educates them on how to keep systems operating that way.

Maintain equipment. It shouldn't have to be said, but equipment must be maintained. Whether or not it is the most efficient equipment, equipment still needs regular care, such as cleaning, inspections, and part replacement, to extend its lifespan. Not taking proper care of equipment can lead to inefficiencies or even larger problems further down the road.

Energy Use Baseline and Setting Project Goals

Baselines for energy use have become more prominent in early design dialogues with clients. The adoption of the LEED rating system, concerns about carbon footprints, and stricter energy codes have all helped to facilitate this new communication and project goals. Currently the two most common energy use baselines are the American Society of Heating, Refrigerating, and Air-Conditioning Engineers 90.1 (ASHRAE 90.1) and the EPA's Target Finder (`http://www.energystar.gov/index.cfm?c=new_bldg_design.new_bldg_design`).

LEED The LEED-NC (LEED-New Construction) rating system uses the ASHRAE 90.1-2004 as the reference standard for baseline energy efficiency. ASHRAE 90.1 provides minimum requirements for energy efficiency of buildings except for low-rise residential buildings. These are the minimum requirements, which are why ASHRAE 90.1 is often adopted as a code, sometimes as a subset of the International Energy Conservation Code (IECC). Your project team should be shooting for better-than-minimum compliance.

A project can earn up to 10 credits toward LEED Certification for providing energy efficiency beyond ASHRAE with Energy and Atmosphere credits EA 1.1-1.10. In June 2007 the USGBC made achieving EA Credits 1.1 and 1.2 for a total of 14% more efficient than ASHRAE 90.1-2004 required. The Energy Policy Act of 2005 also uses this baseline for judging tax credits for those buildings that are 50% better than the ASHRAE baseline.

Target Finder Target Finder baseline data is based on the U.S. Department of Energy (DoE) Energy Information Agency's Commercial Buildings Energy Consumption Survey (CBECS). That data is based on actual operating building data taken from buildings in the survey. The CBECS information only includes energy use data for certain building types. Based on simple inputs about the building and location, Target Finder will report expected energy use intensity expressed in Kilo British Thermal Units (KBTU) per sq. ft. Target Finder is the approved method for setting targets related to the Architecture 2030 program, which has been adopted by the AIA and the United States Conference of Mayors. Figure 6.13 is a sample graph comparing the energy use intensity information from Target Finder for schools in the Kansas City region to schools in the High Performance Building Database (`http://www.eere.energy.gov/buildings/database`) to the Architecture 2030 targets.

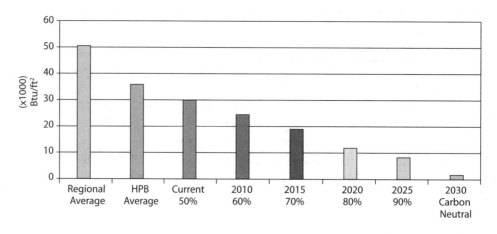

Figure 6.13 Energy use intensity

Energy-Saving Goals in the Lewis and Clark State Office Building

Considering the built environments' impact on greenhouse gas emissions, it is paramount that projects set goals for energy efficiency and conservation. It can be most valuable to set these goals during the predesign or concept design stage of the project. Goals can be tested through simulation during the schematic and design development phases with increasing accuracy, so by the time you are documenting the project for construction, the client will have a good picture for expected energy use.

For the Lewis and Clark State Office Building in Jefferson City, Missouri, an overarching goal was to provide the "greenest" building for the budget. This included a strong goal for the HVAC system to be designed as the most efficient for an office building in Missouri. While there are currently no systems to quantify whether or not the project achieved that goal, it led the team to design using a holistic approach integrating form, systems, and orientation to maximize performance. The building is designed to be 56% more efficient than the ASHRAE 90.1 baseline at the time of design. An outline of the key strategies follows:

- Peak electrical demand is minimized through an efficient, right-sized mechanical system and utilizing daylight as the primary ambient light source during daytime peak use. Occupancy sensors and dimmers limit lighting loads. Operable windows provide natural ventilation during acceptable weather.

- The shape of the building footprint was optimized through iterative energy models to maximize daylighting and natural ventilation.

- Money budgeted for a perimeter reheat system was invested in the building shell, eliminating reheat entirely and reducing gas usage by about 20%.

- The dedicated outside air (OSA) system uses a higher temperature supply air than a standard system, and in combination with the hybrid ventilation air handlers, allows the use of medium temperature chilled water, 55 degrees F rather than 42 degrees F. The higher temperature chilled water is produced more efficiently, either mechanically through a high-efficiency chiller or evaporative using the cooling tower.

- To extend natural free cooling, a chilled water thermal storage tank is charged by the tower during cool night hours to help carry the load during warm days.

- Daylighting controls combined with the thermal storage system significantly reduce peak power use.

- Air handlers are designed for low-face velocity, a 60% reduction in fan power and very quiet operation. Housed and serviced in small closets, they are distributed throughout the building minimizing ducting requirements. Total system pressure drop is one third a typical system.

- Photovoltaics integrated into the standing seam roof provide 2.5% of the building's energy, and a solar hot-water system helps supply domestic hot water.

Using BIM for Energy Analysis

We've established a goal for the energy loads for our project, and we have a preliminary design. Now, we need to test the design so we can begin to inform design changes to the building's features to better optimize our energy use.

It is important to note that energy analysis is a science. Specialists in the field of energy analysis go to years of classes to best understand how different building systems and loads can impact each other and affect the overall building performance. Understanding the information that you are receiving from an energy model is critical to understanding its impact on the building design. Just like the BIM model, *junk in* equals *junk out*, you should never take the simulation results as gospel, but understand why they are giving you those results.

It is also important to understand what to expect in different phases of the building design if you are performing energy analysis. In the earlier stages of design, it becomes more important to use the analysis as a comparative tool rather than trying to measure precise loads. This is because many of the decisions that occur in a building design are still undecided in early stages, and you cannot rely on an exact load count to be consistent throughout later stages of design. However, in the later stages, when the design is more realized, it can become possible to make comparisons in smaller, more precise increments. For example, in a conceptual design process, where you will be studying the effects of larger changes to the building form, the results are more comparative. We might find that a tall, narrow building outperforms a shorter building with a larger footprint with less concern about the actual numbers. However, in the design development or the construction document phases, we might find that increasing the glazing on the west façade changes our load from 55 KBTU/ft/year to 71 KBTU/ft/year, thereby causing an undesired increase in our energy load.

As we have done in other sections, we need to establish our pallet of tools. For energy modeling, we need the following tools:

- The BIM model of our project
- An energy simulation application
- The assistance of a mechanical engineer or energy analyst, if we are unfamiliar with how to perform or interpret the data in the analysis

If you are unfamiliar with the process of energy modeling, remember that to benefit from the use of BIM, you have to take a collaborative approach to the project by using the expertise of consultants.

We will again need to collect some facts from the owner or facilities operator about the building, but those facts will be more specific to our energy modeling application needs, so we will deal with those later.

The BIM Model

For energy modeling to be successful, we first need a solid, well-built model. This does not mean we need all of the materials and details figured out, but we do have to establish some basic conditions. For the sake of our project, we are going to be comparing some design changes to the west façade in the schematic design phase of the project (Figure 6.14).

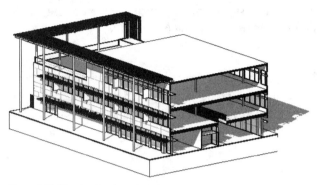

Figure 6.14 West façade schematic design

To ensure our model is correctly constructed to work with an energy modeling application, there are a few things that we need to ensure are within the model to get the proper results. Some of this might sound like common sense, but it is important to ensure that you have the following elements properly modeled or you can have adverse results:

- The model must have roofs and floors.

- Walls need to touch the roofs and floors.

- All areas within the analysis need to be bound by building geometry.

The energy analysis won't be accurate without all of the building elements in place.

We need the ability to transfer the necessary parts of our project from one tool (BIM) to another tool (energy analysis). In some applications, it is currently possible to run a basic analysis out of a BIM model, but depending on your application, this might not be possible. For our project, we are going to use an industry standard transfer methodology: the Green Building XML schema called gbXML. gbXML is a file format that can be read by many energy modeling applications currently available on the market. We will have to define some specific parameters within the BIM model before we can export to this file type.

We need to capture a few key elements from the BIM model and transfer them to the energy analysis application:

- Project location
- Building envelope
- Room volumes
- Any application-specific settings

In the following sections we will discuss why these elements are important to the energy model and how to capture that information in the gbXML file.

Project Location

As we discussed earlier, climate is going to be a large factor in determining the exterior loads on the building. We need to set the location of our project in our BIM application. Our project is located in Kansas City, as Figure 6.15 shows, and is set within our BIM application.

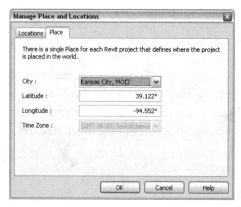

Figure 6.15 Setting location

Building Envelope

Although this might seem obvious in concept, a building without walls cannot have an accurate energy analysis run on it. While the specific wall or roof composition won't be taken into account, each room needs to be bound by a wall, floor, or roof. These elements are critical in creating the gbXML file and defining the spaces or rooms within the building. These spaces can in turn be defined as different activity zones in the energy analysis application.

Room Volumes

Depending on the specific application that you are using, the actual names of these components can change. Autodesk Revit refers to the components as rooms (shown in

Figure 6.16 with Xs in them), but regardless of the term our software uses, we need to establish the volumes within the project. These spaces or rooms must be bound in three dimensions, giving them an area in plan and a height in elevation, and they cannot overlap one another. We will export these spaces to the gbXML file and use them to calculate the energy loads in the project. It is important to be sure that you are creating volumes that fill the occupiable space completely to get an accurate analysis.

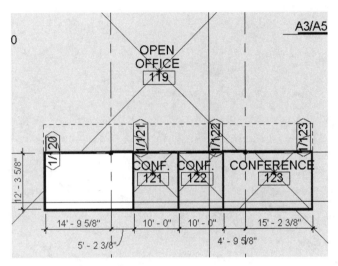

Figure 6.16 Creating room elements

Application-Specific Settings

Every application can have specific settings that will need to be addressed. Although we cannot go into each BIM application's settings, we have shown the ones here specific to the software we utilize. We wanted to show you what needs to be done before you can accomplish an energy analysis.

In Revit, we need to set the location, which we discussed in the previous chapter. We also need to tell the application to calculate the room volumes (Figure 6.17) and the "energy data" (Figure 6.18), as it's called in Revit. This predefines the building type and zip code. The building type we can also set in many energy applications as well as the zip code or building location. However, in Revit the gbXML file will have errors in it if this information is not set first, so we define it here.

After these settings are completed, we are ready to create the gbXML file. This is a simple File > Export routine in most applications.

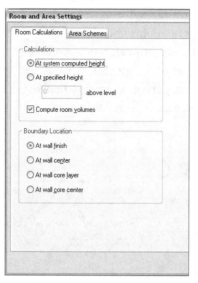

Figure 6.17 Calculating room volumes

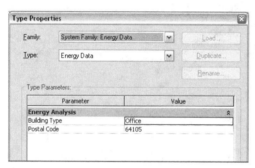

Figure 6.18 Setting location for energy data

Analyzing Energy Use

Now that we have our model geometry and some of the locations and building type settings exported into a gbXML file, we need to import this into an energy modeling application for completing some additional information and the actual analysis results. A number of energy modeling applications are available, and they vary greatly in complexity, interoperability with a BIM model, and their level of detail.

As we've mentioned previously, the right tool for the analysis can vary based on your skill level, ability to digest the results, time available, and the current phase of the project. Following are some of the applications available (Figure 6.19) on the market today along with some pros and cons of each:

IES <VE> IES <VE> (http://www.iesve.com) is a robust energy analysis tool that offers a high degree of accuracy and interoperability with a BIM model. The application can run the whole gamut of building environmental analysis, from energy to daylighting to computational fluid dynamics (CFDs) used to study airflow for mechanical systems. Cons to this application are its current complexity for the user and the relatively expensive cost of the tool suite.

Ecotect This application (`http://www.ecotect.com`) has a great graphical interface and is easy to use and operate. The creators of this application also have a number of other tools (`http://squ1.com`), including a daylighting and weather tool. While easy to use, it can be challenging to import model geometry depending on what application you are using for your BIM model. As an example, Google SketchUp and Nemetschek's Vector-Works can import directly, while applications like Revit can be more of a challenge.

eQUEST The name stands for the Quick Energy Simulation Tool (`http://www.doe2.com/equest`). This application is a free tool created by the Lawrence Berkeley National Laboratory (LBNL). It contains a series of wizards that help you define your energy parameters for a building. It is not currently possible to import any model geometry into eQUEST.

Green Building Studio Green Building Studio (GBS) (`http://www.greenbuildingstudio`
`.com`) is an online service that allows you to upload a gbXML file for a free energy analysis. The service provides quick and graphical feedback of the building's energy performance based on a survey of building use and loads. The survey is not highly detailed, so if the building type or use does not fit into the limited choices available, the results might not be accurate.

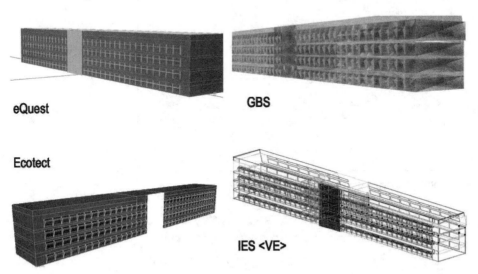

Figure 6.19 Energy analysis applications showing a graphical comparison using the same model

Other energy modeling applications are available on the market. We chose to focus on these four because they tend to be the most popular to the building design community currently. In our own practice, we use a combination of all these tools in design and vary the tool use by the particular phase and desired level of detail in the analysis. We recommend not settling on one, but trying a number of them to see which fits best with your office's needs and workflow.

For our analysis, we are going to use GBS and analyze the project's energy loads. Because we are not in a stage of well-developed design where many of the building systems are highly defined, we are not going to rely on the accuracy of the analysis numbers, but rather on a comparison between one model run and another. As we change the design, was one energy run better than the other? Did our design change improve our energy use?

The final stage in our project before the actual analysis is adding the input parameters for the building construction to the analysis application. Figure 6.20 shows this load data being inputted into an eQUEST wizard.

Figure 6.21 shows this same information being entered into GBS.

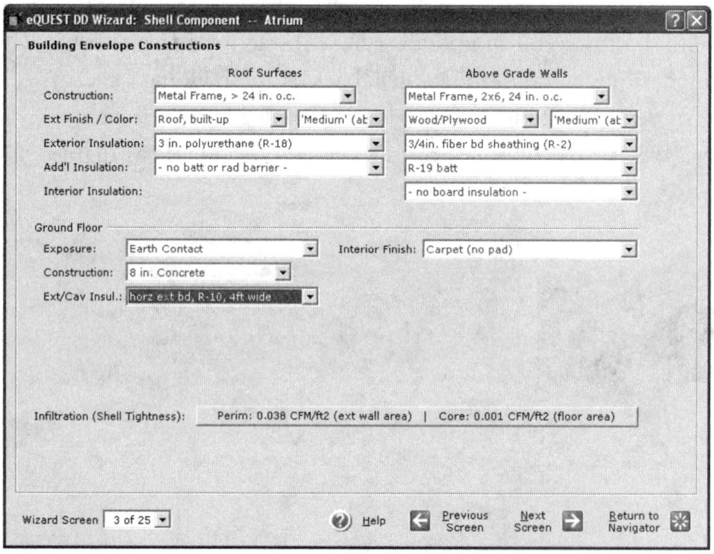

Figure 6.20 Entering building construction assumptions in eQUEST

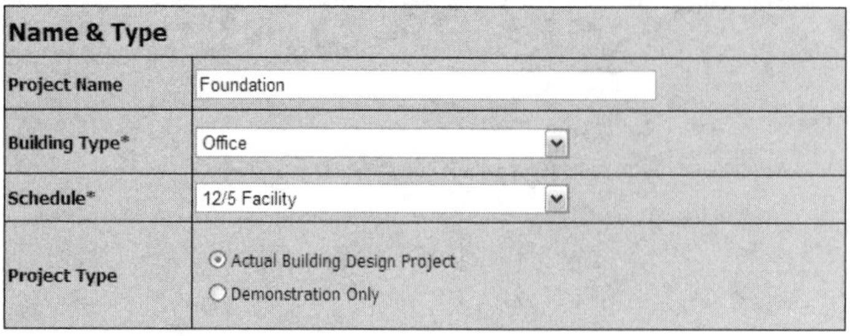

Figure 6.21 Entering load data in GBS

Optimizing the Energy Use

For our analysis, we wanted to compare two design options on the west façade to understand what the relative energy impact would be on the building. Figure 6.22 shows two designs for the build's façade. We've chosen to add a sunshading device to the project, but we want to see what the relative energy impact will be with this design change. Design 1 is without the sunshades, and Design 2 has the sunshades included. We also need a way to prove to the owner that the shades will help supply a cost savings to the overall lifecycle costs of the building. This will help to justify the initial costs of adding the shades to the project.

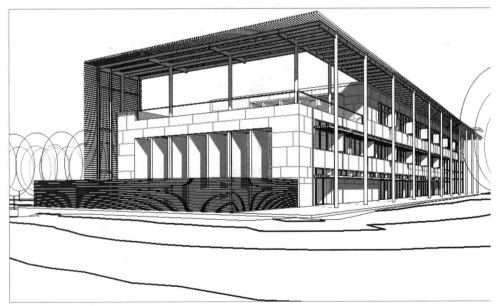

Figure 6.22 Two design alternatives for an energy comparison

With each of these design options, we have exported the BIM model to a gbXML file and uploaded it to GBS's service for energy analysis. The results are shown in Figure 6.23. As you can see, both the building annual energy cost and the lifecycle cost are reduced with the addition of the shading devices. Using this same method, we can continue to make comparative design changes and regularly assess the design changes against our building's energy use.

General Information
Project Title: Foundation
Run Title: Foundation.xml
Building Type: Office
Floor Area: 53,017 ft^2

Estimated Energy & Cost Summary

Annual Energy Cost	$46,929
Lifecycle Cost	$639,168
Annual CO$_2$ Emissions	
Electric	684.0 tons
Onsite Fuel	70.3 tons
H3 Hummer Equivalent	68.6 Hummers
Annual Energy	
Electric	549,811 kWh
Fuel	13.154 Therms
Annual Peak Electric	300.0 kW

Location Information
Building: Kansas City, MO 64108
Electric Cost: $0.057/kWh
Fuel Cost: $1.286/Therm
Weather: Kansas City, MO (TMY2)

Carbon Neutral Potential[1] (CO$_2$ Emissions)

Base Run:	Requires Corporate Acct. & v.3 run.
Onsite Renewable Potential:	N/A
Natural Ventilation Potential:	N/A
Onsite Fuel Offset/Biofuel Use:	N/A

General Information
Project Title: Foundation
Run Title: Foundation.xml
Building Type: Office
Floor Area: 59,967 ft^2

Estimated Energy & Cost Summary

Annual Energy Cost	$31,996
Lifecycle Cost	$435,780
Annual CO$_2$ Emissions	
Electric	329.2 tons
Onsite Fuel	76.3 tons
H3 Hummer Equivalent	36.9 Hummers
Annual Energy	
Electric	264,560 kWh
Fuel	13.154 Therms
Annual Peak Electric	300.0 kW

Location Information
Building: Kansas City, MO 64108
Electric Cost: $0.057/kWh
Fuel Cost: $1.286/Therm
Weather: Kansas City, MO (TMY2)

Carbon Neutral Potential[1] (CO$_2$ Emissions)

Base Run:	Requires Corporate Acct. & v.3 run.
Onsite Renewable Potential:	N/A
Natural Ventilation Potential:	N/A
Onsite Fuel Offset/Biofuel Use:	N/A

Figure 6.23 Analysis results for design options A and B

Using Renewable Energy

As we discussed in Chapter 4, renewable energy is energy from sources that are free and replenishable. According to the Environmental Protection Agency, about 2% of our power currently comes from renewable sources, the largest of these being the burning of biomasses like wood. In earlier chapters we discussed ways to bring down the overall energy demand of a building. Now that we know what our energy demands are, we look at how we can utilize the renewable resources available to meet need.

There are seven recognized renewable energy sources:

- Solar
- Wind
- Biomass
- Hydrogen
- Geothermal
- Ocean
- Hydropower

We can now begin to investigate how to use those seven resources to their fullest potential within our project.

Understanding the Impacts of Climate and Place

The ability to use the most common renewable energy sources, solar and wind, is directly dependent on climate and place. For example, photovoltaic systems and solar hot-water heaters require access to sunlight. Some areas might not have enough sun exposure to rely on either of these systems as the primary power supply. For example, Albuquerque, New Mexico, receives 6.77 kWh/m²/day of solar radiation on average, which is a great supply. Chicago, on the other hand, receives only 3.14 kWh/m2/day, less than half of Albuquerque. In either case, the placement of solar energy capturing systems needs to have access to the sun. At the micro-site scale, existing vegetation or taller neighboring buildings might block solar access.

Wind power is classified by measuring available wind speeds at 50 meters above the ground. The speeds are divided into seven classes, with class 3 or higher considered as having potential for today's wind turbine technology. According to state-level wind resource maps found at the DoE's website, Wind Powering America (http://www.eere.energy.gov), all but the most eastern part of Kansas is in a class 3 or higher wind area, compared to greater than 90% of Missouri that is in class 1. That being said, it is a best practice to measure wind speeds at the micro level because it can be influenced greatly by specific location. For example, if your site is on top of a hill or out in the middle of a prairie, your ability to capture wind is quite high. If you are on the leeward side of a hill, in a valley, or next to a heavily treed area, that potential won't be as good.

There are three other leading renewable energy technologies at the moment that rely on place more than climate: hydro, geothermal, and biomass. Only geothermal is commonly used at the individual project scale. All three, however, can be used for larger scales such as on a campus, development, or the scale of a utility company.

At the utility scale, geothermal consists of taking steam or hot water from more than a mile deep in the earth and using them to generate electricity from turbines. Either could be used directly for heating systems. According to the DoE, most of our ability to use geothermal systems at this scale is in the western States, Hawaii, and Alaska. At the building scale, we can use geothermal energy together with heat pumps and simple heat exchangers for heating and cooling by tapping into the nearly static temperature of the ground just below the surface (~55 degrees F). If you are near an aquifer or surface body of water, you can use the heat pumps or heat exchangers in the same manner, just via water contact in lieu of earth contact.

The ability to use hydropower is directly related to place because it requires a moving body of water. Therefore, the project site must be near a river, ocean, or sea. Although biomass raw materials are easily transported, it is certainly more effective if the project using biomass for a fuel to generate energy is nearby the fuel source, making use of biomass dependent on place. According to the DoE, biomass "is any organic material made from plants or animals. Domestic biomass resources include agricultural and forestry residues, municipal solid wastes, industrial wastes, and terrestrial and aquatic crops grown solely for energy purposes."

Building types have drastically different needs, and those needs change based on building type and climate. In regard to using solar energy, a building with a small physical footprint or one that requires large amounts of energy like a lab building may not have enough roof area to accommodate the solar panels required. So a site-based array might be required to harness enough available sunlight. A site-based array is shown in Figure 6.24. In some hot climate zones where certain building types spend most of their time in a cooling mode throughout the year, a project might not be able to use a geothermal system. This is because the project will constantly be rejecting heat, elevating the surrounding ground temperatures, thereby saturating the geothermal exchange field.

Each of the renewable systems we've discussed capture free resources, but the systems built to capture the energy from the earth, wind, sun, and water can be resource intensive. Over their lifetime, these systems' resource consumption for manufacture will balance out against the resources it took to create, install, and maintain them—especially since there is no greenhouse gas emissions associated with the operation of these renewable energy systems.

Image Courtesy of Brad Nies

Figure 6.24 Parking space shade structure made of photovoltaic panels

Reducing Energy Needs

To get the most out of renewable energy systems, we must use the proper system based on climate and place. There are also a variety of other factors to consider. Efficiency, the amount of space the system needs, maintenance, and so forth are all factors to consider when choosing a renewable energy system.

For example, market available photovoltaic panels range from 8% to 20% efficient, while they generally come in the same size. Using the most efficient version would save materials and time. Wind turbines come with different cut-in speeds. These should be matched appropriately to the wind class that you are working in. Biomass sources should be turned into energy as close to their source as possible. In some cases, moving the biomass to the generation facility can create more carbon and take more energy than it creates. Drilling in certain areas is intensive, and you should weigh its embodied energy against the potential resource gained.

Negative impacts from renewable energy sources are still under great debate. Most of the negative impacts are related to potential habitat disruption. This applies to wind turbines, hydro dams, wave-generation technology, and both scales and types of geothermal systems.

In the case of hydro dams and wind turbines, some people don't care for their look, aesthetics, or noise production. Some claim that the energy to get certain biomass or make photovoltaic panels is greater than the energy potential it creates. None of these claims has been proven unequivocally, and results will vary based on location, efficiency, and other factors we've discussed. Like all choices, there are always going to be trade-offs, but considering the great consensus around our greenhouse gas problem we are currently facing and its impact on climate change, the elimination of greenhouse gas emissions by using these renewable sources for energy generation likely outweighs most of the potential negative impacts. At some point, the energy used to manufacture the renewable systems will be renewable systems, significantly reducing the current embodied energy.

One consistent reason to keep your energy load low is the high cost of renewable energy systems. Paybacks vary from state to state due to the cost of energy from the grid, availability state and federal rebates, and net-metering laws. In California, a residential PV system might take 15 years to pay back, whereas the same system in Kansas City might take 40 years.

Using BIM for Renewable Energy

Choosing the right renewable resource(s) to use in our project is going to be mainly dependent on location and the availability of those resources for our use. After we have investigated potential systems through location, we can use the BIM model to help us properly configure the building orientation, calculate our potential return in energy, and calculate the feasibility of each system. After we have the systems established, we can then tweak the design within the model to optimize the performance of each system.

Take the example of a geothermal system. If we have a few sample wells dug at our building site, we can model the various substrates shown in the sample borings. With this information, we can adjust the location of the geothermal well field to miss potentially difficult soil types or aim for soil types or water sources that allow more heat exchange than others. In each of the stages of design, there are a number of different potential ways to capture renewable energy:

Predesign At the predesign stage, we should know the speed, direction, and frequency of wind on the site; the amount of solar radiation available; and the geothermal potential of our project sites.

We should know the angle to set our PV panels for the best annual average capture of solar radiation, which is normally equal to the latitude of the project. We should also know which direction is solar south so we can orient the building for the best capture of solar radiation and what the surrounding site contains that might cast an early shadow on the building.

We should know the distance to water if looking at a water-based geothermal system, or the geotechnical characteristics and location of rock formation if looking at drilling wells for a local geothermal system.

In all cases, we should be aware of any micro-site conditions related to our project's ability to capture these resources, such as an adjacent building blocking the project from wind.

Schematic design At the schematic stage, we should understand the roof areas, roof orientation, and roof slope we have that can be used for photovoltaic panels or rainwater capture. At this time, we can begin tracking this information relative to the predicted annual energy use of the project.

Design development In design development, we should know the predicted annual energy use of the project and what surfaces will handle PV. This will allow us to assign areas for this integrated system. If we are going to use a wind turbine, we will need to know the building location in relation to the turbine placement so if the turbine is mounted on the building, we can figure height, wind direction, and wind speed.

Because it is probably not realistic to have a site that would use every available source of renewable energy, for our example we are going to focus on the use of photovoltaics to supply a portion of the electrical demands for the project.

As we have begun all of the BIM model analysis, let's start by collecting some simple facts. We already know our location from Figure 6.25, which gives us the longitude and latitude of the building. For solar panels, the optimum year-round panel tilt is equal to the latitude of the building. For our building, the panel tilt would be 39 degrees.

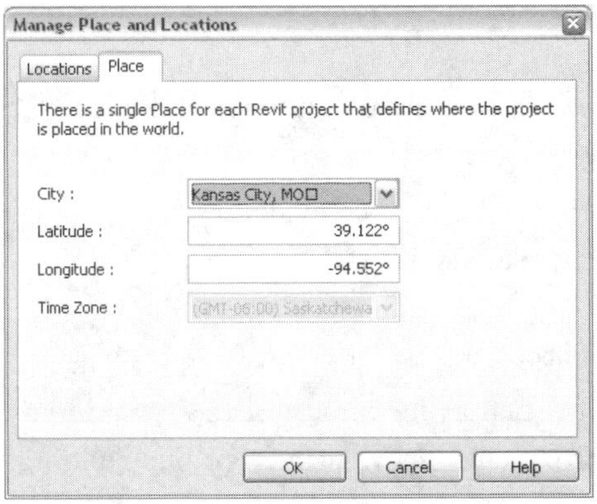

Figure 6.25 Setting location in BIM

Next, we have to define the area we have available for the panel array. In our project, we are going to place the array on the roof. We already calculated the roof area for water, but the roof area for PV is slightly different. In our water calculation, we took the plan area (the area of the roof looking straight down) for our water. For PV, we need to take the *actual* area of the roof. This means that for a 10′ × 10′ roof, if the roof is flat, it is 100 sq. ft. If the roof is on a 45-degree angle, we still have 100 sq. ft. of area available. As for water, we won't be able to utilize all of the roof area for PV panels. Here are some basic guidelines for calculating the area available for PV panels. Remember, these are only guidelines. A PV array should ideally integrate seamlessly into your project design.

- Do not include occupied spaces such as roof decks.
- Use roofs facing solar south with direct access to sunlight. Roofs facing north (in the northern hemisphere) have little or no ability to collect solar energy efficiently.

Because our project roof is flat, we can simply take the area of the roof following these guidelines. Figure 6.26 shows that we have a roof area of approximately 16,200 sq. ft., or 1505 sq. meters. As with our other areas and tables, this can be set up to dynamically change as we adjust the building and roof shapes during design.

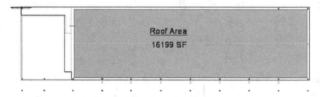

Figure 6.26 Calculating roof area for PV

Analyzing Renewable Energy

Now that we've calculated the basic information about location and availability of energy, we can begin to figure how much energy we can harvest from our solar array:

Find the available sunlight. First, we must determine how much available sunlight we have. To do this, we can look up the total average daily solar radiation given at the U.S. Solar Radiation Resource Map website at
`http://rredc.nrel.gov/solar/old_data/nsrdb/redbook/atlas/Table.html`.

This site prompts you to answer a few questions, such as the month of year you'd like to take the average from and what type of solar panels you are using. For our building, we are looking at a June average with a fixed-tilt panel set to the longitude of the building location. The site results are graphical for the entire United States, as Figure 6.27 shows. From the chart, it looks like our average kWH/m²/day is 4 to 5.

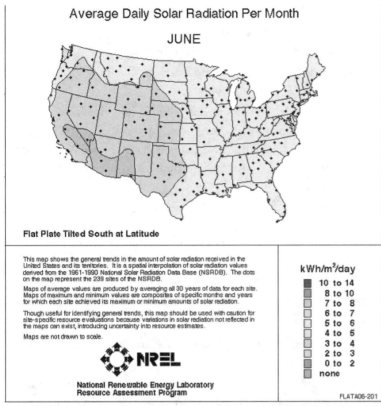

Average Daily Solar Radiation Per Month

JUNE

Flat Plate Tilted South at Latitude

This map shows the general trends in the amount of solar radiation received in the United States and its territories. It is a spatial interpolation of solar radiation values derived from the 1961-1990 National Solar Radiation Data Base (NSRDB). The dots on the map represent the 239 sites of the NSRDB.

Maps of average values are produced by averaging all 30 years of data for each site. Maps of maximum and minimum values are composites of specific months and years for which each site achieved its maximum or minimum amounts of solar radiation.

Though useful for identifying general trends, this map should be used with caution for site-specific resource evaluations because variations in solar radiation not reflected in the maps can exist, introducing uncertainty into resource estimates.

Maps are not drawn to scale.

◯ NREL

National Renewable Energy Laboratory Resource Assessment Program

kWh/m²/day

- 10 to 14
- 8 to 10
- 7 to 8
- 6 to 7
- 5 to 6
- 4 to 5
- 3 to 4
- 2 to 3
- 0 to 2
- none

FLATA06-201

Source: Inputs from the United States Solar Radiation Resource Map website

Figure 6.27 Average solar daily radiation for the month of June across the United States

Determine the total average daily output for the array. Now that we know how much sunlight we have, we need to figure out our daily energy output for our PV panels. We can assume a basic efficiency for a flat film collector of 5%, so our energy collection will fall into the following formula:

```
Total Energy Collected = 4.5 kWh/m²/day x 0.05 x Roof Area in meters
```

For our project, that equals 338.6 kWh/day.

Account for some energy loss in the system. Some energy loss would be typical for any electrical system as current is lost over the loss of the lines, through connections, inverters, and so forth. We should figure on a 65% net gain of power, putting our collected power to 220 kWH/m²/day.

The team can then review this number compared to the energy demand simulated from the energy model. To figure the percentage of power being provided by the array, divide the total average annual demand load by the total average annual capture number. Say, for example, this all-electric building required 70 KBTU/sq. ft. on an annual basis. We know the building is 45,000 sq. ft., so:

```
70 KBTU/ftx 45,000 sf = 3,150,000 KBTU/yr
```

Next convert your KWH to KBTU: 1 KW (electricity) = 3.412 KBTU, so:

```
220 KWH/day x 3.412 = 750.64 KBTU/day
750.64 KBTU/day x 365 days = 273,983.6 KBTU/yr
```

Next figure the percentage of energy provided by the array on an annual basis:

```
273,983.6 KBTU/yr ⁄ 3,150,000 KBTU/yr = 8.6%
```

Based on the quick exercise, design team members know how much renewable energy they can generate with this scheme and how that compares to the overall potential energy load of the building. They can also provide the owner with a cost estimate for the PV installation, the operational cost savings over time, and the carbon offset by going with the renewable source.

Optimizing a Solar Array

Now that the array is established and we have a basic understanding of our power needs, we can begin to manipulate the design to better understand how to optimize the renewable energy potential. For instance, we might decide to:

- Optimize the roof area or slope for greater electrical generation capacity.

- Move from a roof to the site for our panel array.

- We might decide to add more PV in smaller areas like integrated external shading to maximize every available sun exposed area.

- For taller buildings, we could use the southern façade in favorable generation areas, or if the electricity need is much larger than the building physical footprint and we've used available site area.

Regardless of our iterations, it's important to explore the alternative energy available on a project-by-project basis.

Using Sustainable Materials

The use of materials is a constant in the AEC industry. Even if you designed a project that used no energy and consumed no water, you are still using materials. By the way, it took energy and water to make these materials. Our industry is only starting to embrace an understanding of what it takes to get materials and the limitations of the raw resources available for those materials. That embodied energy, though, is only part of the material lifecycle—what happens to the material or product when that end user is finished with it? Can it be reused, salvaged, or completely recycled? Did we need that material to begin with?

When you've decided you need a material or product for a building assembly, what do you know about it? How do you prioritize or justify its use over another material or product for the same situation? Questions are arising about the many diverse impacts of materials. Can you answer them across the lifecycle in regard to the manufacture, installation, use, and end life of your material selections? The following list shows some things to consider during your selection process:

- Does the product or assembly reduce the energy and water consumption of the building over its lifetime?

- Does the product or assembly throughout its lifecycle include any substances or processes that have the potential to adversely affect human health or the environment? Consider the impact on air, atmosphere, water, ecosystem, habitat, and climate. Consider the generation of hazardous by-products and pollution. Take into account the effects of raw material extraction on ecosystems. Factor in the impacts of transportation.

- Does the product or assembly eliminate hazards to indoor air quality, while improving indoor environmental quality and occupant well-being?

- Does the product or assembly perform its intended function elegantly for at least 100 years?

- Is the product or assembly produced with recycled material stock, reducing the demand for virgin raw materials?

- Is the product or assembly made from materials that are rapidly renewable, or are they rare and endangered?

- Is the product or assembly produced in a way that limits the generation of solid waste, and are the materials themselves reusable or recyclable at the end of their useful life in the building? Do the materials disassemble and separate into recyclable or reusable components?

Because decision-making time is always a premium, you cannot always perform a true lifecycle analysis. Numerous material guides, certification systems, and selection methodologies are available to help building professionals collect information and make educated decisions. However, based on our experience they differ in their methodologies and therefore do not provide consistent answers across the evaluation industry. So while they are not perfect, they are continually providing more information on which to base decisions.

At some point in the near future, we hope that these evaluation tools or information databases are directly linked to or integrated within BIM. Next, we continue our look at how BIM helps with sustainable material decisions by illustrating the power of having that information to base decisions on and how BIM can help reduce the quantity of materials. We'll also show you how to quantify some of the metrics needed to achieve credits in the green building rating systems.

Understanding the Impacts of Climate, Culture, and Place

Materials are heavily related to place: the places where raw material are extracted, where they are assembled into products, where they are put together to make a building, and where they go when they are done being used for that building. In between each of those places, the materials are transported—sometimes more than we intended or need them to be. Short of using your dirt from the site to make bricks or harvesting the existing trees on site for wood, even the most benign material in all other concerns about materials has a carbon-based transportation footprint.

In some manner, our ability to transport materials anywhere at almost any time has changed our sense of place too. We can use materials to re-create the style of a faraway place in a feeble partial attempt to bring that culture to a new place. Consider perhaps a Spanish-themed shopping district, or a corporate lobby filled with Italian marble. At the other spectrum, we have thousands of chain restaurants, entertainment districts, and strip malls that look the same here as they do there with no regard to regional specifics.

We believe strongly in selecting as many materials from within the region as possible. Benefits include a better connection to the place, better economics for the local surrounding community, and in most cases, a smaller environmental footprint. Of course, some materials or finished products must come from faraway locations. Some things like carpet might not be available regionally. As long as we remain on a fossil fuel–based electrical grid, other products that increase the energy efficiency of a project can prove to be worth the transportation footprint during the life of the building.

For the University of Texas Health Science Center at Houston School of Nursing project, the BNIM-led project team used a tool called BaseLineGreen™ to evaluate the economic and environmental impact of regional material selection for the project. Base-LineGreen was developed with Pliny Fisk and Rich MacMath from the Center for Maximum Potential Building Systems (CMPBS), and Dr. Greg Norris from Sylvatica. The analysis tool focuses on the measurement of upstream impacts for materials. Upstream impacts within BaseLineGreen take account for toxic releases, criteria air pollutants, and greenhouse gases, within an input/output economic model. BaseLine-Green analysis delivers two types of outputs: upstream external environmental costs and upstream employment impacts.

The upstream external environmental costs are expressed as an "external environmental cost ratio," (EECR). This is a ratio of the external cost of upstream environmental burden in dollars per dollar to market cost of the input to construction. The EECR focuses on three environmental burden indicators: total air pollution, global warming (greenhouse gases), and toxic releases.

The upstream employment impacts are summarized in an *employment impact ratio* (EIR). The EIR is the ratio between the numbers of jobs associated with the input to the market cost of that input to construction. EIR focuses on an economic input/output model of the entire construction sector of the United States economy. This model includes inputs of raw materials, energy, equipment, fabricated products, intermediate products, and services that can be correlated to various geographic locations and scales.

The analysis is done by linking databases from the U.S. EPA and the U.S. Bureau of Economic Analysis with the project specifications. The project team evaluated the material selections during the design phase and made refinements based on the outcome of the initial evaluation. Based on linking those data sets, the project team could see how their material selection impacted the economy at three levels: county, state, and federal. With the feedback from BaseLineGreen, the team revised their selections to enhance regional economic benefit while also decreasing the project's embodied energy carbon footprint. Figure 6.28 shows the results of the two analyses. Note that the team's regional focus also proved to be a big move socially, as statistically it has been shown that having a higher household income provides better human health and longer life expectancy—primarily because it affords an ability to have healthcare. Regional material selection for the project was effectively providing a greater good for the community.

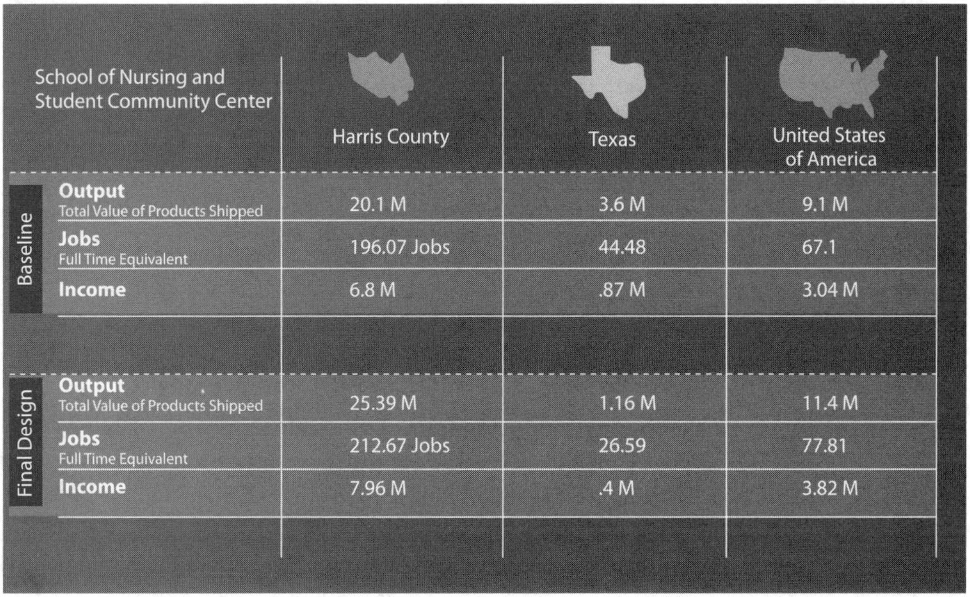

School of Nursing and Student Community Center	Harris County	Texas	United States of America
Baseline			
Output Total Value of Products Shipped	20.1 M	3.6 M	9.1 M
Jobs Full Time Equivalent	196.07 Jobs	44.48	67.1
Income	6.8 M	.87 M	3.04 M
Final Design			
Output Total Value of Products Shipped	25.39 M	1.16 M	11.4 M
Jobs Full Time Equivalent	212.67 Jobs	26.59	77.81
Income	7.96 M	.4 M	3.82 M

Image Courtesy of BNIM Architects

Figure 6.28 Example of the impact from using BaseLineGreen on the UTHSCH School of Nursing for optimizing selection of regional materials and products

Reducing Material Needs

One of the most basic ways a project team can make both the negative environmental impact and the first cost of a project low is to scrutinize and understand the use of materials to a point they can justify the need for each cubic yard or square foot. As explained in Chapter 4, it really starts in the programming phase: does the client need that much space, for the building and for each room?

The project team should continue that line of thinking with each decision about materiality. What will that material or product do for the project and its end users? Will it give them a benefit? Can it provide them with multiple benefits, such as having an exposed structure painted white, which eliminates a finish ceiling and still provides a great daylight-reflecting surface? Perhaps the external sunshades are structural members. There are lots of areas where the team can be creative.

Setting a Baseline

In our project, we have established a goal to use predominately three kinds of materials in the project:

- Reclaimed or salvaged materials

- Recycled materials or materials with a recycled content

- Locally produced materials

While it won't be possible to use only those options in our building design, our goal is to give these preferences. As an example, we are going to focus on our need for concrete in this project. Concrete is one of the materials with the highest embodied energy but currently the most widely used building product available. Embodied energy follows the lifecycle of concrete, from mining and refinement to getting it to the building site and pouring concrete or setting precast panels in place. Portland cement, one of the primary ingredients in concrete, takes a large amount of resources to mine and refine. Portland cement is also the material in the concrete mix that contributes the most to the sum of embodied energy.

A way to lower the embodied energy of concrete is to substitute a portion of the Portland cement with fly ash. Fly ash is a by-product of coal-burning power plants and is an inorganic, incombustible material. Due to the number of coal plants around the country, it can also be a locally produced material additive to the concrete mix.

For our example project, we have chosen a number of locally produced or recycled materials. However, we are going to specifically investigate our use of concrete and use a 45% fly ash in our concrete mix.

Using BIM for Sustainable Materials

Now that we have established our goals, what we can track in our BIM model to help us achieve our desired concrete mix? By getting all of the project stakeholders around the table early in the process, we have established with the contractor and concrete supplier a 45% mix ratio for our concrete mix. For purposes of estimating the overall building cost and the quantity of fly ash in the building, we must calculate the volume of both materials.

As we stated earlier, computers are great at counting. Since we have identified concrete as a material in our BIM model as we were making the floors, walls, foundations, and so forth, we can easily query our model for those elements and derive the volume of each. We can then work with our concrete supplier or contractor to establish how much additional mix will be needed to compensate for any loss in shipment or during the pouring.

Many BIM applications have the ability to create dynamic schedules. These schedules can be created once in the course of the project and will continually maintain up-to-date information in them. In the case of our example, after we create the schedule within the BIM model, we can add concrete elements (walls, columns, floors, and so forth), and the sum of concrete and fly ash in the schedule will dynamically update.

How you create these schedules varies from application to application. In our workflow, we have previously established that we use Autodesk's product, Revit Architecture, so the workflow we will establish will be based on this application.

First, we need to create a schedule and define our parameters. There is no schedule that specifically calculates the properties of concrete, so we will have to make one based on our parameters. To begin, we have chosen a schedule that creates a material takeoff of all the materials currently within the model. This would give us a list of everything we had in the model, such as doors, walls, casework, windows, and so forth. Obviously, this is more than we needed, so we will need to filter out the unwanted materials while adding a table to calculate the volume of fly ash in the concrete.

Our basic table allows us to choose some fields, and we have chosen Material: Name and Material: Volume (Figure 6.29).

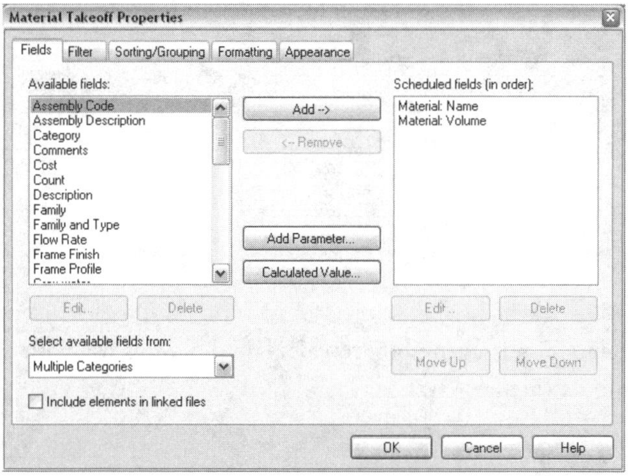

Figure 6.29 Scheduling materials

Now, because we don't have the ability to add fly ash directly into our concrete material, we can choose to create a custom field to do this for us. This is similar to what we might do in Excel or another spreadsheet application. Our formula for calculating the volume of fly ash as a percentage of the concrete is as follows:

```
Volume (of concrete) x 0.12 (amount of Portland cement in concrete) x
45% (the amount of fly ash we are substituting)
```

Figure 6.30 shows how this is manifested in our model.

As we stated earlier, we have to filter out all of the contents of this table except for concrete; otherwise it will appear that we are adding fly ash to everything in our model. By choosing to filter for *only* materials that have concrete in them, we can create a schedule limited to that material (Figure 6.31).

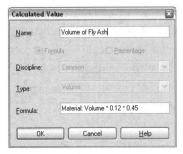

Figure 6.30 Calculating fly ash

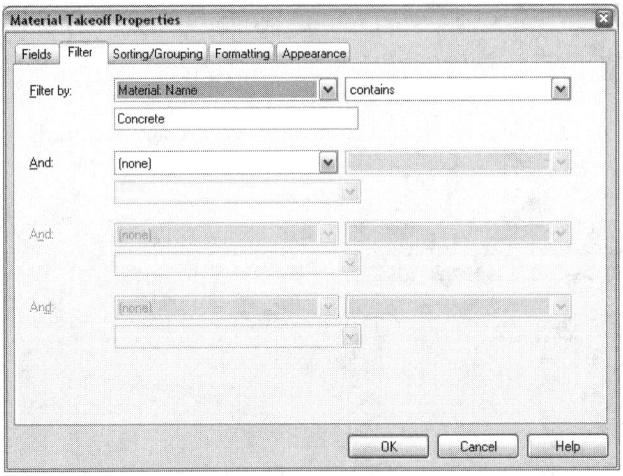

Figure 6.31 Filtering unwanted data

Finally, we select the Calculate Totals check box to calculate the totals for both concrete and fly ash within the model (Figure 6.32).

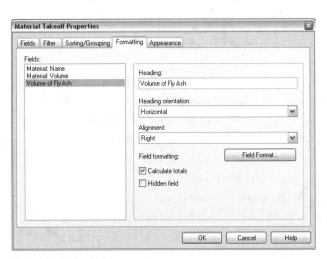

Figure 6.32 Setting final parameters

Now, clicking OK gives us the table that Figure 6.33 shows. This shows the overall volume of concrete in the project and the volume of fly ash. As the building model changes throughout the design process, so will these final numbers, thus allowing the designer to keep the contractor and concrete supplier easily informed about changes.

Concrete		
Material: Name	Material: Volume	Volume of Fly Ash
Concrete — Cast-in-Place Concrete	258.04 CF	13.93 CF
Concrete — Cast-in-Place Concrete	210.28 CF	11.35 CF
Concrete — Cast-in-Place Concrete	239.44 CF	12.93 CF
Concrete — Cast-in-Place Concrete	66.89 CF	3.61 CF
Concrete — Cast-in-Place Concrete	805.50 CF	43.50 CF
Concrete — Cast-in-Place Concrete	230.04 CF	12.42 CF
Concrete — Cast-in-Place Concrete	700.39 CF	37.82 CF
Concrete — Cast-in-Place Concrete	86.00 CF	4.64 CF
Concrete — Cast-in-Place Concrete	272.33 CF	14.71 CF
Concrete — Cast-in-Place Concrete	4286.46 CF	231.47 CF
Concrete — Cast-in-Place Concrete	477.20 CF	25.77 CF
Concrete — Cast-in-Place Concrete	230.29 CF	12.44 CF
Concrete — Cast-in-Place Concrete	191.17 CF	10.32 CF
Concrete — Cast-in-Place Concrete	258.04 CF	13.93 CF
Concrete — Cast-in-Place Concrete	5102.40 CF	275.53 CF
Concrete — Cast-in-Place Concrete	0.00 CF	0.00 CF
Concrete — Cast-in-Place Concrete	537.95 CF	29.05 CF
Concrete — Cast-in-Place Concrete	13.70 CF	0.74 CF
Concrete — Cast-in-Place Concrete	13.88 CF	0.75 CF
Concrete — Cast-in-Place Concrete	13.88 CF	0.75 CF
Concrete — Cast-in-Place Concrete	12.33 CF	0.67 CF
Concrete — Cast-in-Place Concrete	211.37 CF	11.41 CF
Concrete — Cast-in-Place Concrete	19.87 CF	1.07 CF
Concrete — Cast-in-Place Concrete	12.89 CF	0.70 CF
Concrete — Cast-in-Place Concrete	10.96 CF	0.59 CF
Concrete — Cast-in-Place Concrete	10.96 CF	0.59 CF
Concrete — Cast-in-Place Concrete	10.96 CF	0.59 CF
Concrete — Cast-in-Place Concrete	10.96 CF	0.59 CF
Concrete — Cast-in-Place Concrete	10.96 CF	0.59 CF
Concrete — Cast-in-Place Concrete	10.96 CF	0.59 CF
Concrete — Cast-in-Place Concrete	18527.22 CF	1000.47 CF
Grand Total: 31	32843.34 CF	1773.54 CF

Figure 6.33 Final analysis of fly ash

Another Way to Optimize Material Use with BIM

Now that we have established how to track this type of data in a BIM model, what are some other ways we can use this to design more sustainably? Sustainable design is not a prescriptive process. What you design for one project might not be applicable to others. Each design requires a level of thought and creativity to realize all of the potentials.

In a different example, we recently worked on a large office building in the Midwest. The building was not built on an urban site but instead on virgin farmland with a large footprint. Through work with the contractor and survey team, we realized the site had a rock shelf underneath the soil level at varying heights. Using BIM, we modeled the rock shelf and created a relationship between the structural building piers and the shelf. This parametric relationship would make the piers dynamically lengthen or shorten to touch the top of the rock shelf. By scooting the building around by 10′ or 15′ in one direction or another, we were able to optimize the location and length of the piers. A schedule similar to this was used to track the amount of concrete and the volume of the piers during the location studies. By optimizing our piering, we were able to save both money and resources.

The Future of BIM and Sustainable Design

7

"Until recently BIM implementations mainly focused on using 3D models to improve drawing production, but the real promise of BIM lies in its application across the entire project team, especially in the area of improved building performance.

—Technology industry analyst Jerry Laiserin

BIM and sustainable design do not yet have the perfect marriage of integrated parts to make the solutions obvious and accessible. Yet we recognize the need within the design community to inspire better design through communication and knowledge management. This will greatly assist us in trying to get our carbon footprint to zero so that we can create a healthier planet. In this chapter, we discuss what still needs to be done to help better achieve these goals.*

Moving Forward with BIM

BIM is in its infancy. The future of BIM and our willingness to learn from nature can help us move more quickly to a sustainable future: a restored world and a healthy planet.

There is no future, no *next*, if we do not change the ways in which we work, live, and play. If we are open to change, then a few things are inevitable.

Parametric modeling will go well beyond mapping relationships between objects and assemblies (Figure 7.1). Both model and designer will have knowledge of climate and region. The model will know its building type, insulation values, solar heat gain coefficients, and structural components. It will inform the design team with regard to upstream impacts and downstream consequences of their choices. As the building is modeled, the designer will instantly see the impact of the building orientation and envelope choices on the sizing of the mechanical system. It will analyze the design for Americans with Disabilities Act (ADA) compliance and code-related issues. Projected rainfall calculations will be readily available to size cisterns for rainwater use in the building and landscape. It will be a system completely interactive with key building information, so that design integration and data return among all systems is immediate. And after the building is occupied, it will create an opportunity for a postoccupancy and building lifecycle feedback loop.

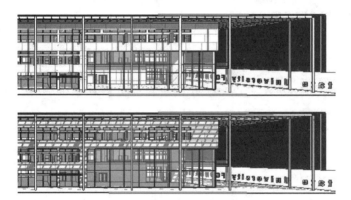

Figure 7.1 A BIM model

However, BIM will not be the solution unto itself. The solution will continue to rely on our abilities to use the tool to its highest advantage. Through the use of BIM, we are able to move from a documentation system that is fragmented and inherently unintelligent to one that is centrally based and able to parametrically analyze model data almost instantly. In our legacy system, individual drawings and lines have no value other than their printed form. With BIM, the intelligence can be interlinked between objects within the modeled assemblies, allowing our team members to be both specialized and integrated. With BIM, the documentation process requires design team communication and integration. If we choose to accept the ultimate design challenge—integration between nature and human nature, between the built and natural environments—we need to rethink our attitude toward practice.

Using BIM as a Tool for Integration

One of the most wasteful processes in the world today might just be the design process as it has evolved over recent decades—an all-too-inefficient progression of transforming the three-dimensional vision (the design) through a two-dimensional abstraction (the drawing set) into a resultant three-dimensional reality (the building). Consider the time spent alone by architects in recent decades debating the craft of a two-dimensional drawing (line weights, composition of a sheet, and the organization of the set). The bulk of the architect's time has been increasingly relegated to information coordination rather than design exploration and quality. While this quantum leap in capacity would qualify as a transformational innovation in and of itself, the true power of BIM's integration capacity as it relates to a sustainable world lies at the front end, during design.

A Fundamental Tenet of True Sustainability

A fundamental tenet of true sustainable design is the integration of all the building systems within themselves as well as with the external economic and environmental realities of the project. When the entire design team is able to share and influence a three-dimensional virtual model (Figure 7.2) in an effort to gauge the impact of one another's work on the whole building, true integration all of a sudden becomes more real and compelling.

Image courtesy of BNIM Architects

Figure 7.2 A three-dimensional virtual model

But this next generation is yet embryonic in the BIM world of today. Some pieces have already been born. Structural and mechanical models can now interact with architectural models, for example, for the purpose of coordination. System coordination can occur more accurately and fluidly within this virtual model rather than the more expensive alternative of on-site field coordination. Still unrealized, however, is the capacity of the software to perform all the aspects of modeling and analysis critical for achieving true sustainable design as we've seen earlier. Instead, versions of the BIM model are exported and then imported into separate virtual worlds (or software packages), which produce information that is then translated back to the design team for possible adjustments to the design. Further still, information regarding the environmental impact of material and system choices is still collected and integrated in the legacy fashion of catalog and manual referencing as they are being integrated into the model. Alternatively, with BIM these parameters could be embedded within the model itself.

As the design and construction community moves more and more into a full and pure BIM world, from design concept to postoccupancy, we can begin to see true interoperability between platforms and applications. The next logical step is the ability to re-create and predict the real, physical environment. This would allow us the opportunity to predict the true bounce of light off a wall or desk surface, accurately simulate the flow of cold or warm air within a room, or visually demonstrate the acoustical vibrations within a room. Today, we can only do so in a snapshot in time (Figure 7.3), but in the future of BIM and simulated natural environment, we can dynamically see this played out over the course of the seasons as the BIM model reacts to its modeled physical environment.

Image courtesy of BNIM Architects

Figure 7.3 Daylighting study of an atrium space at 3 P.M. on September 21

Moving Forward with Sustainable Design

The understanding and acceptance of the global warming phenomenon has gained a lot of momentum in recent years. It has touched mainstream TV, movies, periodicals, and pop culture. Because buildings are a major source of greenhouse gas emissions and the embodied energy of our material and product choices equates to a high-carbon footprint for the lifecycle of a building, we as designers and builders should shoulder the responsibility for implementing change. To keep our planet inhabitable, we need to work at making our built environment more sustainable.

Project concerns will move beyond individual benchmarks for pieces of the building. We will no longer only be concerned with how much recycled content is in the building, but with setting new lows for how little carbon was emitted during the creation and operation of the building. Among other things, we will judge our buildings for the healthy air inside, not just the form and color. We are moving toward a time where design is judged by how well you restore the area you are building, and not by how much you created in the spirit of announcing humanity's presence with the latest invention in larger hammers.

Yet with all of this attention and desire to be more a part of our ecosystem rather than just in it, we imagine that for every owner, designer, contractor, or user who is taking on this challenge, ten more have not even begun to understand the impact of the built environment. So we as industry leaders must continue our own education, innovate new possibilities, and provide knowledge to others.

It is of the utmost importance that we provide education to others through built examples of exemplary green buildings. We should do this in every building type and in every climate. It is up to us to lead by example for total market transformation, and it is not too much to imagine scores of truly sustainable buildings in our near future.

Leading by Example

The U.S. Green Building Council (USGBC) (www.usgbc.org) promised in front of the nearly 23,000 people at Greenbuild 2007 (Figure 7.4) that lifecycle analysis will be a major component of the next version of the Leadership in Energy and Environmental Design rating system (LEED v.3.0). Also, new to LEED v.3.0 is the proposed weighting system so that a project is no longer receiving the same credit for on-site renewable energy as it is for having bike racks and showers. Additionally, four credits will be added to represent challenges specific to a bio-region, recognizing that regional specific challenges and solutions are of high value.

In March 2006, when BNIM Architects' Lewis and Clark State Office Building received its platinum rating, there were only 17 Platinum Certifications in all of the USGBC LEED programs. In the short timeframe of 18 months, 64 LEED Platinum Certified projects existed, tripling the amount in the marketplace. In late October 2007, a new benchmark was set for the second year in a row as the Aldo Leopold Legacy Center was awarded the highest score of any Platinum Certified building with 61 credits, which makes it the greenest building on the planet. Five of the eight unachieved credits were not even applicable to the project because it is not an urban site and there was no existing building to reuse.

Image courtesy of Brad Nies

Figure 7.4 People waiting in line for Paul Hawken Keynote at Greenbuild 2007

The Architecture 2030 program

The Architecture 2030 (2030) program (www.architecture2030.org) is gaining traction. According to 2030, over 250,000 people from 47 countries participated in the 2010 Imperative teach-in in 2007. On October 18, 2007, the California Public Utilities Commission adopted a decision requiring California's investor-owned utilities to prepare a single, statewide Energy Efficiency Strategic Plan for the years 2009–2020. The decision states that all new residential buildings and all new commercial buildings in the state shall be zero net energy by 2020 and 2030, respectively.

As more tools become available to understand the benchmarks and goals for within Architecture 2030, meeting them could likely become a common requirement. In 2007 the authors had a chance to visit the Iowa Association of Municipal Utilities

(IAMU) Office Building and Training Complex, just north of Des Moines (Figure 7.5). The 12,500-sq.-ft. building uses only 28.7 Kilo British Thermal Units (KBTU) per sq. ft., which allows it to meet Architecture 2030 at the 2010 level. The building was completed in 2000, well before Architecture 2030 existed.

Image courtesy of Jean D. Dodd

Figure 7.5 IAMU Office Building and Training Complex

Benchmarks and dialogue about meeting the Architecture 2030 goals have increased rapidly in our own project work (Figure 7.6). Every one of the over 30 projects we were involved with in 2007 devoted time to this issue.

The Living Building Challenge

The inaugural Living Building Challenge Competition started in 2007, based on the Cascadia Living Building Challenge program, (www.cascadiagbc.org/lbc). The competition had two categories: first, the Stepping Stone Award for a project that achieved one or more of the program's *petals* for meeting groups of the required 16 prerequisites, but not all 16, and second, the On the Boards Award for a project that is under design with the intent to meet all 16 prerequisites. According to the Cascadia Region Green Building Council (Cascadia GBC), ten projects were entered for consideration in the On the Boards category. The winner was the Omega Center for Sustainable Living for the Omega Institute. When announcing the winners at Greenbuild 2007, Jason McLennan, CEO of the Cascadia GBC, also announced the Living Site and Infrastructure Challenge, pushing true sustainable design beyond just buildings.

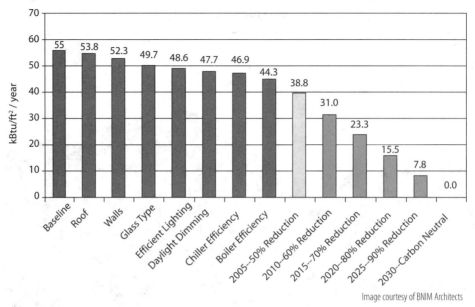

Figure 7.6 An example strategy pathway to reach Architecture 2030 goals

Omega Institute, Center for Sustainable Living

In 2006, the Omega Institute commissioned BNIM Architects to design a new 5,300-sq.-ft. facility on a 4.5-acre site to serve as a new and highly sustainable Wastewater Filtration Facility. The primary goal for this project was to overhaul the organization's current wastewater disposal system for their 195-acre Rhinebeck, New York, campus by using alternative methods of treatment. As part of a larger effort to educate Omega Institute visitors, staff, and local community on innovative wastewater strategies, Omega decided to showcase the system in a building that houses both the primary treatment cells and a classroom/laboratory. In addition to using the treated water for garden irrigation and in a graywater recovery system, Omega will use the system and building as a teaching tool in their educational program designed around the ecological impact of their system. These classes will be offered to campus visitors, area school children, university students, and other local communities.

Preliminary engineering work for the project was completed by Chazen Companies (civil engineer) and John Todd Ecological Design (wastewater engineer). This early investigation was invaluable to the full design team in the early design phases for the building and site. The full design team included BNIM, Conservation Design Forum, Tipping Mar + associates, BGR Consulting Engineers, Chazen Companies, John Todd Ecological Design, and Natural Systems International.

Omega Institute, Center for Sustainable Living *(Continued)*

To achieve the client's vision and goals for the project, the design team first sought to reduce energy and water requirements throughout the basic design of the building and then sought to embrace appropriate technologies in an effort to reduce or eliminate negative environmental impact from the required loads. The team accomplished this primarily by integrating collaborative solutions between all the design and engineering disciplines.

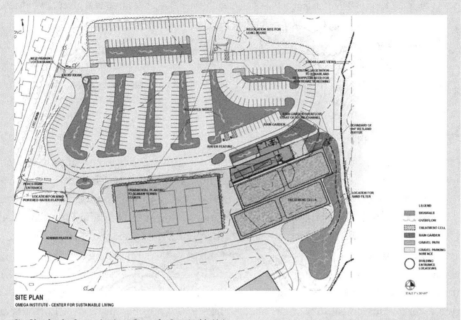

SITE PLAN
OMEGA INSTITUTE - CENTER FOR SUSTAINABLE LIVING

Site Plan for the Omega Institute Center for Sustainable Living

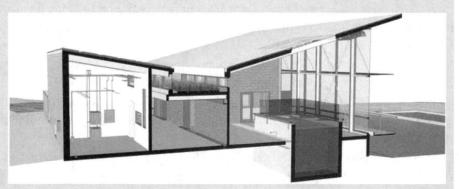

This is a BIM model Section Perspective of the Omega Institute Center for Sustainable Living

Images courtesy of BNIM Architects

Continued

Omega Institute, Center for Sustainable Living *(Continued)*

The building's design is intended to meet the USGBC's LEED Platinum standards and achieve certification as a Living Building through Cascadia GBC's Living Building Challenge. A goal for the project is to be the first living building in the region, if not the nation. To achieve this, the process is relying on a highly collaborative team of experts in wastewater, civil, landscape, mechanical, and structural design with a history of working together on high-performance buildings. Through periodic all-team meetings and ongoing collaboration, the BNIM-led team aims to produce a highly integrated design and ultimately highly integrated building and site, regardless of the living building moniker.

During the design phases of the project, BNIM, Tipping Mar + associates, and BGR Consulting Engineers used BIM. However, BNIM was the only team member to complete documentation in BIM.

Funding Green Design

Funding is going to continue to be a key issue for moving the green building industry forward. Despite the numerous studies, like those mentioned in Chapter 1, that prove the cost of a green building is within 6% of the market rate, building first cost remains a barrier. Research about the benefits of green buildings needs funding too. At Greenbuild 2007 during Chapter day, Vivian Loftness, FAIA, of the School of Architecture at Carnegie Mellon University, provided some startling facts regarding green building research. According to the statistics compiled by the USGBC research committee, only 0.21% of federal research dollars is spent for funding green building research. The top two federal research-funding areas are defense (57%) and health (23%). Loftness also announced that the USGBC itself would fund $1 million worth of research in 2008.

Even more dollars will likely come from initiatives like those of the financial institutions investing billions of dollars in green business strategies to address global climate change. In March 2007, Bank of America Corporation announced a $20 billion, ten-year initiative. In May 2007, Citibank announced a $50 billion, ten-year initiative with a focus on growth and marketplace availability of renewable energy and clean technologies. Investments like these should encourage development of environmentally sustainable business practices through lending, investing, philanthropy, and the creation of new products and services.

Global nonpolitical bound groups like the Clinton Climate Initiative (CCI) (http://www.clintonfoundation.org/cf-pgm-cci-home.htm) will play a large role in the future of green buildings and their funding as well. According to the website:

> *Building on his long-term commitment to preserving the environment, President Clinton launched the Clinton Foundation's Climate Initiative in August 2006 with the mission of applying the Foundation's business-oriented*

approach to the fight against climate change in practical, measurable, and significant ways. In its first phase, CCI is working with cities around the world to accelerate efforts to reduce greenhouse gas emissions.

The 40 cities that CCI is working with include: Addis Ababa, Athens, Bangkok, Beijing, Berlin, Bogotá, Buenos Aires, Cairo, Caracas, Chicago, Delhi NCT, Dhaka, Hanoi, Hong Kong, Houston, Istanbul, Jakarta, Johannesburg, Karachi, Lagos, Lima, London, Los Angeles, Madrid, Melbourne, Mexico City, Moscow, Mumbai, New York, Paris, Philadelphia, Rio de Janeiro, Rome, Sao Paulo, Seoul, Shanghai, Sydney, Tokyo, Toronto, and Warsaw. You can find more information at http://www.c40cities.org. On November 7, 2007, at Greenbuild in Chicago, President Bill Clinton launched a new Green Schools Program. The program will be in partnership with the USGBC and consists of $5 billion available to school districts in America for updating existing schools.

Opportunities for Change

The relatively recent emergence of various modes of integration suggests a promising convergence of thought in distinct yet related disciplines. We might now have the information and tools required to achieve integration in the technological sense, but what we must recover is our understanding of resource consumption and global regard for the environment. With tools and wisdom intact, we can effectively work toward realignment with a sustainable planet, a living planet, even a restored planet. It is first and foremost a call to humanity to learn from nature—*essentially a will to change.*

The use of BIM and an integrated design approach affords us tools that begin to better predict the impact our designs will have on the earth. By creating the building virtually, before we create it physically, we can accomplish the following:

- Reduce labor through higher productivity
- Reduce conflicts between disciplines and trades
- Reduce schedule time for construction
- Reduce costs associated with complexity
- Reduce information/intent lost in translation between designer and fabricator
- Reduce material waste
- Reduce errors and omissions
- Increase the ability to rapidly test numerous options of varying complexity
- Increase the ability to quantify and test variables
- Increase precision in fabrication
- Increase productivity and efficiency
- Increase communication and integration
- Increase opportunities for breakthroughs and restorative solutions

All of these goals lead to more sustainable solutions for the built environment and are possible to achieve through the use of BIM. However, while these are all excellent goals, they are also vague and not well quantifiable. When is a union between BIM and sustainable design achieved? What specific elements of design should we as an industry focus on to elicit the greatest impact on our built environment?

The Next Steps for BIM

We can use BIM in a number of ways for a more sustainable world, and as the processes become more integrated, many of the solutions will become more transparent. To achieve this goal, we must focus on the improvements and innovations that can have the largest and most immediate impact. It is simply not possible to improve all things at once. We want to be able to focus our current efforts on the areas where they will have the largest initial impact. The following list is where we feel innovation should be first focused to help us all reach a more sustainable built environment:

Interoperability between software packages BIM is a great source for building geometry. It can contain the structural, mechanical, and architectural thoughts and ideas for a building translated digitally into a three-dimensional vision of the finished project. However, it has a long way to go to become an analysis tool. One tool cannot be all things— the primary and most obvious need to achieve better sustainable solutions with BIM is better interoperability between software packages. Analysis packages already exist for things like costs, labor, energy, comfort, daylight, and life cycle analysis, with more likely to come. The ability to move the building geometry and necessary ancillary data from the BIM model to an analysis package is critical. Based on our own projects and performance analysis, we have found that 50% of the time it takes to build and analyze an energy model is spent simply re-creating the building geometry in a new application.

Figure 7.7 shows a comparison of time between two energy modeling applications. The first bar demonstrates the time to re-create the building geometry; the second bar represents the time to add information to the energy model (such as building loads, occupancy, and so forth); and the third bar represents the time for the computer to run the analysis. By simple elimination of the first step, the possibility exists for twice the number of design iterations for energy calculations alone.

The ability to move uninhibited from the BIM model to the analysis package is only a start; even greater value will come from the ability to go back to the BIM model with changes from the analysis package.

More input from the designer in the BIM model With the building trend leaning more and more toward a sustainable solution, the knowledge needed by the designer is changing. It is no longer enough for the designer to simply select whether a wall should have glass. The type of glazing, its orientation, and the amount of time it is in the shade or receives direct sun in the building's respective climate are all critical components to good design.

Analysis Time

■ Geometry Manipulation   ■ Adding Load Data   ☐ Simulation

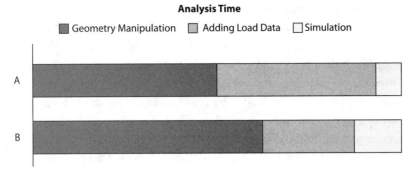

Figure 7.7 Energy analysis time comparison

The designer needs the ability see the thermal and visual properties for glazing in a building design to see how it affects the quality of the space within the building. Another example is the flow rate of different toilet types to calculate cistern sizes for capturing and reusing rainwater. This is true for a number of other systems that make up our buildings today. Currently, BIM does not contain properties to track energy, water, and light efficiencies. Being able to input those metrics directly into the building design will become necessary in future iterations of our design tools. This is only possible today if the designer also knows enough about the BIM application he or she is using to customize it to contain that information. Figure 7.8 shows the properties of a commercial toilet where flow rate and a check box for graywater have been added that allows those elements to be scheduled and tracked.

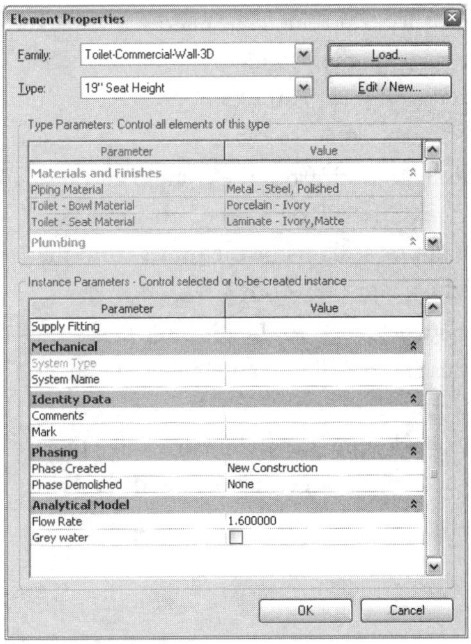

Figure 7.8 Element properties

Right now, there are a number of locations in the marketplace to look up this information. Most major manufacturers of building materials have sections on their websites that deal with their sustainable practices. Additionally, there are other websites that help to combine this type of data for you. Two examples are the International Glazing Database (http://windows.lbl.gov) and the USG's website for wall and ceiling materials (http://www.usgdesignstudio.com). Both sites are created to help inform a design team about light transmittance, reflectance, and other material properties that have until now been underprioritized in the design industry. Some of the material properties that should be integrated into elements and/or materials within the BIM model are as follows:

- Light reflectance
- Light transmittance
- Solar heat gain coefficient
- R-value (or U-value)

These four values would help create informed energy and daylighting models directly from the building information model.

Integration of carbon accounting Currently, there is no integrated software solution to track a building's carbon output as the project is being designed. A building's carbon footprint is currently a major component for measuring sustainability because the carbon left behind by a building embodies the construction process and occupied life of the project. Here are some factors contributing to the carbon footprint of a building:

The embodied energy of the materials that create the building This is a sum of the energy it takes to harvest raw materials for a product, the energy it takes to make the product, the energy it takes to relocate the product to a place where it can be assembled, and the energy required to transport the final product to the building site for installation.

The emissions from constructing the building. Both from the equipment on site and the off-gassing of any cut or applied materials. Examples of off-gassing might be the fumes from the drying of paint or sealants or the fumes from the glues used to bond medium-density fiberboard or plywoods.

Emissions from the fuel it takes to get the work crew to the job site This amount can make a strong case for fabricating building components off site and bringing them to the construction site for erection. It typically takes only one trip to get a material to site, whereas the work crew makes the drive five times a week. If the distance is substantial and the project large, that can add significantly to the building's carbon footprint.

After the building is completed and occupied, other factors add to the carbon load, such as the following:

- The drive time and distance of the occupants of the facility
- The amount of energy or efficiency of the systems within the building as they operate over time

Being able to track the carbon load of a building as we select a site (urban vs. suburban), building materiality, and lifecycle costs can help us to make more informed decisions about where we choose our resources and why. Many times, we simply don't have the information on hand to make decisions about these components and the decision is ruled by the building's first cost.

A schedule of quick calculations BIM is a database. As with any database, it has the ability to track and count elements and report information based on calculations. There are several calculations that are currently unavailable directly from the BIM model that would directly benefit the design team. We've listed some of them here:

> **Roof area calculations** By calculating the roof area in a plan (Figure 7.9), you can directly tie this number to rainwater tables for the region in which the building is located to derive the amount of rainwater that can be collected from the roof area. You can then plug this number into a formula to size cisterns to capture and reuse the rainwater. Additionally, many municipalities will tax a building based on the nonpervious surfaces they have created. This tax is then used for stormwater management.
>
> You can also apply this same concept for calculating the area and orientation available for photovoltaics on the roof.

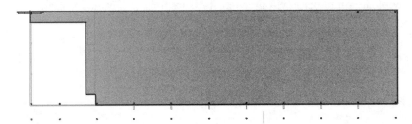

Figure 7.9 Roof areas

> **Window-to-wall ratio** Reporting a calculation involving the window-to-wall/aperture ratio for each primary building orientation (Figure 7.10) is another key calculation that aids sustainable design. This calculation helps the designer keep the design climate responsive by balancing the heat gain and usable daylight from each façade.

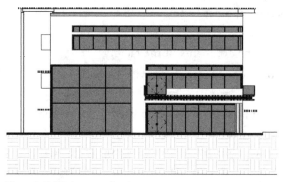

Figure 7.10 Window-to-wall ratio

Minimizing the Western Sun

In a recent project that our office worked on, the energy modeler on the team requested that the west façade have only 17% glazing. This number was a calculated value to maximize the light in the space and minimize the harmful effects of the afternoon western sun in the Midwest climate. The design team had to create their scheme and then manually calculate the percentage of open area on each façade.

Interactivity with weather data It's already possible within a BIM model to set the location of a project by longitude and latitude (Figure 7.11). The next step would be to tie that location directly to weather data available online and directly download a number environmental statistics for the specific location.

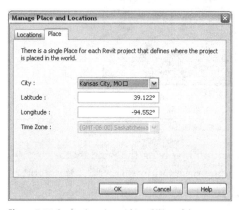

Figure 7.11 Setting Location within a BIM model

The end result is allowing the model and designer to learn from environmental factors such as wind, rain, and sun, as shown in Figure 7.12. This can also be the first step in creating the physical environment around the building within the model environment.

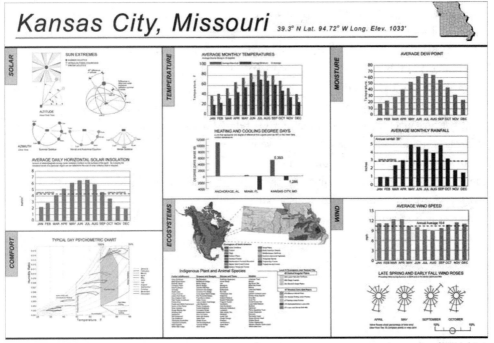

Image courtesy of BNIM Architects

Figure 7.12 Understanding local climate helps reduce negative environmental impact and increase user comfort.

Opportunity

The combined future of BIM and sustainability can help us move faster and more elegantly to a restored world and a healthy planet. There is no future, no *next*, if we do not change the ways in which we work, live, and play. Without overstating the connection between BIM and sustainable design, a few things are inevitable.

Parametric modeling will go well beyond mapping relationships between objects and assemblies. Both model and designer will have knowledge of climate and region. The model will know its building type, insulation values, solar heat gain coefficients, and impact on the socioeconomic environment it resides within. It will inform the design team with regard to upstream impacts and downstream consequences of their choices.

As the building is modeled, prompts will inform the designer of the impact of the building orientation and envelope choices on the sizing of the mechanical system and comfort of its inhabitants. Projected rainfall and solar radiation calculations will be readily available to size cisterns and renewable energy systems. The future BIM model will be a system completely interactive with key building information, climate information, user requirements, and triple bottom line impacts, so that design integration and data return among all systems is immediate and symbiotic. Then once the building is occupied, the BIM model will create an opportunity for a postoccupancy feedback loop.

If we choose to accept the ultimate design challenge—integration between nature and humankind, between the built and natural environments—we will need to rethink our attitude toward practice.

The relatively recent emergence of various models of integration suggests a promising convergence of thought in distinct yet related disciplines. We might now have the information and tools required to achieve integration in the technological sense, but what we must recover is our understanding of resource consumption, global regard for the environment and social equity. With tools and wisdom intact, we can effectively work toward realignment with a sustainable planet, a restored planet, even a thriving planet. It is first and foremost a call to humility to learn from nature—*essentially a will to change*.

Index

Note to the Reader: Throughout this index **boldfaced** page numbers indicate primary discussions of a topic. *Italicized* page numbers indicate illustrations.

daylighting, **157**
energy modeling, **186**, *186*
massing, **141–142**, *142*
materials, 114, **201–203**
overview, **76–78**
renewable energy, **193–194**, *195*
water harvesting, **169–170**, *170*
Loftness, Vivian, 218
longitude and latitude in declination, 137,
 137–138
loose insulation fills, 149
Los Altos Project, 11
losses
 boilers and furnaces, 118
 in renewable energy analysis, 199
Love Canal, 6
low-flush toilets, 102
LSG (Light to Solar Gain Ratio), 149
luminance, 153

M

MacMath, Rich, 202
magnetic declination, 79, 137, *137–138*
maintenance
 in energy modeling, 181
 water-use equipment, 168
man-made efficient systems, **115**
 electric lighting, **119–120**
 equipment, **120–121**
 mechanical, **115–118**, *116–118*
 plumbing, **119**
massing
 BIM for, **143–147**, *144–146*
 building, **139**
 building envelopes, **148–150**, *150–151*
 building form analysis, **147–148**, *147*
 climate, culture, and place, **141–142**, *142*
 resource needs reduction, **143**
master-builders, 54
materials
 BIM database, **39–40**, *39*
 construction use statistics, 30, *30*
 in daylighting, 156
 free resources, **114**, *115*

Heifer International Center, 71
 landscaping, 102–103, *103*
 resource consumption needs, **96–98**,
  97–98
 sustainable. *See* sustainable materials
 USG website for, 222
McCownGordon Construction, 71–72
McDonough, Bill, 12
McLennan, F. Jason, 23–24, 215
mechanical efficient systems, **115–118**,
 116–118
mechanical, electrical, and plumbing (MEP)
 integration, 72–73
migrating to BIM, **43–45**, *43–44*
Missouri Botanical Gardens, *108*
Missouri Department of Natural Resources
 (MoDNR), 68
models
 BIM. *See* building information modeling
  (BIM) and methods
 energy. *See* energy modeling
moisture data, 83
moisture sensors, 119
Montana State University Epicenter project,
 24, **59**
monthly data
 rainfall, **83–84**, *84*
 temperature, 82, *82*
Montreal Protocol, 6
mutual respect in integrated design teams, 61

N

National Climatic Data Center, 85
National Construction Employment Cost
 Index, 31, *31*
National Geophysical Data Center's
 (NGDC) website, 137
National Institute of Standards and
 Technology, 59
National Renewable Energy Laboratory, 84
National Resource Council Canada, 160
National Wilderness Preservation System, 5
Native Americans, 2
natural daylight. *See* daylighting

natural gas heating, 118
Natural Resources Canada, 18
natural systems. *See* free/local resources and natural systems
Natural Systems International, 216
natural ventilation
    orientation for, 133, *133*
    wind, 103–105, *104*
needs reductions
    efficiency, **98–100**, *99–100*
    energy modeling, **180–181**
    massing, **143**
    materials, **96–98**, *97–98*, **203–204**
    orientation, **134–135**, *134*
    renewable energy, **195–196**
    water, **101–103**, *101–103*, **167–168**
negative impacts
    offsetting, **125–126**, *125*
    renewable energy, 195–196
    sustainable materials, 203–204
negotiated guaranteed maximum price delivery method, **69–71**, *70*
Nelson, Arthur C., 56
Nelson, Gaylord, 5
net zero results, 125
neutral results, 125
Nevada water supply, 166
NGDC (National Geophysical Data Center's) website, 137
Nicklas, Michael H., "Student Performance in Daylit Schools", 154
Nixon, Richard, 5
Norris, Greg, 202

O

occupancy in graywater models, 174
offsetting negative impacts, **125–126**, *125*
oil spills, 6
Omega Institute Center for Sustainable Living
    design, **216–218**, *217*
    Living Building Challenge, 215
    water treatment, 168
on-demand water heating units, 119

On the Boards Award, 215
online data for water harvesting, 169
operable windows, 104, *104*
operations
    negative impact offsets, **125–126**, *125*
    water-use equipment, 168
Oppenheim Lewis, 11
opportunities
    for change, **219–220**
    future, **225–226**
order of operations in sustainable solutions, 76
    building type, **91–96**, *92–95*
    climate. *See* climate factors
    culture, **76–78**, **87–90**, *88–89*
    efficient man-made systems, **115**
        electric lighting, **119–120**
        equipment, **120–121**
        mechanical, **115–118**, *116–118*
        plumbing, **119**
    free/local resources and natural systems, **103**
        materials, **114**, *115*
        rainwater, **106–107**, *106–109*
        sun, **107**, **110–113**, *110*, *112–113*
        wind, **103–106**, *103*
    negative impact offsets, **125–126**, *125*
    place, **76–78**, **90–91**
    renewable energy, **121–124**, *122–124*
    resource consumption needs, **96**
        energy, **98–100**, *99–100*
        materials, **96–98**, *97–98*
        space, **96**
        water, **101–103**, *101–103*
organizational culture, massing, 87, 90, 141
orientation, **131–132**, *132*
    BIM model, **136–137**, *136–138*
    and building type, **139–140**, *140*
    climate impact, **132–134**, *133*
    daylighting, **110–111**, *155*
    energy efficiency, 99
    project goals, **135**, *135*
    resource needs reductions, **134–135**, *134*
    sun angles, 80
"Our Common Future", 10

location factors, **169–170**, *170*

for materials, *96*

needs

analysis, **175–176**, *176*

reductions, **101–103**, *101–103*, **167–168**

optimizing, **178**

rainfall factors, **170**, *170*

roof areas, **172–173**, *173*

runoff strategies, **67**

site factors, **171**

treatment onsite, 168

Water Efficiency Credits 3.1 and 3.2, 168

water-free urinals, 102

weather. *See* climate factors

Weather Maker tool, 84

Weatherbase site, 82–83, 85

wetlands, 107, *109*, 171

White, E. B., 75

Wilderness Act, 5

William McDonough + Partners, 24

wind

charts, 105

data, 85–86, *86*

as free resource, **103–106**, *103*

for renewable energy, 122, *124*, 193, 196

Wind Powering America site, 193

window-to-wall ratio, 223, *224*

windows

daylighting, 155

natural ventilation cooling, 104, *104*

"Windows and Classrooms: A Study of Student Performance and the Indoor Environment", 154

"Windows and Offices: A Study of Office Worker Performance and the Indoor Environment", 154–155

wood decking, **114**, *115*

worker performance, daylighting effects on, 154–155

workflow, **46**

workshops for integrated design teams, **65–67**

World Commission on the Environment and Development, 10

WorldClimate website, 170, *170*

Wright, Frank Lloyd, 127

X

xeriscaping, 166

XML schema, 185–187

Z

Zimmer Real Estate Services, *124*

Redesign how you design with BIM.

BIM is big, Revit® is red-hot, and it's time to join the revolution. Go from concept to completion with these practical, in-depth guides.

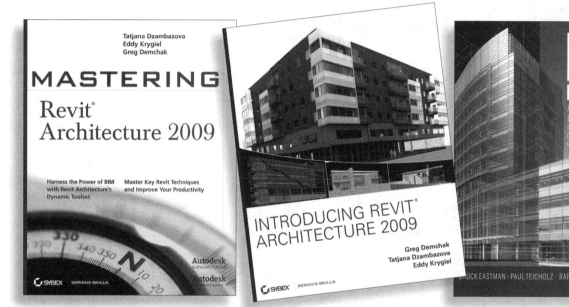

978-0-470-29528-1 • Available September 2008

978-0-470-26098-2

978-0-470-18528-5

Also available

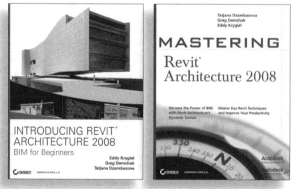

978-0-470-12652-3

978-0-470-14483-1